In Hitler's Shadow

IN HITLER'S SHADOW

Tim Heath

PEN & SWORD
HISTORY

First published in Great Britain in 2018 by
Pen and Sword Transport
An imprint of
Pen & Sword Books Limited
Yorkshire - Philadelphia

ISBN: 9781526720016

Typeset in 10.5/12.5 point Palatino by SRJ Info Jnana System Pvt Ltd.
Printed and bound in the UK by TJ International

Pen & Sword Books Ltd incorporates the Imprints of Aviation, Atlas,
Family History, Fiction, Maritime, Military, Discovery, Politics, History,
Archaeology, Select, Wharncliffe Local History, Wharncliffe True Crime,
Military Classics, Wharncliffe Transport, Leo Cooper, The Praetorian Press,
Remember When, Seaforth Publishing and Frontline Publishing.

For a complete list of Pen & Sword titles please contact
PEN & SWORD BOOKS LTD
47 Church Street, Barnsley, South Yorkshire, S70 2AS, England
E-mail: enquiries@pen-and-sword.co.uk
Website: www.pen-and-sword.co.uk

or

PEN AND SWORD BOOKS
1950 Lawrence Rd, Havertown, PA 19083, USA
E-mail: Uspen-and-sword@casematepublishers.com
Website: www.penandswordbooks.com

To my mother and father Jean and Trevor, and to all
of my family and friends for their support and encouragement
throughout the writing of this book.

Contents

'I walked through what felt an eternity of darkness and into the half-light of hell.'
Weiner Katte, 15-year-old BDM girl, Aachen, 1944.

Introduction

The idea for this book as a companion volume to *Hitler's Girl's – Doves Amongst Eagles* was not an idea wrought purely from the acceptance of what was my first book. The Hitler's Girls project had been a very extensive one. Spanning over four years, it was not possible to include everything within a single volume. There was still much that remained to be told, including some of which I felt was of such historical significance, that it could not be consigned to obscurity.

The Second World War brought about many unique challenges for young girls and women in Nazi Germany. It is clear from the narratives within that they overcame these challenges no matter how hard they were. They accepted the fact that they would have to rise above doing so without question. The level of responsibility placed upon their young shoulders would be impossible for most modern female youths to contemplate. Although methodically nurtured to serve a regime that brought terror, death and destruction to the world, one cannot help but admire their tenacity and bravery.

In the realm of Third Reich historical literature, one has to be aware of the fact that the line between admiration and glorification can easily become blurred. And what of the young girls, all former *Jüng Mädel* and *Bund Deutscher Mädels* (BDM) who had effectively reached the end of the Second World War alive? 'Victory! War is Over!' the world's press announced, yet the reality for many German girls and women would be the complete opposite.

The peace that followed the end of the Second World War was tenuous. Germany was in ruins, her infrastructure crippled, facing an uncertain future. Her position in Europe, however, was of such importance both economically and politically, from both East and West perspectives, that her rebuilding and eventual rearming was inevitable. Many of the former BDM girls who had survived the war faced difficult individual journeys.

In Hitler's Shadow examines further unique material relating to the girls in Third-Reich Germany. It forms the social nucleus of a journey these girls and women had to take, however brutal that may have been. These women, who have chosen to remain silent for decades after the war, now have voices that are louder than the shot from a rifle. As youths vulnerable to the evils of fascist indoctrination, they believed in what they followed, they served, and some even fought and died. Those who became the spoils of war for soldiers inebriated with hate were not broken by the abuses they suffered. As those German women found guilty of war crimes were rightly treading a path to the hangman's noose, others would walk forward into a new era to begin new lives.

My association with the women who have contributed to my work has been uniquely unforgettable. We shared an understanding, yet there is still much to learn and understand. The social structure and politics of Nazi Germany were both contradictory as much as complex. If we have learned anything, we have learned the fact that dictatorships are rarely beneficial to the societies over which they preside. Yet dictatorships still flourish in our modern world. Generally, they are both nourished and nurtured by those too weak or too afraid to challenge them. They will remain an integral part of human nature until the end of humanity itself. Individual governments around the world have an obligation to their societies. They have to learn to preserve their individual cultures, customs and identities. They must also learn how to best satisfy the wishes of their people. Above all else, they must listen. If they fail to do so, then hate, prejudice, segregation and violence will be the inevitable outcome. For many reasons, the world today is as uncertain a place as it has ever been. We can only hope that any emerging evil never prevails again to the extent that it did in the twentieth century. If this work achieves anything, I would hope that it somehow serves as a warning to those who refuse to listen.

1

The Road Out of Hell

Having commandeered a Luftwaffe truck under the pretence of collecting an ammunition supply, under the cover of darkness the Dann brothers, Franz and Josef, worked furiously to prepare for one of the most dangerous journeys they would ever make. Franz tossed a full petrol can into the back of the vehicle, along with a large canvas tarpaulin. They referred to a map that had been hidden under the passenger's seat in the cab. Studying the map by torchlight, they agreed that the only viable means of escaping from Berlin was via a road to the north-west of the city, through Nauen. As far as the two brothers could ascertain, the road was still open, but its condition was unknown and there would be many dangers along the route. There was a possibility that the road was mined, which would force them to abandon the truck and continue on foot. They might have to leave the road to travel cross-country towards the American lines on the Elbe.

As the two brothers prepared, Anna and her mother and father waited anxiously, shivering in the chill night air. The flashes of exploding artillery shells danced in the dark skies all around them and the sounds of war were coming ever closer. Anna recalls:

> I was petrified and just wondering if we would get out of this alive. If caught, we would be shot as deserters or traitors and strung up from lampposts. My brothers decided we would take the truck as far as we could go and that me and my mother and father would remain in the back, underneath the canvas cover which had been put in there for us. It was not going to be a pleasant journey, but there was just this one chance we might survive this war if we succeeded.
>
> I recall Josef putting a pistol in his belt and pulling his jacket over it and Franz doing the same. They both agreed that if anyone tried to stop us they'd shoot them dead, that's the way it would have to be. Father was also given a pistol to use if the time came. I remember the

truck pulling off and it lurching from side to side and the bumping, which shook us up in the back and scared us as it felt as if the truck was going to crash or something. There were bomb craters – in fact there were many bomb craters which had to be carefully negotiated. For us in the back of the truck, there was nothing we could do but pray that we would make it far enough away from Berlin to be safe from the Russians who were closing in from all sides. I remember our progress was slow as we were travelling in the dark with no headlights on, and Franz had to guide Josef as he drove by hanging out of the window.

After what seemed some time, the truck suddenly shuddered to a halt and we could hear voices outside. I could hear Franz and Josef speaking to men outside and I heard Franz shout, 'This is a Fuhrer order! Do you want me to inform the authorities themselves that you are being obstinate?'

Huddled under the canvas, we heard and felt the bang as the small ramp at the back of the truck was dropped. A light was shone into the back, though at the time we couldn't see it as the canvas tarpaulin blocked it out. There was more talking about general road directions then the ramp was slammed shut again. Franz later told us that we had encountered a German patrol of what he described as 'rag-bags' – displaced soldiers from flak or artillery units that had just fallen back and they were heading east into the city. They probably never even made it there, I don't know.

It seemed we had been driving all night. We had to make frequent stops, to negotiate bomb craters, damaged or abandoned vehicles and tanks, and to go to the toilet of course. The fear made you want to urinate almost constantly. The truck stopped for the last time not long before dawn. There were vehicles strewn across the road and all burned out. My brothers helped us out of the back of the truck, and I remember my legs hurting and bruised from the bumpy ride. In fact, we had bruises all over after that journey.

The sky was becoming lighter, and with the prospect of daylight would be the danger of attack from the air. We would have to continue the journey on foot from now on – across fields. Franz and Josef had torn up two large sections of white sheet and we would raise them over our heads once we spotted the Americans. It was crazy, as any Germans we might now encounter up this way we might have to kill if we were to make it through to the Americans. The road, even in the dim light of early dawn, was littered with corpses that were crawling with maggots. The stench was so horrific we covered our noses and mouths and walked on past vehicles with charred bodies hanging from them. This was no shock to us by then, as we had lived with death for so long, and had seen so much, that this was normal by now. Death had been our constant companion – it neither shocked nor repulsed us anymore.

Suddenly, the Dann family, weary from their night of travelling, spotted movement ahead in the early morning gloom. A large group of figures emerged into view – they were German soldiers. At first, they drew up their rifles menacingly, but the family shouted to them, 'Lower those damn weapons, we are Germans from Berlin.'

There were a few seconds of silence as if each side was trying to work out whether the other was telling the truth. As they approached, still with their weapons half pointed at the Dann family, they drew a sigh of relief. They had a *Leutnant* with them, who immediately began to babble, 'The Americans and British are behind us now … what of Berlin? What has been happening there? Our reports have been confusing.'

Franz addressed the officer and replied, 'Sir, Hitler is probably dead by now if the Soviets have got him and the Soviets are in Berlin. If you go there you will probably die. There is nothing but death. The Soviets have made incursions into Berlin now, and may God be with all those people there. The Soviets are raping and killing – you must believe us.'

The officer looked down at the ground, rubbing his chin with his hand before replying, 'Then the war really is lost? Now what are you people proposing to do with yourselves? Are you deserters?'

Josef Dann barked at the officer, 'Sir, we are not deserters, we are survivors. I for one was not going to remain in that hell and see my mother, father, sister and brother perish before that red storm of murder. The Ivans were killing everything that moved. Women and girls who ran were shot in their backs, and those who did not run, were raped. Men were beaten to death or left crippled.'

The officer looked at the bedraggled Dann family, then looked down at the ground and Anna recalls him whispering 'fuck' to himself. Anna's father, who had kept silent to this point, then said to the officer, 'We are walking to the Americans as we will be safer with them than going back to that hell back there (he points towards Berlin). If you are going to shoot us as deserters, then get on with it – go on, do it now if that's what you want.'

The officer displayed the hint of a grin and replied, 'We will not kill German citizens. We are Wehrmacht, not SS, but if you have any weapons on you then we want them, and then you can do what the hell you want.'

Franz and Josef reluctantly handed over their sidearms to the officer, then the group of German soldiers begin to trudge off in the direction of Berlin. The officer turned around and shouted, "I hope that you find what you are looking for, but things will be no better where you people are going!'

Anna recalled how the officers last remark gave her cause for concern: 'It made me think that maybe the Americans and the Western Allies would also treat us badly. We were going into the unknown and the unknown is a frightening thing, isn't it?'

The family walked on but a little over an hour had elapsed before they halted as they could hear the distant sound of engines approaching. The noise of engines grew louder until, just above the treetops, six P-38 Lightning fighter aircraft roared overhead. They flew along the treeline above the road, then four of these American fighters flew on while two peeled off, banking back around. Anna recalls what happened next:

> I thought, hooray, they have seen us and I began to jump up and down and wave at the planes as they began to turn. Franz, Josef and mother and father shouted in a kind of panic, 'For God's sake stop that right now Anna!'
>
> As I looked around at them, feeling slightly dejected at being shouted, at there was a crackling sound followed by a series of small explosions. By the time I had turned my head back to the direction of the planes, I felt like concrete had just slammed against me and I was sent flying into the ditch at the roadside. Bewildered, I gathered my senses to find the rest of my family lying on top of me. They had thrown themselves at me and we all ended up in a pile in the ditch. Those American planes had fired their guns at us. The planes circled for what seemed an eternity, but must have been only seconds, before they roared off and their engines again became a distant drone fading out over the fields and trees.

Franz was very angry. 'Those fucking Americans, what are they doing shooting at people like that?'

Josef replied, 'They think we were soldiers, and we are or at least we were!'

Franz replied, 'Well Anna is no fucking soldier and there she was in the middle of the fucking road waving, for God's sake!'

Father interrupted by saying, 'Okay' you two, that's enough. We have enough problems already, but the next time no silly ideas Anna, okay?'

I replied something like 'I'm so sorry father' and I was very sorry. In fact, I burst into tears as I felt I had nearly got us all killed. What the hell was I thinking, and I vowed if ever there was a next time, I would not do anything so stupid.

Events as described by Anna above were commonplace over German territory at that time in 1945. The German Luftwaffe (Air force) had long ceased to have been the once all-conquering force of the early years of the Second World War. Blighted by a chronic shortage of experienced pilots and eventually fuel, the Allied air forces now dominated the skies over Germany. It was foolhardy to attempt to move around in daylight unless the weather conditions did not permit flying. Anything that was not British or American that moved on the roads or in the fields during the daylight hours could be subjected to sudden attack by marauding Allied fighter-bomber aircraft.

Anna continues:

To make matters worse it started to rain. The rain soaked through our clothing and Franz complained that we should have brought the canvas sheet with us as we could have made a shelter with it. As the rain poured down, the road became horrible to walk on, and as it soaked through our clothes, we became quite cold. Franz and Josef said that there was a small farmhouse nearby and that we would have to get off the road and go across the fields from now on. We would go to the farmhouse and see if anyone was there and seek shelter.

The walk was by now taking its toll on the Dann family Anna's mother was becoming ever slower, to the point where Franz suggested that he carry their mother on his back. Their mother remarked 'don't be ridiculous I will be alright,' but clearly, she was not. It would take some persuasion to make her see sense. The family stopped for a few minutes in the pouring rain. The trees had no leaves on so there was no shelter at all. Anna took her ankle-high boots off and removed her socks. 'There was some blood on my socks and as I removed them, I could see my feet were blistering and covered in sores. The rain was not helping. You can't keep your feet dry in such conditions, so I had to put the wet socks and boots back on until I could dry them somehow.'

The Dann brothers pointed to a house on a gently sloping hillside. 'There is the farm over there!' They walked the last few torturous steps up to the farmhouse, which appeared to have been abandoned and had been for some time. The front door was wide open, looking as if whoever had lived here had left in a hurry. The house was dark throughout. The family stayed together and checked all of the rooms to see if anyone was around. Anna describes the scene:

It was eerily quiet, apart from the rain lashing down outside. Once we had agreed there was no one around, Franz and Josef went out into the outbuildings to check them over. They came back with armfuls of wood and began to stack it into the fireplace. Franz then lit the wood he had found in the barn outside with some matches he had had the good sense to put in a watertight tin in the bottom of his small pack. The fire took some time to get going, but once it was going, the warmth was delightful and I took off my wet socks and boots and placed them by the fire.

As the room slowly warmed up we put our other clothes bit by bit in front of the fire. We pulled some blankets off the beds upstairs and wrapped ourselves up in them and we huddled together using the sofa as a back rest. Franz agreed that one of us should be awake to keep an eye out just in case, and that he and Josef would take it in turns to keep watch while we got some rest. I must have fallen asleep in seconds as I rested my head on my knees. The next thing I know I wake up on the sofa deliciously warm and snug, not wanting to move. It was dark outside again. Mother and father had boiled some water from a nearby stream as my brothers still had a small amount of coffee in their rations. We all drank the piping-hot coffee,

even though I didn't particularly enjoy coffee, especially
without sugar. I drank it down and felt it warming my
whole body. We needed some food as we had only a little
dry bread. Down in the cellar beneath the house we
discovered bottles of alcohol and some pork was hanging
from a hook on the ceiling – we also found a little cheese.
The pork was checked and it looked fine, so we cut pieces
off and ate this with the bread and cheese. It wasn't much,
but we hadn't eaten hardly a thing for nearly four days so
felt immediately better for it. We then discussed what our
next move should be. We could either stay here or carry on
walking until we meet the American soldiers. There was
a danger they might shell the house thinking there could
be flak or artillery guns hidden there in the surrounding
buildings. So we thought it wise to wait for first light then
just to keep walking, but in the meantime we would rest.

Father decided to leave a note for the owners in case
they ever came back. He wrote a short note explaining we
had sought shelter, used some food and that hopefully we
could come back to pay them at a later date when things
were better and safer for us to do so.

The Dann family's decision to leave the farmhouse at first light
the following morning was indeed a wise one, as many such
properties encountered by the invading Allied forces would be
fired on or shelled to ascertain whether any enemy forces were
inside. Barns were often used by the Germans to hide their deadly
88mm flak guns, which were being used in a ground role, where
they would be covered with straw or any other foliage, then await
any unwary foe.

The Dann family left the farmhouse at dawn the next morning.
Franz and Josef had cursed that they had left the map behind, but
Franz had his compass that they could use to ensure they were
heading in the right direction. As the family set off across the
fields, the cold morning air chilled them. Yet again, the clear skies
meant that at least there would be a respite from the rain that had
plagued them the previous day. While walking across the boggy
fields, strewn with the corpses of livestock, the distant drone of
approaching aircraft again broke the silence. Anna recalls:

It was that feeling of instant terror again. Taking no
chances, we lay flat on the wet ground and awaited them
to pass. The planes roared over very low. As they passed

over, I glanced up at them. These planes were big, with single engines, not like the ones we had seen previously with two engines and two tails. They passed over our heads and carried on without turning. They could have seen us easily as we were out in an open field, though we were lying down on the ground.

When the noise of the planes had faded away, they were replaced by another more eerie sound: the sound of creaking and grinding metal on tracks. This was a sound I knew very well – it was the sound of tanks coming. I was very afraid at this point. In fact, we were all very afraid. We took out the two sections of white sheet and tied them to a stick each and walked steadily forward down the field towards some woods and the oncoming monsters. Franz and Josef said, 'When we see them [the Americans], put your hands up straight, don't run or do anything stupid and we will be fine.'

The first I saw of them was a tank, which came into view then immediately halted like a dog spotting a hare in the grass. Its commander dropped down through the hatch out of sight into the tank. We had raised our hands and the two white flags, and in a line, we moved slowly towards the tank. Soldiers began to appear from around the sides and out of the woods. They had their rifles pointed at us and were gesturing for us to keep our hands up. My heart pounded in my chest as they approached. They grabbed my two brothers first and searched them for weapons, before making them lie down on the ground with their hands on the backs of their heads. They searched mother and then my father and they found the pistol he had hidden in his coat. They threw him to the ground and one of them kicked him. We all screamed at them to stop hurting father and they shouted back. We did not understand, but they sounded very angry. They grabbed me and looked through my clothing too, and, realizing I was only small, they then gestured at me to sit down cross legged. They talked among themselves and one of them was shouting with his hand cupped over his mouth.

A man then came forward, clearly an American soldier, but he could speak fluent German. In fact, his German was perfect and beautiful. We were excited and began to all babble at once and he said, 'Hey, hey, hey, calm down, I am going to talk to you, but one at a time okay.' He first spoke with Franz and Josef and they told him they had been with a flak unit and it was they who led us away from Berlin. Father told them he had not been involved in the fighting, even though he had been threatened to report for *Volkssturm* [national militia] mobilization. He was asked about the pistol he had in his coat and he explained he was carrying it to protect his family.

The American then asked about the situation in Berlin itself and we all explained how bad it was. The soldier wrote down everything we told him, including about the rape and murder being carried out by the Russian forces there. I don't think he believed us at that time. The American then turned to me and asked, 'Hey kid, are you okay?' I nodded to him and he said something about not being shy. He said, 'You look like you've been through a lot. Do you want to tell me as it might help other Germans in your situation?'

At that point I don't know what came over me, but I just burst into tears again. I cried harder than I had ever done in my life. All the stress and pain and the sadness spilled out of my body. The American I was sure was going to hug me, but one of the other American soldiers pulled him away and said something to him. Once I had stopped crying, I told him I had been a member of the *Bund Deutscher Mädel*, though I had done no one any harm. I also told him that Franz, Josef, and my father and mother were good people, and they would cause no trouble. As he stood up, he patted me on the head and explained that the medics would check us over, and that once they had given us a check-up, we would be given some food and drink. Then the army intelligence people may want to talk to us.

The Americans were true to their word. We had a medical check and our cuts and bruises were treated, and we were given some hot food and there was so much of it. Franz and Josef underwent a long interrogation, where they handed over their identification papers, which they had kept just in case. The papers confirmed that they had belonged to a flak battery. Even so, they were stripped almost naked and searched a final time. At that point, our future was uncertain and we wondered where we would be taken from here and what lay ahead for us. We did not want to go back to Berlin and had few options.

Germany was in chaos, and until order had been restored, we could do nothing other than wait and see what the future held. Father suggested we try to get to Schwerin where he had sisters, and maybe we could stay there until we had sorted ourselves out. But how would we get there and what do we do in the meantime? We would need regular food and water and somewhere to stay, but where do we go. We were now homeless refugees in our own country.

We stayed in a kind of refugee camp for displaced persons for a week or so. The British Red Cross supplied the people there with food and medical aid. The camp was not that pleasant to live in, though, and it soon became unsanitary as latrines filled up and had to be replaced. Usually the toilet area was no more than a pit, and when this became full, petrol was poured into it and it was set alight to destroy bacteria, and then filled in and another pit dug. Just being able to have a proper wash was a real hardship, and we often walked off across the fields and washed in a stream as it gave us more privacy.

We became restless in the camp and Father said we must make our way to Schwerin, a beautiful town in the north of Germany, to his relatives there. Schwerin was not that far and would take around two hours if we had motorized transport, but we did not. So, we set off on foot again. We made sure we had some food and water and carried some blankets with us. We managed to get a lift part of the way from a British army truck. It was so surreal to be walking along a road and a British army truck come along and stop and ask you where are you going, then jump in the back. The driver was only a young lad and he had a mate with him in the front, but told us to say nothing about giving them a lift or he could get into big trouble.

'We're not supposed to fraternize you know, orders from above you see, so if anyone asks, you didn't get help from us.' He smiled as he spoke, but we understood – there was still much anti-German feeling at this time.

The Brits dropped us off at a lonely junction and the young man driving pointed and said, 'Schwerin is over there. You people take care now, God be with you.'

We watched the truck disappear from view around the bend in the road and trudged off towards Schwerin.

We stopped after thirty minutes of walking for some water and to have some food. We had bread and cheese and some corned beef that had been wrapped up in a piece of cloth. We laid it out and then shared out the food equally and sat at the edge of the road eating. It was serenely peaceful and we sat there eating in silence. Father interrupted the silence by saying, 'God, I just want to know what is going to happen and how we are going to get on in life?'

My brothers tried hard to reassure both Father and Mother that somehow we would be alright – we had no choice, we had to be alright, didn't we? We made it to Schwerin and it appeared that the war had never taken place here. We arrived at my aunt's home late in the afternoon and they welcomed us in and we sat down while my aunt made us all a hot drink. We were in a right state, but we managed to have a wash one by one in a metal tub in front of the fire, and once we had all bathed we got rid of our dirty clothes as my uncle said he could get us all some clean clothes the next day.

Everybody helped one another in Schwerin and that was how we were able to get back on our feet again. Father was able to get a job working with a blacksmith and he also did other odd jobs like chimney sweeping and gardening. I was given a job in a small bakery in the town, a job I soon came to really enjoy. All we needed now was a home we could call our own, but sadly we would not find that home in Schwerin.

My brothers became restless after a few weeks and they decided to go to Roblingen to find work there. They knew we would be safe now the war was over and we all had to get on with our lives. They promised to write us a letter as soon as they arrived. They hugged and kissed us and off they went. We received a letter from them a month later, telling us to come too as soon as we could as we could easily get work. My concern was that there would be little there for us, but it turned out to be a good thing for us. Franz and Josef had found good jobs on a construction project, and although it was hard work, the pay was very good. They had found us somewhere to live and had even paid some rent for us. Father and Mother both found work and I went to study art, as it was something I always wanted to do.

After much effort, hard work and study, I left Roblingen for Vienna, where I became an art teacher. I became friends with a fellow teacher and we fell in love and were married two years later. We had three children, and I have to say, we have lived a very good and rewarding life.

Of course, Nazism did return to haunt me on a few occasions. I once had a student's parents complain to the school where I worked that they did not think it appropriate for their child to be taught by a Nazi. This was always a problem, having to justify yourself and try and explain to people who were not there under the National Socialists that not all of us were Nazis. As our children grew up and left home, we had put our savings into buying a house in France, and that is where we retired and would live out our life. Do I have any regrets you might ask?

Well, of course I do. We all have regrets over something in our lives. I wish Hitler had never been born. When he came to power, he promised us prosperity and to make our nation great again. As young people, we should have questioned more, but had we done so, how could we have changed anything?

Sophie Scholl tried to defy the Nazis via non-violent means, yet look what they did to her – they executed her for treason. In the Third Reich, anyone could inform on you if you expressed political reservations, which instilled a fear that made people conform, even if they did not agree to things. Unless you were there and living in it you cannot possibly understand what it was like. At the same time, I feel that, had the Treaty of Versailles not been so harsh, maybe fewer Germans would have chosen to follow the Nazis. This is a lesson in some ways, but have we learned? I think not.

Look at what has happened in Iraq since 1991, and then 2003 when the Americans and British decided to go in there and remove a ruler by force, which has plunged the whole of the Middle East into chaos and uncertainty. The truth is we have not learned lessons from the past, and if we don't learn, then the past will repeat itself. To this day, I still fear Russia and still think they are a potential enemy, but that is my own personal opinion and does not mean that I would go around killing Russians just because I don't trust or like them. I experienced their brutality in April of 1945 and it does not leave you. Even the smell of war stays in your skin. No matter how hard you scrub and keep washing, you can still smell rotting bodies, blood, smoke, cordite and masonry dust. I could smell it for months afterwards.

I have no regrets. I did not participate in, or condone, the killing of Jewish people. I was horrified when the true scale of the murders was made public. When we were young, we heard many rumours, but we had not seen anything first hand. Those who lived near the death camps would have smelled them, and rumours combined with strange smells would have told you that something was not right, but what if you had discovered the truth? Would anyone have believed you and would they have cared? We in the *Mitte* [centre of Berlin] lived with just the usual smells of an urban environment, though there was a death camp discovered not far from the city of Berlin. All I can say is that I hope that nothing ever happens like that again, and if my story serves as a lesson or a warning, then that is good. Me and my family were some of the very lucky ones – not everyone lived happily ever after, though everything we did have after the war we had to work very hard for. My opinion now is, that if adults and politicians want to fight, then let them, but do not involve the children or the young in these fights.

2
Fighter Girl

Monica Vanessa Kieler Dorsche was, perhaps, one of the most unique of all the German women I had the pleasure of talking with. She was born in Germany, though her family was of South African descent. Her parents emigrated to Germany well before the outbreak of the First World War. Her father, who fought in the First World War, like many returning soldiers, soon became despondent about Germany's fortunes. They were a relatively wealthy family in comparison to most Germans, supporting the rise of Adolf Hitler and the Nazi party from its inception and appearance on the world stage. Monica recalls:

> My father had served as a reconnaissance aircraft pilot during the First World War, so I guess aviation was passed into my blood. I had always been interested in flying since I was a little girl. I always said when I grew older I wanted to learn to fly. We witnessed the rise of National Socialism in Germany. The privations which had brought about the Nazi party cannot entirely be blamed upon the German society at that time. Many Germans were suffering the crippling effects of the Versailles Treaty: there was hyper- inflation, borderline starvation and a high rate of unemployment among the working classes. My mother, father and extended family generally supported the National Socialists. My parents had interests back in South Africa in diamond mining. I know that from this they paid contributions into the funding of the Nazi Party. This was by no means unique among wealthy German families, unless, of course, they were not supporters.
>
> I joined the League of German Girls, or *Bund Deutscher Mädel*, before it had even become compulsory. I found the discipline, camaraderie and ethos of fitness quite enjoyable. We were politically active in some instances as we wore swastika badges on our uniforms. We were also expected to explain what National Socialism was in class

at school, and explain the differences between the old Germany, as it soon became known, to that of the new Germany. I did very well in school, having aspirations to study and travel upon leaving. I attended Munich University, studying architecture and design, yet the yearning to fly remained unabated. It was my father who arranged for me to have my first taste of 'leaving the earth behind' as he put it.

My first aerial experience was in an unpowered glider aircraft. It was one of the most memorable experiences I have ever had in my life. I was not anxious or nervous – I just desperately wanted to learn to fly one of these things. Of course, there was a lot to learn about flight control, atmospheric conditions, safe flight parameters, what you must do in an emergency, etc. – the list was quite extensive. I was the only girl on that occasion, as it was mostly boys who wanted to learn to fly. The male arm of the Hitler Youth had glider schools, with the specific intention of training them towards single or twin-engine aircraft. Any pupil lacking the required aptitude was quickly dismissed, as flying was a dangerous occupation. I absolutely loved it, but became impatient at being the passenger and wanted to learn to take the controls and fly by myself. The overall theory was quite intensive, as one might expect. I excelled with the examinations, soon grasping the rudiments of reading flight instruments and learning the controls, such as ailerons, rudders and flaps. My first few flights were at very low level, sometimes no higher than 100ft off the ground and as a passenger.

My first flight, where I took the controls of the aircraft, was scary, but the excitement was immense, I loved it. With father bankrolling my lessons, I was soon flying solo, soaring above the beautiful Wasserkuppe ranges. It was breathtaking, to the point where it was easy to become distracted and forget everything. Concentration had to be maintained at all times as there were many dangers, even with gliding. Anticipating thermals, smooth control, keeping an eye on your altitude instruments – there was little time to admire the views properly.

After nearly a year of sports gliding, I wanted to fly higher and faster. I wanted to fly a powered aeroplane with an engine and do some real flying. The best way to achieve this back then was to get your pilot's licence and apply for work as an air-mail transport pilot. The more hours of flying you accrued prior to application, the better your chances. The problem was that there was still a very chauvinistic attitude to women with abilities. The males did not like the idea that women could fly an aeroplane as good or if not better than what they could. They would refuse to fly in the aircraft at your side. It was only after an argument I had with one obstinate male colleague, plus the intervention of my father, that things were resolved. They stopped being asses and I was allowed the opportunity to get on with a job I wanted to do and loved.

I worked in Africa as a mail pilot and also took photographers up in the air to photograph the wildlife. This was extremely lucrative work if you could get it, and if you were good, the wealthy photographers would book you again. I took one fellow out as he was hoping to film a herd of giraffe. We found not quite a herd of them, but enough for him to want to film them. I made several passes over the animals at quite low altitude, but he kept on gesturing 'lower, lower', to the point where it became annoying. So, I thought, right, I will give you lower! I knew the limitations of my aircraft and what I could get away with safely. I climbed several hundred feet, keeping the animals in view, then pushed the stick forward into a dive, gathering speed rapidly. I levelled out something like 35ft above the ground and the animals. I looked across at the photographer. He had dropped his camera in the foot well and his knuckles were turning white from gripping the sides of his seat. He was pushed back into his seat with a look of sheer terror on his face. I had to really bite my lip to prevent him seeing me smile.

When we landed back at the airstrip, which was just a dirt runway nestled between some trees, and before the propeller had even stopped turning, he had undone his harness and leapt out of the aircraft.

'What the bloody hell kind of stunt was that for God's sake!' he roared, in that typically British upper-class accent.

He walked away shaking his head, and I am pretty sure the seat of his pants were moist. I hasten to add he never hired me again. During my time abroad, I flew many aircraft of various kinds. I even flew a stunt aeroplane and learned a few tricks with it. The speed and agility of these small monoplanes were astonishing.

With the clouds of war gathering over Europe, I decided it was time to return home to Germany. The years of flying in Africa were both beautiful and memorable. I had accrued over 152 flying hours by the time I left Africa, and hoped to continue flying back in Germany.

When I returned to Germany, it was a completely different one to the one I had left. I went to a few air-mail company offices, asking for work as a pilot and they almost laughed in my face. I threw my credentials down on the table in one office and shouted, 'Well, have any of you done better than this?' There was silence, so I said, 'Oh well, I thought not!'

I turned and walked out of the office. Talking to my father about it that evening he explained that I must not go around rocking the boat. Hitler wants his women to concentrate on marriage and motherhood and that policy is policy.

'But I want to fly, Father,' I replied, 'I certainly have no intentions of marrying and having children just yet.' I felt very dejected that the regime my father had helped with cash injections along its way to power had somehow dismissed women from what were now predominantly male occupations. Oh, I was angry! I was very angry about it. My father tried to calm me down and said he would have a word in a few ears, but he had no influence over the new policy in Germany.

'I cannot be seen to be bribing people as it is dangerous,' he said.

Of course, I understood, and was going to return to Africa, but with the threat of war on the horizon, Father convinced me that this would be a bad idea. When war was declared in 1939, few of us believed it would drag on for six long years. In the event, the length of the Second World War proved advantageous to my ambitions to fly again. A protracted war, culminating in the ever-higher loss of life, particularly German men, meant girls and women would soon be called up to fill the gaps. We had entered into what soon became a war of rear-guard action and our military forces were haemorrhaging manpower on a daily basis.

By late 1943, I had enrolled into the Luftwaffe auxiliary services, working on the new radar detection systems.

I was involved with the *nachtjagd*, or night fighters, as you know them. We would basically vector them onto the RAF bomber streams as they attacked our cities by night. This was an extremely demanding job, requiring skill, attention and resourcefulness. Our pilots' lives depended on our utmost accuracy and precise communication. Many young girls fresh out of the League of German Girls enrolled into this line of work. Few of them could withstand the pressure, and many came and went. Those that went or were taken off this duty, were often placed in other areas such as the flak auxiliary. This, though, was equally hazardous work

It was amazing when a pilot radioed in a successful interception of an enemy bomber. We often received letters from them thanking us for our work. I once had an invitation to dinner with the pilot of a Messerschmitt Bf 110. I was amazed at how articulate our pilots were. They had impeccable table manners, and although they could speak little of their operational activities, they told us some amazing stories of the night air battles over our cities.

I dined with the one young pilot frequently and I know he had romantic intentions, but there was an age gap between us. He was 20 and I was 27. He always brought me flowers to our dinner meetings. One evening he said he had a surprise for me, but we would need to take a train and have an overnight stay in a hotel. He had booked us separate rooms, of course, which I thought was very sweet of him. The next day, he revealed his surprise – it was a visit to his airfield. When we arrived, he took me around the hangars so that I could see the mechanics and armourers working on the aircraft. There were Messerschmitt Bf 110G aircraft with these masses of radar antennae [FuG Lichtenstein radar] sticking out from their noses. They had huge batteries of powerful guns, some of which fitted to fire upwards.

'How do these work?' I asked. He went on to explain that the idea was that once vectored into the bomber stream, they would find a target via radar. Once identified as an enemy, you had to fly beneath the enemy bomber then open fire on its underside.

'Wasn't this dangerous?' I enquired.

He smiled and said, 'Well yes, it is dangerous, but it's more dangerous for the enemy than for us'. He then said to me, 'But don't tell anybody I told you this, as it's operational information and I could get into serious trouble.' I assured him I wouldn't say a word and we left the hangar.

Parked out to the west side of the airfield, beneath some trees, were Messerschmitt Me 109G [Gustav series] aircraft.

'You can sit in one if you would like,' he said, and my face must have lit up like a fire.

I could not get over to it quickly enough, and climbed up on the wing and jumped into the cockpit. The instruments were much the same as a civilian air-mail monoplane, but the performance and handling would be staggering in comparison. I grasped the control stick and felt the rudder controls with my feet. Everything seemed to be in the right place: throttle lever, gun button, gunsight – it was marvellous.

'God, I would love to have a go at flying this thing,' I remarked.

'Hmm, the Gustav is a good aeroplane, but it is a vicious beast too. We have lost more pilots to this aeroplane than any other type.' I was intrigued.

'In what way?' I asked.

'Well, it's a very powerful motor in a lightweight airframe and the undercarriage is narrow. If you give it too much power on take-off, it has a habit of oscillating or pitching a little like a boat on a rough sea. Many pilots panic increase the throttle input, which exaggerates the problem. They try to get off the ground too quickly and the aircraft rolls over onto its back, and then the inevitable happens. The consequences are often fatal.'

I was fascinated, and imagined myself taking off in this aircraft.

'What are the weapons?' I enquired.

'A 20mm gun and two machine guns, all in the nose, but more weapons can be added if necessary, though this hinders performance.'

It was all very exciting, and after dinner in the mess with officers, we spent the night in the hotel. In the morning, we parted as I had to get my train back and resume my duties. We promised to write and keep in touch, and I begged him to be careful. I kissed him on the cheek and left to get my train back home.

We continued to keep in touch, but as the war progressed, I saw him less and less. It was a day in late 1944 that I received a letter back that I had written. The envelope was marked 'missing', so I made some enquiries. The authority was not permitted to give me any personal information, so I wrote a letter, which they said they would forward on to his family for me. I received a letter some weeks later stating my friend had been listed as missing. He had not returned from an operation and his whereabouts were still unknown. I received a second letter a month or so later confirming him as dead. The wreckage of an Me 110 had been found in a forest by the army and remains of his *ausweiss* [identity book] were found. The news came as a huge shock, and I thanked God that I had not allowed myself to fall in love. I was still very upset as he was such a nice young man. I found out much later, after visiting his parents, that one of the other things that were found in the wreckage of his aircraft was the small black and white photograph of myself that I had given him. It was partially burned, but a miracle it had survived. The family asked if I wanted it back, so I took it along with a photograph of him. I still have it now and will never part with it.

By late 1944 and into early 1945, the Luftwaffe was really struggling. Every available man who could fly an aeroplane had to report for fighter duty. A few women were selected for the purpose of delivering fighters to the fighter units. I had heard about this and so I put my name forward. The authorities were reluctant at first as they considered my experience on radar duties as being more important. I argued that getting aircraft to the fighter units was of far more strategic importance than me sat on my arse in front of a radar screen. I begged them to let me do it and told them, if necessary, I could do both. I handed in my flying log, detailing the aircraft I had flown on mail runs and the flying hours I had accrued, and had an anxious wait for a decision.

My father was not at all happy about the idea. In his opinion, I was putting myself in unnecessary danger. I explained that the flights would be short, localized hops, delivering fighters with an escort. The idea would be to take a brand-new aeroplane along, with a group of other pilots. We would fly very low to local destinations where we would deliver them and sign them over.

The dangers were obvious, as the Allies were gaining air superiority over German territory. The chances of running into Allied fighter-bomber sweeps were a real threat. We would have an escort, of course, but this would be no guarantee of our safety. The aeroplanes were not in short supply, but the Luftwaffe fighter arm was rapidly running out of pilots to fly them. After a few weeks, I received a letter informing me that my application had been granted. Before our work could begin, we were schooled in various aspects of what to do if we encountered an Allied fighter patrol. We also had to identify silhouettes of enemy aircraft. Anyone who failed to identify all of the selected enemy aircraft profiles correctly were rejected. There could be no room for error in this work. I also had to undertake intensive parachute training in the event I had to bail out of an aircraft. This took some mastering, but after six weeks I was proficient enough to continue to the next phase.

The first fighter aircraft I had to deliver was, ironically, a Messerschmitt Me 109G-5 fighter. It felt as if the spirit of my young pilot friend was with me. I recalled the conversation we had that day at the aerodrome: 'Don't give it too much power on take-off and beware of the narrow undercarriage, which can be a problem on take-off and landings.'

Climbing up into the cockpit felt like climbing into the seat of a racing car. The engine was started and I pulled the hood shut. I checked my instruments and the pressure gauges as the engine roared into life. The vibration seemed to go right through my whole body. You felt the power of that 2,000hp Daimler Benz engine. I was the fifth Messerschmitt to taxi out onto the grass runway. I levelled my boy up and slowly opened the throttle – the momentum amazed me compared to the mail aircraft I had flown. In comparison, they were unwieldy and sluggish. I held the revs as I felt the tail rise slightly, then increased my speed and the Messerschmitt rapidly left the ground behind.

Once airborne, I retracted the undercarriage and made a couple of orbits of the aerodrome as the other aircraft got airborne. We set course for our destination, escorted by three Focke-Wulf Fw 190s. The 190s stayed behind and high above us as we flew over the German countryside.

As instructed, I looked behind and to my left and right every few seconds, while keeping an eye on my instruments. The flight was uneventful, and less than twenty minutes later, the 190s swooped down in front of us to guide us in to land. One went in to land while the other two orbited the aerodrome as we followed. Once the 190 was clear, we were called in to land. I was first, and this was the scariest moment as most accidents in the Gustav were as a result of a poorly executed landing.

'Reduce height, level him up, reduce speed, check instruments, check air speed …' the instructions running through my brain. Making corrections to my rudder and flaps, I eased back very gently on the stick to bring the big nose of the Gustav up slightly, so that the tail wheel would touch down first, followed rapidly by the main wheels. The runway vanished from view below the Gustav's nose. I shut off the throttle and the Gustav touched down with a bump. A few gentle hops and he was slowing down. Slower, slower, slower … then I had to just taxi him in off the end of the runway. I had landed what was often referred to as the 'rookie's coffin' by Luftwaffe fighter pilots.

I checked everything was off before climbing out of the cockpit. The Gustav fitted me very well as I was only of small stature, but many pilots hated it because they said it felt cramped. I climbed out of the cockpit and watched the other aircraft come in. I was interrupted by an officer with a clipboard with an attached document. I had to sign my aircraft in, and then I could go and get a hot drink in their mess.

As I turned away to walk over to the mess hut, there was a tremendous crash. I spun round to see one of the Gustav's cartwheeling down the grass runway in a ball of flames. By the time it stopped, it was burning fiercely, its pilot trapped inside. The fire service soon had the blaze out, but the pilot was dead by the time they got him out. The pilot had made the mistake of landing too fast and trying to get the thing down too quickly. It was a sobering lesson for the others who were still airborne and waiting to come in to land. They were vectored to one of the satellite airfields to land, escorted by the two 190s.

In the mess I drank down the hot coffee, and was congratulated on an excellent landing and questioned on where I learned to fly. So there I was, I had delivered my first aircraft safely, had witnessed a fatal crash, and now I was in the mess being congratulated by career fighter pilots.

A ride home came via a Luftwaffe truck, and not the most comfortable ride at that. When I arrived back at my station, I phoned my father and told him of the day's drama. I made a few other flights, which again were only very local hops. We did not see any enemy aircraft, though we had a couple of false alarms due to misidentification.

My last flight was the most memorable for a number of reasons. I was to take one of the brand new Focke-Wulf Fw 190 Ta 152 aircraft over to the aerodrome, which by this time was operating the new jet-powered Messerschmitt Me 262 fighter aircraft. The idea of delivering piston-engine fighters to a jet station puzzled me. I guessed I would find out why when I landed there. Again, the routine was as much as normal. The flight was made early morning, just as the sun was rising. I signed for my aircraft and climbed up into the cockpit. This was a treat of an aeroplane, a pure thoroughbred. Unlike the other variants of the 190, this one had the Junkers Jumo engine, not the older BMW radial.

During the pre-flight brief, we were told the aircraft has an emergency escape system should we encounter an enemy patrol. It operated a nitrous oxide injection and MW50 [water methanol] injection system. When activated, this gave the engine a truly massive power boost, where the aircraft could reach over 500mph in level flight – quite astronomical I thought at the time. We were instructed, that should anything go wrong or we were in imminent danger, to return to the factory aerodrome immediately. The Ta 152 was a pleasure of an aeroplane and I found its characteristics were superb, and here I was about to take off in one and deliver it.

I found it an easier and more forgiving aeroplane and was airborne in no time. Again, carrying out a few orbits of the aerodrome while the other aircraft cleared the ground, we then set course with our escort, which included Me 109s and Fw 190 fighters. Someone wanted to make sure our precious cargoes were delivered!

We were only approximately ten minutes into what should have been a fifteen-minute flight. One minute we were flying in an empty sky, then all hell broke loose. The first I saw of the enemy aircraft were specks in the distance at my twelve o'clock. Before I could even call their position, our escort had spotted them. The closing speeds were immense and one of the enemy aircraft, which I could clearly see were American Mustang fighters, gave me a squirt of machine-gun fire. The tracers passed harmlessly over my cockpit hood. Forgetting what I was told in case of an emergency, I accelerated into a hard, corkscrew climb. At the top of the climb I levelled the 190 out and rolled. As I levelled out from the roll, I could not believe my luck – there right in the gunsight was a big fat Mustang. I don't know, call it instinct or stupidity, but I stayed on his tail for a few seconds and depressed the gun firing button, but nothing happened. I cursed, realizing that as the 190 I was flying was not yet an operational fighter, the guns had not been loaded with ammunition – the magazines were empty. Had the big 30mm cannon and two 20mm guns been loaded, I would have shot that Mustang down.

I pulled a hard-left manoeuvre, diving for the ground and the treetops. As I levelled out just above the treetops, I noticed Mustangs trying to close in on my tail. I pulled up again using the climbing corkscrew manoeuvre, rolled and levelled out, and activated my emergency boost system and headed back to the departure airfield as instructed. The power boost was like a kick up the arse from Thor himself – my airspeed was soon indicating 460mph! The pursuing enemy disappeared from my rear view in seconds. The engine temperature began to rise, so I shut off the boost and at the same time I saw the departure airfield.

The airspace around it is alive with our fighters, which scrambled to take off after hearing our warning. Thirty of our fighters flash past me, while others began orbiting the aerodrome to cover our landing. I get the 190 down safely, bar a few skips and bumps, and open the hood and jump out.

There are plumes of smoke in the direction that I have come from, but only two other aircraft from my delivery flight return. The others were unable to escape in the panic and were shot down. Their pilots failed to bail out and were killed. When the other aircraft returned, and all of the operational pilots were safely down, I thought that was it, until we were ordered to take off again.

My manoeuvres with the Mustang had not gone unnoticed and I had been reported for serious misconduct. I was told by a senior officer that I could face a court martial as I was working under military jurisdiction. I was called in to explain myself in front of the commanding officers of the aerodrome.

'What on earth do you think you were doing up there? Do you realize you could have been killed? This is not a game we are playing here. Consider your licence revoked with immediate effect. You are to return home while we deal with this matter and make a report to the relevant authority.'

The outcome was uncertain, and my mother and father, when they heard of the news, were furious with me.

Father shouted, 'You bloody, silly fool! Do you think it's funny that we might have had to arrange your funeral? For God's sake girl, what is the matter with you? Now you will be in trouble with the authorities and God knows what their decision in this matter will be.'

I was, of course, called in for a disciplinary hearing, but to my surprise some of the fighter pilots airborne that day, who witnessed what I had done, had come forward in my defence. My flying licence was still revoked and I would not be permitted to continue delivery flights. I was given a stern telling off and told I could resume my job on radar if I wished. After that incident, I had more fan mail than a pop star from the fighter pilots. They all wanted to take me out for dinner and I found it quite amusing. No official record of the incident exists as I have tried to find documents on it, but to no avail. We were not permitted to take photographs of our work either, so I have no souvenirs of that time. The only thing I have relating to the incident is a letter sent to me afterwards by one of my many admirers from the Luftwaffe. The pilot did not know my name, so it was simply addressed to my station. The words written above on the envelope were simply 'To the Fighter Girl'.

This has to be a truly remarkable story from one remarkable lady. Had the guns of her aircraft been loaded on that memorable day, she may have been famous for being the only German female pilot to have been credited with shooting down an Allied aircraft. What an accolade that would have been, but Monica was always modest about her endeavours. The only photograph I was provided of Monica was one of her with an aircraft taken somewhere in the United States after the Second World War. She had continued to fly and had even taken part in air-racing events after the war.

The bug for flying never left me at all. Having flown some very powerful piston-engine fighter aircraft, which included the Me 109G and Fw 190, I wanted to fly more. I became addicted to the element of speed. Air racing was always a popular sport and in the USA it was followed religiously, attracting huge crowds in the 1950s. The prize money could be pretty big too. It was a cheap sport back then, and after the Second World War you could buy a brand-new P-51 Mustang for just a few dollars. Many were leaving the factories just to be broken up as unwanted surplus or sold abroad. Providing you had a flying licence and a couple of good mechanics to back you up, you could enter the air races. It was not an expensive sport at all in those days. There were dangers, of course, and not much room for error. Having saved money from doing tourist drops and flights, I bought a P-51 Mustang virtually new for twenty-five dollars. The machine-gun armament had been removed of course!

It was a magnificent looking aeroplane, fitted with a Packard Merlin engine. The idea was to strip the weight down of the aircraft as much as was possible. Seat armour plating was removed and discarded, as was anything else that added weight but was not a necessity. The Packard Merlin was already a very powerful aero engine in its own right. Power could be increased by adding nitrous oxide injection to the engine. It took a sound mechanical mind to fit and set up, but if you set it up properly, it was magnificent. If you did not get it right, it could blow your engine up!

I suffered a fire on take-off once, but it was nothing serious and was down to a leaking fuel line, which was repaired easily. As for the races, they were an adrenaline rush. Most competitors were flying decommissioned Second World War fighters. I only ever saw one German aircraft at the races, and that was an Me 109G Gustav. I even asked if I could fly it after telling its owner my story. He still wouldn't let me fly it though.

I won a few races. We were all so desperate to win, that we did some foolhardy things. You had to be prepared to push your aeroplane to its absolute limit of performance. There were crashes and people got killed, but it was a wonderful era, it really was, and I have some fond memories.

Monica passed away long before my book was published. I hope that, in some small way, this chapter provides something of a tribute to her remarkable career, from BDM girl to ferry pilot/fighter girl.

I also hope that it serves as a tribute to all the German women who served in this dangerous field of operations during the closing stages of the Second World War.

3

Theresa Moelle: Homecoming

Theresa Moelle, having returned home with her adoptive family after her ordeal during the fighting in Berlin, began the process of trying to get back to normality.

It was not easy as we had to support ourselves as a family. The house had to be cleaned and repaired and this was a lot of hard work. We still had the farm outbuildings and fences to sort out too. For a time we would have very little to live on, but we would be okay in the long term. I had also taken on work at another nearby farm, helping the owner with repairs and tending his few animals as we all had to help one another. The Germany we were now living in would need cereal crops, vegetables, milk and meat, and we knew we could achieve this goal.

Labour was never a problem as there were by now many hundreds of former German soldiers wondering the countryside looking for work of any kind. These were men that had lost everything, their mothers and fathers, wives, children and homes. I suggested we take some of these men on and give them shelter in return for labour. They could help to repair buildings and fences, and help plant seed for new crops and tend livestock. Once we were able, we could employ them on a paid basis. Walter Moelle was very surprised by my suggestion, raised his eyebrows and smiled, saying, 'What a wise head you have on those young shoulders of yours. That is a wonderful idea, Theresa.'

The American and British forces were constantly passing through our area, sometimes staying overnight in the fields, but they were mostly very good and we hardly knew they were there.

Firstly, we had to gather in what livestock we had still remaining from the fields and to dispose of the dead animals, which we did by burning and removing anything else that shouldn't be there. As I had suggested, we had recruited a group of good men. They were grateful for having somewhere to stay and for the work with which to keep their minds occupied. The barn was nice and watertight, so we turned this into a billet and put some mattresses in to ensure the boys would be comfortable in there.

We managed to round up chickens and cattle and a few pigs that had been roaming free in the fields, and we repaired the fences and enclosures. The animals had not fared too badly. Those that had not been machine-gunned by the Allied planes had been feeding on grass, which was a lot more than what we had. After much hard work, we were beginning to see the rewards. We had cows producing milk, hens for eggs, chickens for meat, and pigs that we hoped might breed to produce some pork. We were also growing potatoes and a small amount of wheat, from which we could then make flour for bread. In fact, it was like the war had never happened.

After a while the Moelles had one rule that we were expected to obey, and that was that we should not talk of the war. They were both of the opinion that the war was now over and we did not need to discuss it any further. I talked about the war with the labourers, or boys as I called them, who had all served in the *Wehrmacht*. We understood one another and we told our stories between us, usually in the barn in the evenings. They told of many horrors particularly in the east, and it was the only time I had talked about the war since its end. I heard one of them say that Hitler and Eva Braun had shot themselves in their bunker and that they chose to die like cowards, below ground.

I became quite friendly with the one young man who was to me quite beautiful. His name was Raif. Raif was from Berlin and had lived there all his life. He had lost all of his family in the bombing, so he had nothing at all. As he talked, his brown eyes would well up with tears. His emotions touched me and I wanted to hold him in my arms, but I couldn't in front of the other boys. I guess it must have become obvious I liked Raif, as the others would torment him every time I came to chat with him and the others. The attraction I felt towards Raif grew, and every time I saw him or was near him, I felt that butterfly feeling in my stomach.

I remember one day out in the fields, we were moving cows from one paddock to another. As we drove them through a small gateway, I slapped the one cow on its arse to try and make it move quicker. The cow gave me a sharp kick with one of its back legs, which caught me on the right shin. It was not that hard, but it bloody hurt. I dropped to the ground holding my leg. Raif and the other boys were all laughing at me.

I shouted, 'You blonde *arsch*' at Raif.

A blonde *arsch*, or blonde arse in English, was a slang term the Luftwaffe flak boys used for a homosexual.

Raif shouted back, 'I'm no blonde *arsch,*' and continued to laugh.

I grabbed the first thing I could, which I thought was a lump of dirt, but turned out to be cow shit. I threw it at Raif and hit him in the chest with it. The next thing he is looking around, finds cow shit, and throws some back at me. The shit is sloppy, cold and wet. I am on the ground trying to cover my face with my arms, when the other boys join in, and there we are all throwing cow shit at each other.

On returning to the farm, we had some explaining to do, as to why we were all covered in cow shit. Whenever Raif smoked a cigarette I would ask him for a couple of puffs, which seemed to amuse him. He would quickly look around to see if anyone was watching, then pass me the cigarette.

Things came to a head with Raif when I could hold back no more. I wanted him to know that I liked him, so I suggested that we meet at 11.00 pm one evening when everyone else would be in bed. It felt wrong having to sneak around, but the one evening we planned to meet. Everyone was in bed well before the planned meeting time. I threw on my coat, but decided shoes would make too much noise on the wooden flooring, so went barefoot, creeping out of my room, down the stairs, and through the kitchen, where the large fire still flickered. I turned the lock to the back door, crept out, and then ran down the lane to the stream at the bottom where we had arranged to meet. I waited for some minutes until I could see a figure in the dark coming down the lane. Raif appeared out of the darkness. We stood looking at one another dumbstruck – we did not know what to say.

Raif broke the silence by saying, 'Look Theresa, I really like you and every time I see you I just want to hold you and I want to give you a kiss.'

I smiled at him and asked, 'Have you ever kissed a girl before?' He replied 'yes.'

'Was she pretty?' I asked jealously.

'Not as pretty as you and it was a long time ago,' he replied shyly.

I had seen men and women kissing in the cinema, but had not kissed a boy before – well, not properly anyway. So, we stand there awkwardly for a few minutes and I decide to take Raif's hand and pull him towards me, fearing we would be standing there all night if I didn't.

We hugged for a time and then he looks into my eyes and says, 'Right, shut your eyes and open your mouth like you do when you yawn or something.'

So I do as he says, and he then presses his mouth around mine and we kiss, and I'm thinking, 'Oh my God, this is really nice!' In fact, I wanted to carry on, but we had to get back, and with quivering knees we both made our way back up the lane. Raif went back into the barn while I crept in through the back door, back through the kitchen and up the stairs where I jumped back into bed. My sisters were blissfully snoring away and I soon fell fast asleep with a happy heart.

We met like this a few more times and each meeting was more intense as our desires increased. I think Mother and Father had their suspicions of what was going on, but they knew I was not daft. Raif and I had fallen head over heels in love and the next time, I thought to myself, I would give myself to him properly.

We met again, only this time I told Raif to meet me in the barn at the far end, where grain and straw was stored. We met in the barn; there were few words and we undressed. I don't know, it just felt so nice to be so close to a man I loved and I wanted this so much. He muttered something about birth control and that we must not have any babies, well not yet anyway. Then he pulled out this small silver packet, which contained this rubber thing. I stepped back from him as I had never seen a condom before. I put my hands over my mouth and burst into hysterical laughter. He was stood there stooping like a monkey fumbling around with this piece of rubber. I was crying with laughter and all the time Raif was saying, 'Shh, be quiet as someone will hear.'

The laughter stopped as he kissed me again and we both lay down on the straw, when he told me he loved me, and that I was beautiful. He stroked my face and ran his fingers through my hair. Without a word, he then positioned himself above me kissing my mouth, neck and shoulders. It felt wonderful and it sent shivers through my whole body. He asked me if I was alright doing this and I whispered 'yes.'

I wrapped my legs around his back and asked him to be gentle. There was some initial discomfort for a few seconds as I had never had sex before, but it was like 'Oh my God!' This was what they called making love and here I was doing it – a funny thing to think when you're doing it.

We both climaxed fairly quickly, and afterwards Raif rolled off onto his back and said, 'You were beautiful.' We got up and got dressed. Raif had the condom held firmly in his fingers. He was looking around puzzled and wondering where he could throw it away.

I told him, 'No, don't you dare throw that thing away in here as someone will see it.'

I then began to laugh hysterically at him again. I told him to throw it away into the stream outside and we watched it as it bobbed away on the water.

We sat down beside the stream and Raif lit another cigarette. He took a few puffs and I pulled the cigarette from his lips and drew hard, taking back the soothing smoke before placing it back in his lips. We sat and talked for a few minutes. Raif held my hands and looked me in the eyes, and then he says, 'Look Theresa, I love you. I want to be with you and one day I would love to marry you. I want the blessing of your father and mother as we shouldn't be sneaking around all of the time.'

I reassured him and said that we should both speak with mother and father in the morning and discuss this with them. I had only just turned 18, but I was sure they would be alright; in fact, I imagined that they would be very happy, if a little shocked. We parted and I made my way back to the house, while Raif went back into the barn. I opened the door leading into the kitchen and carefully closed it. As I turned the lock, I noticed someone standing behind me – it was my father. He was stood with his arms folded and shaking his head at me. I was just about to say sorry to him and try to explain myself when he said, 'No, don't say anything, my child, just come and sit down.'

I sat down at the large kitchen table and he pulled up a chair beside me.

He said, 'Look, I know you have been seeing someone, one of the boys. Maybe you should bring the lucky fellow up to the house tomorrow evening and we can talk. I want you to be happy as I love you as my own, and you know that. But we must do these things properly. Now off to bed with you and no more sneaking around in the middle of the night.'

He kissed me on the cheek and made a sniffing noise, 'Have you been smoking those dreadful cigarettes again?' he asks, and I say, 'No Papa.'

He knew that I was lying, but he left it there and I went off to bed.

The next morning I got up early, got dressed, and went to the barn to find Raif. When I got there the other boys were busy washing themselves outside with water from the well. I asked, 'Where's Raif?' The boys replied he had got up before them and had gone, but they didn't know where he was. For a few minutes I began to panic. I didn't know where to start looking for him. I thought perhaps he had second thoughts about us being together, as we had talked about the previous night. I had visions of him leaving without a word. I just got down by the stream to look in the fields at the bottom of the farm, when I heard Raif shout, 'Hey, Theresa!'

I turned around and there he was coming up the lane, holding some wild flowers that he had been out picking.

'Here,' he says, 'I have picked some flowers for you. I love you so much, and do so more with each day. I don't want to have to be away from you.'

I explained what happened with Father when I was sneaking back into the house the night before, but assured Raif all would be fine. In the event, we had our little meeting with Mother and Father before dinner. Father gave Raif his blessing to marry me with a handshake, but he also laid down some rules.

'There is to be no more sneaking around at night time, do you both understand? We are still under occupation and I don't think it is safe for you both to be messing around outside at night.'

We agreed to his terms. We were both so excited. I know I was only young at the time, but war had matured us all, especially those of us who had witnessed the horrors of war first hand. We just smiled at each other and held hands across the table – everyone was happy. Father told Raif that he could remain on the farm, and when things permitted, he could have a share along with me. It would provide us with support and an income all our lives, should we so wish. Mother and Father would not be able to run the place forever, while my sisters all wanted to go to proper schools again and university, and maybe go on to see some of the world.

Our meeting was interrupted by my youngest sister, Heidi, who came bursting in through the door, almost out of breath, saying 'An American tank has just driven through one of the cattle fences we had not long repaired, and was now parked up in the field.'

We all got up and made our way down to the field behind the barn to see what was going on. When we got down there, the crew of the tank was busy filling up their water bottles from the stream.

One of our boys tried to reason with them saying, 'We have only just repaired this fence you know. Why didn't you just drive up the lane and through the other field where there is no fence?'

There was a violent response, as one of the Americans shouted, 'Fuck off, you Krauts!' He shouted in German and then another American just walked over and punched one of our boys in the face, knocking him over. Immediately both me and Raif stepped forward, but then I pushed Raif behind me and I was now face to face with the angry American.

'Well, go on then,' I shouted, 'Why don't you hit me?'

I think the German-speaking one told him what I was saying. I didn't care. I told him that I was not afraid of him, and I was certainly not afraid of any tank. I stood my ground until the Yank turned his head away and spat a stream of spit from the corner of his mouth. I could smell the reek of tobacco on his breath. There were a tense few minutes before the Americans climbed back aboard their tank, reversed, then drove back out the way they had come.

We were very angry about this, as we now had to repair the fence again where these idiots had driven through it. An hour later, a group of Americans arrived at the house. We thought we were all going to be arrested, or get beaten up or something, but it turned out one was an officer. He had been told of the incident earlier and had come to apologize. He asked if there was anything he could do. He even offered to have the men responsible sent back to repair the fence, but Father just said, 'No thank you, we don't need anything. All we need is to be left alone to get on with our lives.'

Father gave the officer some eggs as a gesture of good will. They shook hands and that was it. Incidents like this were rare, but they did happen. In all, however, things were nowhere near as bad here as they were in Berlin itself.

The following Sunday was a blissfully warm day. In the afternoon, me and Raif went out for a walk in the fields. I wanted to tell him more about myself, or rather my past. Walking hand in hand in the sunshine, I told him I had been conceived out of wedlock and when I was born I was put into the care of a religious order. My earliest recollections are those of being raised within this very strict, loveless Christian religious order. It was not idyllic; in fact, it was totally emotionless and no one seemed to really care about you. No one ever kissed you or gave you a reassuring hug. It seemed each day I was paying for sins that I had not committed. In fact, even when Walter and Greta Moelle adopted me, I still felt that I was paying for sins I hadn't committed, even well into my teens. As a result, I know I had been a very difficult child and had picked up bad language and had a bad temper.

I had joined the *Bund Deutscher Mädel* as I felt it would be an escape and maybe a way to find my own place in what was then Hitler's new society. I thought it was a good thing at first, but it was a good thing that soon became a nightmare.

Raif asked if I had ever tried to find my birth mother and father, and I told him, 'No, I had not, and I had no desire to ever do so. My family is here now and you are now part of it.'

I also told Raif all about what had happened in Berlin, and the part that I had played in the fighting, or rather defence. I also told him about my head injury and the nightmares that were plaguing me almost every night. Raif was very good. He just stopped and hugged and kissed me, telling me he loved and adored me and he understood everything clearly, which I knew anyway. He looked at the scar on the back of my head and I recall him saying, 'Those bastards probably fractured your skull.'

It was the summer of 1949 when we married in a small chapel, not far from our farm. It was only a very simple ceremony, but that did not matter to us; we were very much in love and adored each other. We loved my parent's farmhouse and having my parents around. Our bedroom was up in the attic, which was lovely, as we could lie in bed and listen to the wind and rain on a stormy winter's night, and listen to the owls on summer evenings. It was really beautiful and idyllic.

However, I felt we needed change. We spoke with the owner of the little farm I had worked on after my return home. He agreed he would rent it to us with a view to us buying it later on. I asked Raif about this and he thought it might help us both if we had a fresh start in a new home. The labourers could continue to help my mother and father and, because we were not taking a wage anymore, they could have more pay for themselves. We had a meeting with my parents and they were quite happy for us to go and start afresh, as they say, and they could visit us anytime they wanted as it was only a short distance away.

It was one day in the summer that Father said visitors had called at the farm, looking to speak with me personally. He had told them where me and Raif were living and that they should call the next day. The visitors turned out to be the family of the girl I was with in Berlin in April of 1945 during the fighting. I was not sure I would be able to tell them the horrible truth, to sit in front of them and tell them how their Anneliese was gang raped and murdered by Russian soldiers. I was dreading their visit, but my parents told me I owed it to them as it may give them some closure. At the time, I was not even aware that Anneliese's body had not been recovered. I recall the blow to the back of my head as I tried to help her, but nothing more.

When they arrived, I swallowed hard and wanted a cigarette, but I couldn't smoke in front of my family.

I agreed that I would meet them and speak to them on my own. When I had the first glimpse of Anneliese's mother, father, sister and brother as they arrived on our doorstep, I thought, my God, how am I going to do this. We sat down and Raif brought some tea in for us. We sipped some of the hot tea. I swallowed hard and I began to recount what happened that day when the Russians began to enter the city.

Recalling how we had been fighting and that I had destroyed a tank with a *panzerfaust* [anti-tank weapon], I then told them that the Russians began to appear from everywhere. If you ran, they would fire at you, and the dreadful things they were doing to girls and women they captured. I told them what happened to Anneliese and me after I tried to get the Russian soldiers off her.

Telling Anneliese's family all of these things really upset me, and by the end of our meeting, we were all sobbing our hearts out. What hurt me most was that her family said that her body was never found. Under the circumstances, I can see why. There was so much artillery fire coming in and tanks moving around, and bodies became buried deep under rubble. In many cases, bodies just vanished in all of this or became totally unrecognizable. Her father said he had begged her to stay home and not join the Hitler Youths fighting in the city, but she would not listen and she ran away. I did not know what to say to them other than that I was sorry.

I bid Anneliese's family farewell, but I did ask them to feel free to visit us again if they wanted to. I never saw or heard from them again after this meeting. When they left, Raif spent some time consoling me. I couldn't stop crying as it really hurt having to relate that horrible ordeal again. That night, the nightmares returned, only with an increase in their violence. Raif, as usual, was awake and waiting for me to wake up, as I was thrashing around and shouting so much. I woke in a hot sweat and fighting to get my breath, and I began to cry again. Raif was holding me and trying to wipe away the droplets of sweat that were running down my face. He would say, 'It's okay, it's okay, it's over now' and he would be hugging me, trying to reassure me.

We went downstairs into the kitchen and he sat with me as I drank a cup of hot tea with sugar. I was shaking like a leaf, so Raif had to hold the teacup to my mouth. Even with his help, the tea ran down my chin. It took almost three quarters of an hour for the shaking to subside.

I asked Raif, 'Darling, please, I need a cigarette,' and we went outside where I smoked two cigarettes, one after the other.

Raif was worried about me, but back then the condition I was suffering from, and had continued to suffer from into my old age, was not recognized. Only in recent years has post-traumatic stress disorder been addressed and treated, usually in soldiers returning from combat. The nightmares were something I would have to learn to live with and I coped with them with my Raif's support. He had fought too and seen some terrible things. I had never forgotten that and he had his own nightmares, but these were not very often, thankfully. Things on the farm were going really well and we were supplying small amounts of milk, eggs and meat locally, and were expanding further. We were making a living and money, which meant that we could pay our labourers a decent wage from the money we made. Me and Raif had been trying for a baby for some time. The one morning I awoke feeling really ill and was sick. There was no other explanation for this sickness other than the fact that I must be pregnant. The doctor visited me one afternoon and examined me, and with a further appointment at a hospital, confirmed I was now expecting our first child. We were overjoyed, but it meant I would have to give up heavy work for the time being, which I did not mind as I was feeling so tired.

Our first baby was a beautiful 7lb 8oz healthy boy we named Christopher. We had another child, a daughter, two years later, and we named her Isabelle. We did not have any more children, though traditionally, German families were large, with many children.

We saw the world change and relations between Russia and the West deteriorate. We saw the Berlin Airlift and we saw the Berlin Wall. We lived in fear of a nuclear war right on our doorstep, yet we also lived to see the collapse of Communist Russia and that Berlin Wall torn down – well some of us anyway.

The world is still far from at peace though, isn't it? Everyone asks about the death camps and did I hate Jews and things like that. To be honest, I never really met many Jews, and could not really understand what it was that Hitler hated about them so much. The Nazi system instilled hatred in young children and young children are easy to influence. If you tell them that man over there is the bogey man, stay away from him, nine out of ten of them will heed that warning and that was what it was like. Those with a direct involvement have no excuses, but whether we followed blindly or with our eyes wide open, we have to accept responsibility for the murders committed under the National Socialist regime, it is as simple as that.

My children will not carry that burden of guilt as they are the new generation. There are those still looking to blame, but I say, don't blame the new generation of Germans, only blame us if you must. I did not fight for Hitler or Nazism. I was there in Berlin fighting for the people: the women, the old men, the children, the babies and my friends.

If you are faced with a choice that says, okay, let this enemy into your city and they will rape the women and children and kill young and old men alike. Alternatively, you can fight them and maybe you will kill that many, that the others might give up and go away. What choice do you make, especially if you are trapped and have nowhere to run? I hope that no one has to make that kind of decision in their lives, but, like I have said, the world is still an uncertain place. People are still fighting and dying, innocent people mainly, and that will never change, will it?'

Theresa's husband, Raif, died in 1980. As one can imagine, this was a painful episode in her life, as they had spent so many hard yet rewarding years together. Theresa's children took over the small farming business after their father's death, allowing their mother to enjoy a peaceful retirement. Even in her retirement, Theresa continued to lead a very active lifestyle, which included horse-riding and walking with her grandchildren.

My last meeting with Theresa, back in 2005, was a memorable one, yet both of us felt that this occasion would be the last time we would ever see one another – we did not know why, it was just a mutual feeling. It was also strange that, for the first time, we did not talk much about the war. Much of the conversation was focussed upon the breakdown of my own eighteen-year relationship.

Theresa, always trying to be cheerful, quipped, 'If I was 40 years or so younger, you would certainly not be sitting here alone!'

Before we parted, Theresa gave me a photograph of herself taken while relaxing in the fields near her home in 1944. She also placed in my hand perhaps the only memento she had of her battle in Berlin as a young girl. It was a brass 7.62mm Russian rifle cartridge case. She explained that she picked this up shortly before her return home, and that she wanted me to have it. Before parting, she gave me a hug. We exchanged a customary kiss on the cheek as I wished her a safe journey back home, reassuring her that I would be in touch soon. I watched her get on her coach, waving her off until it disappeared from view.

It was just two weeks later that I received the sad news, via an email from daughter Isabelle that her mother had passed away peacefully in her sleep one evening. To me, she was a wonderful character, who was honest, straight speaking and caring. I consider myself honoured to have known her and to have shared so much valuable time with her. I, along with her family, will certainly never forget her.

One quote she made that I felt compelled to include here, was one that she made to a young neo-Nazi skinhead who had heard that a former BDM girl was coming to give a talk at a school near her home. Theresa recalled:

> I was invited along to the school to take part in a talk back in 1994 that dealt with tolerance, humanity and understanding. When I came out, there were these young skinhead boys hanging around outside. One of them strides up to me and shouts, '*Sieg Heil*!' and he is giving me the Nazi salute.
>
> He says to me, 'You were a hero.
>
> I replied to him, 'and you, my boy, are a bloody fool. I was no hero – I was a victim!' They didn't know what to say after that. People were laughing at them, but it served them right.

4
Flight Through the Sewers

Dora Brunninghausen, who turned 22 years old as Berlin began to fall, has a unique perspective on the battle for the city. She had volunteered in her own words 'to help defend the city and its people'.

Dora had been working as a clerical assistant for an NSDAP [Nazi party] office in the city. The round-the-clock bombing campaign, coupled with the approaching Allies from the west and the Russians from the east soon, curtailed any notion of normality in Berlin. Dora recalls:

> With the continuous bombing, I could not continue with my daily job of two years as an office clerk. It was impossible to work in any normal context. The offices were soon moved below ground into a specially prepared bunker, where we could work in safety. Before our transfer to the bunker, we had to run to the air-raid shelter, leaving all of our work and documents up in the offices. This happened on a daily basis and throughout the day. Our office took a hit from a bomb on one occasion, but luckily no one was hurt as we were not in the building. After that, the decision was made to go below ground.
>
> My work changed from the usual administrative duties to helping with the production of propaganda material. I recall numerous visits from Josef Goebbels, who was minister in charge of propaganda. He would call in to have a look at the work we had produced. He would thumb through the papers at my desk, his hand under his chin deep in thought. He always appeared jovial and optimistic and would say things like, 'Yes, this is excellent … this will do the job.'
>
> He once asked me if I would like to join him for dinner. He said to me, 'When this war is over, and we have secured a great victory, you must permit me to take you to dinner. I wish to thank you for all of your endeavours.'

He then kissed my hand, smiled, and off he went with great enthusiasm. We all knew of his reputation for wining and dining women into bed, so in a way I hoped he would forget about it.

As history now tells us, the great victory he was so enthused about did not happen. Goebbels and his wife Magda would poison their six children then kill themselves. I heard all about it after the war as some friends confirmed everything for me. The charred corpses of Goebbels and his wife were soon discovered and were photographed in all their gruesome glory.

We knew that the Russians were about to launch a full-scale assault on Berlin. Our forces had failed to stop them at the Seelowe Heights, and all we could do now was prepare for the defence of the city. The *Volkssturm* had been mobilized, and what forces we had available in the city, prepared numerous defensive positions. Vehicles were used as barricades, and alleyways used as ambush points along with cellars and bombed-out buildings. I was competent with weapons, as I had been taught basic marksmanship with a rifle and how to throw grenades. I had learned this just before leaving the BDM. In the event of the mobilization being called, I offered to join the Werewolves.

The Werewolves were merely groups of Hitler Youths – both boys and girls – who had been taught guerrilla warfare and sabotage tactics. A Werewolf could operate as a single individual or as a group, it did not matter. Most of the girls operating as Werewolves were former BDM leaders in their twenties. There were much younger girls who joined in with the Werewolves, though.

There were no joining criteria by the last stages of the war – if you wanted to fight you found a weapon and you joined in. My parents were beside themselves with worry and we shared heated words before I saw them for the last time until the end of the war. They did not want me to join any fighting. My mother was in tears and wailed, 'In God's name, let the soldiers fight, that's their job, not yours. I don't want to lose my child in this dammed war.' I tried to explain to them that we would have to fight anyway, as the Russians will show us no mercy for what our people had done to them. I felt at the time that I had no choice and that we needed every available person to fight and keep them out of the city. I begged Mother and Father to go down to one of the air-raid shelters and stay there. They would be safer there than inside our now heavily damaged home. Reluctantly, they left, but only after I told them some of the things that had been going on in Warsaw. German families were being massacred by Russian forces, and raped and murdered in revenge for what German forces had done in the east. I was frightened, but I was also determined to survive any way possible.

I took some clothes from our home. I put on a shirt, some work trousers, two wool jumpers and a winter coat, and attached one of my father's leather belts around my waist. I pulled on my boots and said a farewell to my parents, telling them that, God willing, I would see them again later.

I then set off for the mobilization point to collect a weapon and take orders of where I was to go. There was a sensation of surrealism about the city. I can't explain, but it was just a weird kind of feeling that all this was not really happening. As if it was all a bad dream. We had been convinced over the years within our Hitler Youth organizations, that this would never happen. No enemy would ever fly over the Reich capital and no enemy soldier would set foot on Reich soil.

As you will be aware, Berlin was bombed almost into oblivion. The Soviets began to shell the city as soon as their artillery was in range. The noise became incessant, to the point that people were sometimes driven mad by the constant explosions. I recall an old man running past us up a street, waving his arms and shouting 'mercy, mercy!'

We [the Werewolves] were instructed to form into groups and join the defences in the city. It did not matter where you went, as long as you took a weapon and had the intention of killing Russians. A small group of six of us was led by a soldier of the SS Charlemagne Division. He talked very little. He had an abrupt attitude and just barked orders at us.

'We're going here, we're going there, do this, do that!' etc.

Central Berlin came under very heavy bombardment from the Soviet guns. You had to crawl along the ground, weaving your way through demolished buildings, through sewers and over rotting corpses. If you didn't, you would have almost certainly been hit by shrapnel. I could hear shrapnel ricochet off walls above me, spraying me with dust in the process. We found a position beneath a partially collapsed building, which offered cover and safety. We then checked our weapons and waited for the enemy to come. We knew they would come, it was just a matter of time.

It's funny the things you think about in such situations. Will I ever see Mother and Father again? What will happen if we lose this battle? God, I'm hungry … God, I'm thirsty. We are all afraid of the unknown, apart from the SS soldier who is as ambivalent as ever. He doesn't speak. Even now, he just looks forward, clutching his rifle, waiting to kill I guess. We are afraid to talk in case he scolds us for doing so. But we gesture to one another with hand signals, 'are you okay?' and 'yes, I am fine.'

I almost drift off to sleep in my thoughts, and I dream I am sitting by a river. It is summertime, so peaceful, with the soft sounds of water and of birds singing up in the trees. The serenity of dreams were soon shattered by the war as the SS man starts shouting hysterically, 'Fucking bastards … there they are … fucking shoot … shoot!'

Gathering my senses, I clear my eyes and see enemy coming through. They are probably only 250ft away from us. We fire our shots into them. I see some of them drop down dead. The SS soldier throws a stick-bomb over, and we hear it explode seconds after. We come under heavy rifle and submachine-gun fire.

The SS man is shot through the forehead. He staggers a few yards, before falling backwards like a drunken man. He is dead before he hits the ground, yet his legs refuse to acknowledge this. His eyes are wide open and staring, as if he is still alive. In the confusion, we scatter and I become separated with one of our boys. He shouts at me, 'For God's sake, run and stay close … follow me and don't lose your weapon!'

In blind panic I follow, yet I keep stumbling on the rubble. Sharp stones slice into my knees and shins. We squeeze through small holes in the sides of buildings and then come to a courtyard. The boy lifts up a circular drain cover on the ground and says, 'Quick, get down here. Just hold onto the ladder and move as quickly as you can.'

I hand him my rifle and begin to climb down into the darkness below. The boy then drops down onto the ladder, pulling the cover back over the hole. I look around as he makes his way down the ladder. I realize that we are below the city and we are in the sewers. The smell then hits you and your eyes contest with the darkness, desperately trying to gauge your surroundings. The boy says his name is Karl and that he is 14 years old. Karl insists we will be safer down here in the sewers than up above ground.

I ask him, 'Will the Soviets come down here, do you think?'

To which he replies, 'Yes, they probably will, I'm not sure, but if they do, we can hit and run and hide down here.'

I continue by telling him he has big plans for such a little man. He was annoyed by my words, saying, 'I am not a little man!'

Either way, and despite a six-year age difference, we will have to learn to get along and try to get back to our lines.

As we travel deeper into the sewer system, the smell becomes increasingly worse. Karl says we must cover our mouths and noses with pieces of clothing, or anything, as the gas down here can be deadly. Your eyes become accustomed to the dark to an extent, but the deeper we go the harder it is to see anything. Karl stops and takes something out of his pocket. He has a candle and lights it and we can now see around us. The candlelight flickers, and shadows dance around the walls. It makes me nervous, as it would be hard to distinguish a waiting enemy from a shadow down here. The damp walls, the stream of water to our side, and the pathway snake off into the gloom ahead.

We move on and hear the rumble of the war above us. Berlin's sewer system is not that deep below the ground, so we keep as quiet as we can. There are rats down here and I don't particularly like rats.

Karl says, 'It's not the rats that you have to be worried about down here. If it rains, we could be drowned by flood water – we must be vigilant.' he says.

We see something floating in the water, and as Karl moves the candle closer, we can see it is a rotting corpse, crawling with maggots. We can't tell whether it's a man or a woman. There are many corpses down here, or parts of them, and the rats are eating the corpses.

I begin to tire, so we agree to find somewhere to rest up. We don't know what time of day it is and can only guess. We find somewhere where we can actually sit down. Karl pulls two lumps of stale bread from his pocket, offering me one. I thank him, and am so hungry, that I eat the bread, despite the fact that it is actually disgusting. The bread is beyond stale and takes much effort to break with your teeth. As I eat the bread, I see things moving down by my side and soon realize that they are rats fighting over the crumbs of bread I am dropping. They show no fear whatsoever. Two of them are locked into a battle for a small piece of my bread. They squeak and wrestle and tumble into the filth below. The rats are our constant companions as we try to rest. These rats have grown fat feeding on rotting human flesh.

The cold seeps into your skin and then your bones, along with the damp. Karl is shivering and huddles ever closer to me. In the end, I put my arms around him and we keep as warm as we can. We have to make sure our weapons are close to hand at all times, and uneasy sleep descends.

We are woken by odd sounds and voices. The voices are down in the sewer, but we can't see anyone, or tell which direction the voices are coming from. We are ready with our rifles when the dull yellow glow of a torch lights the tunnel behind us. Are they Germans or Russians? We can't just fire on them without knowing, can we? If we startle them, they may kill us accidentally if they are Germans. What do we do? Listening intently to the voices as they grow nearer, we soon understand these are not Germans, they are Russians.

Karl whispers, 'I will aim at the one with the torch. I will shoot, then we run like hell. We can't see properly to shoot them all down here, so when I fire, run and don't stop. Go and find a way out.'

Before the yellow beam can hit us, Karl squeezes the trigger of his Mauser. There is an almighty crack that echoes down the tunnel. The gunshot is deafening, but the Soviet holding the torch crashes into the putrid water dead, his light extinguished in the process. I run with eyes straining to ensure I don't fall off the path and into the stream of filth just feet away. I hear gunshots behind me. Flashes light up the tunnel enough for me to see my way forwards. I am running, but where am I running to? Is Karl still behind me? Fear and panic set in and you have to pull yourself together, clear your mind, and try to think logically.

All seems silent behind me now there are no more gunshots or flashes. I decide to keep going and, as the darkness increases, I use my hands to feel my way along the wall. There has to be an access point somewhere here. That is what I will look for. Finally, I discover an alcove in the wall where there is a metal service ladder against the wall. I decide to wait for a few minutes to see if Karl is behind me somewhere. I hear something coming along the tunnel and I ready the rifle into my shoulder. The noises were shuffling noises and definitely not rats.

I shout, 'Karl, is that you? Who is there ... show yourself'

There is no answer, but I know I am not alone.

I shout again, 'Who is there? God damn you.'

I hear peculiar grunting noises and waste no further time. I aim my rifle to where I heard the noise and fire a shot. In the flash, I see for just a split second the heavily clad, bearded figure of a Soviet soldier with some kind of gun in his hand. There is the crash of water as he falls into the stream of sewage. That was the first and last time I had ever killed anyone. I sling the rifle around my shoulder and, with a pounding heart, I climb the ladder. There is still much noise above and I'm worried as to what will happen. There is a cover over the exit to the shaft, which is 15ft up the ladder. I am not sure if I will be able to move the metal cover. I hold onto the ladder with one hand and push it as hard as I can with the other. The cover slowly lifts, revealing a shaft of daylight. I look out through the gap and there is no one around. With one hard push I lift the lid and it falls back with a loud clatter against the ground. I climb out and there are explosions all around – lots of smoke and dust.

The air feels warmer compared to that of the sewer and its scent somewhat sweeter than that of faeces and dead bodies. The problem is, I don't know exactly where I am. I can see no discernible landmarks and I cannot stay where I am for long. I stay low to the ground, climbing piles of rubble that were once buildings. I see the rotting remains of a human arm sticking out from the mass of stone. The strangely sweet scent of decaying human flesh meets the nostrils. There must be many bodies buried in this rubble.

A shell lands nearby, the blast throwing up rocks and masonry, hurling it into the air. I lie flat and cover my head as best as I can. I feel earth and small stones falling on my back and legs. I look around and can just about make out the top of the Tiergarten flak tower. If I can get there, it will be safer than being here. There are no people around, just the incessant noise of artillery and the occasional crack of 20mm cannon fire. Staying as low to the ground as I can, I make my way towards the flak tower. Again, I feel stone, glass and metal cut into my legs, as at times I am forced to crawl along the ground. My hands are lacerated and covered in drying blood. The pain does not register as the adrenaline pushes me forward. I think of Karl, the young kid back in the sewer. Was he able to escape or was he killed? Either way, if it wasn't for him I would have probably been either captured or killed. Neither would have been good for me.

After what seemed an eternity of pain, I reached the flak tower. I was spotted and four people came out and dragged me inside to safety. I was shocked to find many civilians inside the tower. It was a formidable structure and could withstand attack from most artillery the Soviets had at the time. It was many people's goal to get to this place, as it was probably the safest building in the city.

My legs were in a terrible state, many of the cuts now septic. These had to be cleaned up properly to prevent further infection. I was brought some lotion and knew that I would have to squeeze out the puss from the wounds. I gritted my teeth and squeezed out the thick yellow-green fluid. I cleaned the wounds as best as I could, then a middle-aged woman helped to dress them. My hands were in a poor state too, covered in septic cuts. The woman helped clean my hands and then she bandaged them for me.

One of the other women asked me how I made it here. I told her and she said, 'You are one very lucky girl. Many soldiers would have died trying to do what you have done.'

It was April 30th, if I recall correctly, that some form of surrender was offered by the Soviets. The only reason for this was the fact that they could not destroy the tower.

They tried air attacks and even brought in 203mm-calibre artillery guns in an attempt to destroy the tower, but to no avail.

The garrison commander of the German soldiers in the tower negotiated the surrender. The surrender of the tower and its occupants would take place at midnight. This surrender was just a trick to give the soldiers in the tower enough time to make their escape. This information we learned afterwards.

Shortly before midnight, the soldiers left the tower, disappearing into the darkness. Many civilians followed them, but what was the point of trying to break out when the Soviet forces were everywhere. We moved out of the tower a short distance to another small building that had been partly demolished. There we waited for the Soviets to come. When they appeared, they began to ask questions like 'where are the soldiers?' We told them we didn't know where they had gone, just that they had left the tower shortly before midnight. We were searched and it was a good job I left the rifle behind in the tower. I had ammunition in my pockets, which I took and dropped behind my back. This did not go unnoticed, and in seconds I was thrown to the ground with this Soviet soldier sat on top of me.

'What were you doing with ammunition in your hands?' he shouts, putting one hand around my neck.

I tell him I don't know how they got there, but I know they are suspicious of me. The other civilians just stand watching, powerless to help when one young man says, 'Why don't you get off her and leave her alone. She can't do you any harm as she has no weapons.'

As was the usual response, the man was beaten up. The Russian probably did not even understand what he had said, but I think he guessed from the tone of voice. The Russian got off me and I was dragged off away from the others for questioning.

The questioning was accompanied by the usual threats of death or torture. I told them that I found the coat and took it because I was cold, and that I did not notice it had bullets in the one pocket. They asked where I found the coat and I replied 'in the tower.'

This seemed to satisfy them and they were quite calm after that. In fact, the one officer was quite nice to me and said, 'They say we are beasts, that we are not human, but we are. You could have been shot today but you were not.'

He asked if I have any family and I told him I had a mother and father in the city, but didn't know where they were as we got separated. He then asked if I had a husband or boyfriend. I told him I hadn't. His German was excellent. The only thing that betrayed him was that Slavic twang that they all had to their voices. Had they known the truth I would have probably been shot, or even raped and then shot? Either way it was a miracle I was not sexually attacked, as many German women suffered that fate.

The officer then said he would personally escort me and place me back with the other civilians. I would be held with them until order was restored in the city. Before he left, he did something which I consider totally odd. He lifted my bandaged hand, kissed it and said, 'I hope you find your mother and father soon, and good luck. If you ever need my help just ask for Lieutenant Ziernowski.' He smiled and that was the last time I ever saw him. I was reunited with Mother and Father two long months later.

After the war, in the 1950s I did try to find that Russian officer. I was not sure what I wanted to say to him, but just wanted to let him know I was alright. I sent two letters to the Soviet authority in the east of Berlin, but I received no reply. I also tried to find out who Karl was, as I never knew what the kid's surname was. Do you know, I spent months trying to find out, but it was like he never existed at all. My son tried sourcing information on his computer and we made enquiries to the *Rathaus* [mayoral authority] in Berlin. We could find no trace of him at all. Many records are incomplete, even today. I recall his face and his image still lives in my memories today. Maybe he got away, but not knowing is the worst thing.

My life was not too bad after the war. Western Germany was slowly reorganized and steadily regained its basic infrastructure. I later resumed employment as a clerk, but under far different circumstances. I have lived a happy life with few bad memories. I know I was one of what was known as the Werewolves. I killed a man, I can't deny that. Had I not shot that man dead in the sewer, he would have killed me or done maybe worse things, I don't know. I do feel regret about it now, as I do about many things in my past. I met my husband and we settled down to life, having just the one child, a son. When my son was born, I had never really thought of a name. But then I reflected back to Berlin and the escape down through the sewers while lying in my bed.

My husband asked, 'What are we going to name our fine boy then?'

I looked up at him and replied, 'Karl, we will name him Karl.'

5

Blood and Dust

During the compiling of research material for *Hitler's Girls: Doves Amongst Eagles*, I received an email from one of Kirsten Eckermann's old friends. Her story is particularly powerful, so I felt compelled to include it in this volume.

Kirsten had known Wiener Katte for some years. They had been more or less neighbours in Berlin, until Wiener and her family moved away to Aachen following a family bereavement. Both girls had been in the same BDM troop, remaining in touch by letter after Wiener moved out of Berlin. Aachen, as explained in the first volume, was the first German city to be captured by the Allies. The fighting that took place there was some of the bloodiest of the Second World War. It is a battle that has fascinated military historians ever since. Wiener's account is a rare view, requiring a strong stomach to read some of her words:

> I was 15, but felt like I was going 50 at that time. I felt hungry, old and tired, and I was just sick of the war. We had endured bombing and you get used to bombs. You don't always get used to death. Seeing death every single day, some say, desensitizes you to it all, but it doesn't always.
>
> As the Americans drew ever nearer to Aachen, the aerial bombings increased. We were attacked from the air for days on end. Once the bombers left, the American artillery started. For some weeks previous, I had been assigned to work with a medical team. I had always been very good at first aid and had been given advanced training. I could treat most things, from cuts, gunshot and stab wounds, to broken limbs. How do I begin to describe it all to you?
>
> I knew Aachen well, as when we moved from Berlin it became my home. I made many new friends there, and from my friends I soon knew all the alleyways and all the shortcuts around the city like most kids did. When

war came, this local knowledge would prove useful when being sent out on various duties. Many posts for treating the injured were set up around the city. Ours was set up in an abandoned beer house in one of the side streets near the city centre. We had been preparing the post for some weeks and had built up what we thought were adequate supplies of morphine, bandages and medicines. The upper part of the beer house was where the injured would be taken after treatment until they could be transported out. The lower rooms were to be used as a makeshift surgeon's quarter and morgue. A large red cross was painted on the roof in the hope that no enemy aircraft would bomb the post. Some voiced their concerns at this, arguing that it may encourage the enemy to bombard the building.

We were told that any walking wounded, who could still throw grenades or fire a weapon, after treatment would have to re-join the defences. Anyone refusing to do this duty could face being shot as a traitor. Many civilians had fled the city before the battle, but there were many thousands still remaining. A number of around 5,000 *Volkssturm* were said to be in the city, but I would say there may have been more than this figure. There were many girl and boy Hitler Youths ready to take an active role in the defence. Just how many there were I cannot say, but quite a lot. Many had volunteered of their own free will to leave their families and help defend the city with the soldiers. They knew exactly what they had to do.

I was spared any combat role because they wanted me to assist the medical teams, as I was highly proficient at this task. I was not too bad when it came to seeing blood and things. They didn't want girls who would faint or be vomiting all the time at the first sight of blood. I knew in my heart that what was coming was not going to be pleasant. I would see terrible things; I knew that and I prepared myself mentally for it. There were weapons in the beer house that we would use, only if we really had to, but, unless instructed, we were not to touch them.

I remember the many heavy air raids over the years. Yes, they were very frightening, as some were particularly heavy attacks. I will never forget the rumble of thousands of bombers in the sky above, the whistle of the falling bombs, the explosions, the screaming, the fire, the death, the mutilated bodies, and the continuous anti-aircraft fire.

War is the stuff of nightmares. There is no glory whatsoever in it. Aachen had been subjected to heavy aerial bombing prior to the American attack. All you could do was go below ground in the shelters and wait for the all clear. The American artillery fire was just as heavy and intense. The shells came in thick salvos in a kind of rolling barrage. Clusters of exploding shells would creep towards you, forcing you to take cover. Once in a hole or inside a building, you then closed your eyes, held your ears, and prayed that a shell did not land on you. I also learned that when you covered your ears, you must open your mouth, as this helped to equalize the pressure during the blast. If you didn't do this, your eardrums could burst.

Artillery was something I came to fear more than the bombs. Whenever we went out and tried to move around the city, from nowhere artillery fire would come in. Artillery shells would come in so fast, that many had little time to take cover. I recall soldiers digging holes in the ground and offering to help them.

The one said to me, 'Why do you want to help us? We are digging holes that have to be deep enough for us to stand up in. I can't help but feel that we are all digging our own graves. Do you want to help dig yours too?'

The soldiers often said things like that, but then they were probably afraid or missing their families. After a while, you could tune your senses to artillery shells, and you could tell if you needed to take cover or whether it was safe to keep going. The shells that landed nearest to you were often the ones that you did not hear until it was too late. These made a loud rushing sound as they came in. You would hear this noise and a split second later the explosion would come. The danger came from the blast wave, incendiary effects and the shrapnel. Bombs killed sometimes without leaving a mark on the victim, but artillery shells caused devastating injuries. Many who should have survived died from shock. A person can survive losing an arm or a leg quite easily if they are treated rapidly and correctly. In some cases, the damage looks far more extensive than it actually is. The victim sees this then assumes the worst, then goes into shock and sometimes dies.

Despite the air attacks which occurred from 2 October, many of the military defences around the city were left intact. There were many SS soldiers in the city. The SS were confident that they could defend their positions and showed a different attitude to other soldiers. The SS were far more aggressive. One said, 'Let them come, they will soon be going home to their mothers in wooden boxes.'

Before the fighting really began, I wished some of my BDM friends well and to take care, and we would see each other again soon. We hugged each other and I watched them disappear into the gloom – some were carrying weapons. I say gloom because thick smoke hung over the city, which even in broad daylight made it seem almost dark. We could hear the fighting taking place in the form of machine-gun and rifle fire, and then the artillery started to come in again.

I was sent out quite a number of times to take messages and to collect more supply items. My knowledge of the city meant I could easily use shortcuts to get around, and take cover where necessary. When the fighting did start, the first victims of shell fire began to trickle in. Several were helped into our post by other soldiers, who dropped them off then ran back to the fighting. Soon men were being brought in with horrific injuries. Some had arms or legs blown off or pieces of their heads missing. Some come in with their intestines spilling out onto the floor. You wonder how they made it this far. The director, as we called him, shouted across to me, 'You come over here and take hold of this!' He handed me the tourniquet tied around this young German soldier's left leg.

'Pull it as tight as you can Fraulein, and I do mean tight. You must keep it tight to stem the bleeding, alright?'

I looked at him and nodded in acknowledgement, pulling as hard as I could on the tourniquet. The injured soldier's left leg was a mess, looking as if it had been shredded in a meat mincer. Nothing below the knee could have been saved. The soldier moaned and mumbled incoherently as he was pumped with morphine. The damaged portion of leg was wrenched down flat onto the makeshift operating table, making a horrible crunching sound. I could see splinters of bone in the gore. The medic doing the surgery then came over and examined the man's badly shredded leg. He says, 'This has got to come off.'

In just seconds, he runs his scalpel blade around the circumference of the injured man's leg. He then cuts just below the knee with a bone saw. He saws right through the bone and the mangled leg comes away. The leg is literally thrown to one of the orderlies with the words, 'He will not be needing this back, now get rid of it.'

He shouts, 'Keep that tourniquet tight, Fraulein!'

He is now working frantically, removing and pulling bits of skin and flesh into place. Another medic comes across and begins to stitch. My fingers are beginning to turn white as I maintain my grip on the tourniquet. In a few minutes the procedure is over. The medic tells me to release the tourniquet, so I let it go. The soldier's stump of a leg is bandaged and he is taken away to hopefully recover.

After this, I am feeling a little sick and I ask to go outside for a minute. I stand by the door, but instead of blue skies and fresh air, all there is, is smoke. I gulp in the putrid air, the smell of which is of corpses, blood and smoke. I look down on the ground and all I see is blood and dust.

'*Blut und staub willkommen in Aachen.*' [blood and dust, welcome to Aachen] I whisper under my breath.

More and more soldiers are brought in and with them some *Volkssturm*. I am called back inside to help again.

'Fraulein, get me bandages, more bandages,' another medic calls out to me.

My hands and my legs are trembling and I fight to control it. I hand the bandages to the medic who begins to work on a man's head wound. Blood is still pouring down the man's face, but the wound is nothing serious. Other soldiers come in, covered in blood, and I have the job of dealing with them. I clean their wounds and check to see how bad they are. If they are not serious, I clean and bandage them up. The men are then told to report back for duty immediately. The soldiers then stagger out of the door, disappearing into the gloom.

One young soldier has an injured arm. He is in terrible pain, and the only way I can get at the wound is by cutting off the sleeve of his jacket. There is a piece of bone sticking out from the forearm, an open fracture. I clean the area of the wound as best as I can and bandage the whole forearm. As I work on him, he just looks at me.

He then asks, 'What are you doing here? You shouldn't be here. You should be with your family, not in this hell.'

I say to him, 'I am here because I want to be here. I can't hide away like a frightened rabbit doing nothing.'

He asks me my age and things like that. The kind of coffee-shop small talk I would later encounter when boys tried to ask me to go out with them.

I shout to the director that he has an open fracture of the right arm. The arm is bandaged and placed in a sling. The arm will need surgery, but until this can be done, he must wait. The problem is there are now so many cases waiting for surgery that there is no room. They take their chances hiding in nearby buildings until they can be dealt with. No one can be transported out as it is too dangerous.

One *Volkssturm* man has a gunshot wound to his head. The bullet has torn away a chunk of skin along with a piece of skull from the top of the man's head. The chunk of skin hangs loosely to the side of his head, a portion of bloody brain clearly visible. He was conscious when brought in, but quickly dies on the table. The doctor shouts for the body to be removed. The body is taken down to the cellar, which is being used to store the dead.

We are soon overwhelmed as children are brought in. I see a little boy with both legs blown off. Frantic efforts are made to save his life, but nothing can be done. He dies in his mother's arms. The mother had carried his body under fire for a quarter of a mile to our post. She is covered in her son's blood and she is crying out, '*warum? warum?*' [why? why?]

She is taken out of the post. I feel tears running down my face and wipe them away with my sleeve. The doctor puts a hand on my shoulder and asks me, 'Fraulein, *bist du in ordung?*' [girl, are you alright?].

I say, '*Ja, mir geht es gut.*' [Yes, I am fine].

The doctor gives orders to treat only the non-seriously injured from now on, and that we have no choice and no time. Another distraught woman comes in screaming with her child in her arms. The child is young, maybe 5 years old, and it has a five inch long piece of shrapnel lodged in its head. The steel shell splinter has entered through the right side of the baby's head just above the ear. The child is a bluey pale colour and quite lifeless, and when examined, has already bled out [bled to death]. The woman is totally distraught and hysterical. One of the medics shouts, 'For God's sake, deal with her and get her out of here.'

I gently talk to her and manage to coax the woman into handing me the body of her child. I write down the mother and child's names, then I take the child's body down into the cellar. I carefully place her little body down on the stone floor. For a minute or so I am knelt down beside the child's body, thinking to myself 'what life has this little one had, it has not really lived at all, has it?'

I stroke the tiny forehead with my hand and then make my way up the cold, stone steps out of the cellar. I sit with the dead child's mother, holding her hands trying to comfort her. Then I am called away as there is still so many people to have to deal with.

There is much commotion and, as instructed, the very badly injured are now left where they fall at the mercy of the artillery. I recall what my dear father said to me as I became a BDM: 'It is all very well selling your soul to the devil my girl. But will you have the funds to buy it back when all of this is over?'

He didn't agree with me joining the BDM and was dead against it, but events were beyond his control. I now began to understand the meaning of what he said to me. I felt as if I had sold my soul to the devil, and here I was in hell itself.

The days and nights blurred into one another – I would try to snatch sleep where possible. I would be so tired, yet found it difficult to sleep. Lack of sleep soon affects you in many ways. You cannot think as quickly and rationally and it slows down your reactions.

Food was becoming scarce. We existed on whatever we could find, and we also ate meat from dead cats and dogs. I heard stories of people even eating rats, mice and birds, if they could catch them. Small birds could easily be caught by putting nets up in the trees. I saw one man who had managed to catch a small bird in a net. It was alive, fluttering about. Holding its body with one hand he grabbed its head with the other and just wrenched its head clean off. The wings still flapped after its head was pulled off. He then pulled out the few feathers and cut off the small morsels of meat from its body and he ate it raw.

I recall one man trying to coax a stray dog to come to him so as he could catch it and kill it for food. The dog would come so close, then it would run off a distance and stand looking at the man as if mocking him. I watched the dog and the man playing this cat-and-mouse game for some time. Then they both disappeared up a street with the man chasing the dog shouting 'come here you bastard!'

We had supplies of bread, but this soon became stale, so you had to moisten it with water as it became as hard as bricks. It was not pleasant, but you ate whatever you could. Near the end, the body of a soldier is brought forward, but left outside our post. I go to see why he has been left and see that he is very badly burned. His skin is red and black in colour all over and barely recognizable as a human being. He looks just like a large piece of roasted meat. His comrades said something about a flamethrower or petrol, or something like that. The smell reminded me of roasted meat. It was disgusting, and one of the smells that, even now, I can still recall. The soldier is still alive but only just. There is nothing we can do for him, though. I try to moisten his lips with cotton wool and some water. Just a few minutes later one of his friend's pulls out his pistol. With tears in his eyes he aims the gun at his friend's head and squeezes the trigger. A shot rings out and one man's suffering is now at an end. I feel sick and I can't watch this anymore and go back inside the post where the stone floor is now slippery with blood.

An old woman comes and gives me a small amount of milk in a cup with some very stale biscuits, '*Kinder, haben diese.*' [Child, have these] she says. I say '*danke.*' [thank you].

The old woman shuffles off back outside just as the artillery fire intensifies. As I sit eating one of the biscuits, I watch the old woman shuffling along when there is a huge explosion. I drop the cup of milk and the biscuit and watch the scene in almost slow motion. The old woman is no more. She is blown into a thousand pieces, yet her small, brown hat lies on the ground undamaged. My head is buzzing as I get up and walk outside. It feels as if there is an electrical shock coursing through me. I stumble over to the old woman's hat and pick it up off the ground. I hear people shouting, yet nothing registers, and I don't remember what they were shouting.

A tank, followed by a mass of infantry, roars into our position. All around me people are holding up their hands in surrender. The tank is green with a large white star on it. The Americans have taken the area we were in. Guns are pointed at us as German soldiers are kicked onto the ground, beaten, and searched for weapons and paperwork. There is so much shouting, swearing and commotion. I sink to my knees and just stare at the ground, nausea coursing through my stomach. I look up and begin to gather myself and to regain my composure.

I slowly raise my head to see a gun barrel pointing at me with a bayonet at its end. The bloodstained blade points menacingly at me. I slowly lift up my hand and, grasping the soldier's bayonet with my fingers, I gently move it away from my face. I look into the young American's eyes and he looks frightened, he's just a boy. I speak to him calmly and I say '*nein*' [no], shaking my head from side to side. I think he understands what I am saying as he nods in agreement. He points his rifle and bayonet away from me.

We are now in the custody of our American captors and, after the initial kicking and beating and searching, things calm down. They later question me and ask me what I was doing and why was I covered in blood? I told them the truth, that I was assisting the doctors. The doctors told them that I was with them and I probably helped save the lives of many. The doctor later told me what he said to the Americans: 'that girl is braver than most men. She was surrounded with death, went out under fire to get supplies and deliver messages, and doing everything she was told to do without question.'

Later that day, one of our officers arrived to give instructions to the soldiers who were now all prisoners of war. He talked with them for some time, asking them to comply with all Allied Command wishes. He went around them shaking their hands. Then he walks over to me and says, 'I have heard that you have been exceptional. I have heard things about you that make me proud. I have forwarded many recommendations during the last years of this long war. Few have been so deserved as yours. It probably matters little now that the war is over for us.'

He then takes out this small packet from his pocket, hands it to me and then holds out his hand. He shakes my hand. There are no more Nazi salutes, just a hand shake. He says he will document his gratitude if it is possible, but this may be difficult now the war has ended for us here in Aachen. He tells me to keep the packet out of sight in my clothing, as someone will probably steal it off me for a souvenir if it is discovered on me. He then smiles and walks off on his way, accompanied by American soldiers.

Later on, in a quiet moment, I take out the small packet from a pocket in my skirt to see what was inside. I initially thought it was some kind of a letter or money. Opening the packet up I slide my fingers inside. I feel that there are some kind of medals inside. I tip out the contents and they fall into the palm of my hand. I can see there is an Iron Cross Second Class and a War Merit Cross 2nd Class. The ribbons are neatly folded inside the packet. The Iron Cross Second Class was awarded to German soldiers for acts of bravery in the field of combat. It could also be awarded to civilians for acts of bravery during war services. The War Merit Cross, without the swords, was issued to non-combatants involved in war services. I looked at the medals and I couldn't help but smile to myself. I just thought 'good God, here we are, the war is now over for us and I am given medals.'

I then put them back into my pocket. I understand that to have had these presented to me, even in this quite 'unofficial' capacity, was quite something, maybe even unique. I don't know if any other girls were ever given them. I don't even know if the ones I was given were ever documented. I still have them today, but have never worn them of course. After the war, we were not permitted to wear any insignia or medal with the swastika emblem on, though de-Nazified versions of both these awards were later introduced for veterans.

The Americans treated us with a great deal of suspicion for some time but things became friendlier. Some were nasty to us, others were not, and this is how it was I guess. There were still some random incidents of shooting in the city even after the surrender. Die-hard German soldiers had managed to arm themselves, shooting dead some US soldiers. It was pointless and I was afraid it might antagonize the Americans.

Most Americans I came into contact with were very polite and respectful once they got talking to you. There were always a few that were not, but you will find that in society today things like that don't change, do they? It was not long before I was being given bars of chocolate, drinks of tea and coffee, and good food items. The American photographers wanted to take my picture and I was happy for them to do so. I seldom smiled for the photographs, so they would always gesture for me to smile. If they could speak German they would say in that funny accent of theirs 'c'mon, smile sweetheart.'

From that point to the end of the war, I was classed as a displaced person. I had to have an identification photo taken of myself holding a black board with 'Katte Wiener 15A' written on it in white chalk. My photo, along with hundreds of others, was posted up so that families could trace their lost children or relatives. Many pictures would be posted of men, women and children who would never be found. Many of the dead became buried under tons of concrete and rubble. Sometimes their remains were unearthed months or even years later during rebuilding projects. It was just heart-breaking.

Some of the girls I knew were also missing. There would be mothers asking me if I had made any contact with their daughters. I told them we wished each other good luck before the battle and that was the last I saw of them. They then asked if I knew where they had gone and where they might be. I had to tell them the truth: I just didn't know. I knew enough to realize that if people did not return home after some weeks, that they were probably dead. When the mothers left, I started to cry. I felt bad that they had all probably been killed and wished I had been there fighting with them. Maybe I could have helped them, I don't know, but it's one of many ghosts I was left with.

Today, the ghosts are still with me as faces that I would never see again in my life. The young man having his leg sawn off or the boy with his legs blown off. The old woman who gave me milk and biscuits, only to be blown apart seconds later, and the dead baby with a steel shard embedded in its head. They are all frequent visitors to my sleep.

I was reunited with my family around a month later. Mother and Father, along with my sister, had remained in Aachen. They had found refuge with other families in the basement of a shop to the east of the city. Our home, like many others, was nothing but a pile of rubble. We stayed in a camp for less than one month before going to stay with my older sister and her husband. My sister's husband had been a radar operator, and when captured, he was treated really well as the Americans needed technical information from him. While we stayed with my sister and her husband, the Americans frequently visited the house, carrying suitcases of paperwork for him to look at. He was later given a job working in West German intelligence for his former enemy. Strange how life works out, is it not?

As I grew up in a new town in West Germany, I was not sure what kind of job I wanted to do. I was not sure if I could pursue a medical profession. My family persuaded me to take exams and try for a career as a doctor. I studied and finally passed after my second attempt.

I stopped eating meat after the war. This was mainly due to the soldier that had been burned almost to death by a flamethrower gun. My mother and father cooked some roast pork once, and as soon as I smelled it, I was sick, as the smell reminded me of the smell of that poor man. They tried cooking beef, but I was sick with that too. I have not eaten meat since, though I can eat fish.

The nightmares I have are things that I will always have. There are no cures for things that are imprinted into your mind. You forget over time, but your subconscious reminds you in your sleep. Aachen was a very unpleasant experience, but then war is not a pleasant thing, is it?

I went back to where we used to live in Aachen in the 1960s, just to see what had changed. I discovered many of the old buildings still bearing the scars of war. I could still find pieces of shrapnel on the ground in places. As I walked I held a piece of shrapnel in my hand, contemplating how lucky I was to have survived. I was able to achieve much after the defeat of National Socialism. Of course, I was a BDM girl, so I have to accept that this implies some degree of guilt for all the terrible things done under the Nazis. I never considered myself a Nazi. I was like my friends, patriotic and hopeful that Hitler would bring us prosperity and lead us from the dark years of the Versailles Treaty. The dream soon became a nightmare.

Before leaving Aachen after my last visit, I knelt down on the ground, lifted the brown soil with my fingers and caressed it. I said to myself, 'This is no longer blood and dust. The earth here is no longer wet with the blood of those killed or injured in the fighting.' I said a prayer and kissed the ground goodbye.

I still feel as if I am being crushed beneath a mountain of guilt. I had sometimes wished, as a young girl, that I was not even human. Humans really are disgusting and they do disgusting things.

I made the journey to London in May 2006 to meet with Wiener Katte, who was accompanied by her children and grandchildren. They had come to England to see some of the sights, and during their two-week stay we arranged to meet. It was another memorable occasion, the language barrier being broken by Wiener's granddaughter Milla, who acted as interpreter for us all.

During the meeting, we discussed many things. Wiener's memory was as sharp as that of a 20-year-old. Yet she still appeared greatly saddened, if slightly troubled, by the past. She explained:

It's so strange that all the places we used to go to on our BDM summer camps are still there. The rocks we sat on the streams and rivers we splashed about in. Yet when I see these familiar places it makes me sad. The reason for this is that I can see my sisters there in my memories, but all my sisters are now gone. These are all just reflections, or ghosts, within my mind. I recall the little BDM sporting tournaments and how my sisters would shout 'come on Kattie' when I was in the lead in running races. In fact, the nickname they gave me was Kattie. There were times when we were playing around some of my sisters would make a 'meow' noise like a cat, as my surname was similar to the German word for a cat [katzchen]. Sometimes they would keep doing this out of habit. It used to make me laugh. I love and miss them so much.

The tears begin to well up in her eyes as she talks. She then gestures to Milla to pass her, her handbag. Milla hands her the bag and she takes out several tissues and wipes her eyes. Then she takes something else out of her bag, clasping whatever it is in her slightly trembling hand. She slides it across the table to me and there is that sound of metal against wood. She looks at Milla, quietly whispering something into her ear. Milla then says to me, 'She wants you to have these as they are a piece of her, which she wants you to have. We don't want them and they represent something that we would rather not recollect now.'

Wiener removes her hand and on the table before me is the Iron Cross Second Class and War Merit Cross Second Class as presented to her by the German officer in Aachen. She says, 'Please take these from me and my sisters. If they were all here now every one of them would want you to have them.'

I am in momentary disbelief at this most unexpected of gestures. I pick both crosses up, holding them in my hand and look at them for some minutes. It is possible the German officer that presented these crosses to Wiener was prepared to break certain protocols. He rightly felt very strongly that she deserved these decorations when he heard of her endeavours during the battle. As an officer, he would have had access to such decorations, ready to be presented to deserving individuals, which, in a sense, were under his command. Had Germany won the battle for Aachen, Wiener would have, without doubt, received fully documented recognition with her awards. It was heartening to think that, as a young girl, Wiener performed duties that today would be considered heroic in their context. Despite the horror, the death and the destruction that this young girl was witness to, she remained remarkably steadfast throughout the battle, and in the process she helped save many lives. Many females were presented with the Iron Cross Second Class and the War Merit Cross Second Class during the course of the Second World War. These ones in my opinion are very significant. Neither being awarded to an adult, but a 15-year-old girl, and that is a powerful statement. I then ask Milla to thank her grandmother as this means a lot to me, and they are things that I will always treasure. I carefully place the crosses in my pocket.

We finish our cups of coffee. It is now late afternoon and it is time for me to leave for home. Milla very kindly offers to drive me to Paddington Station, where she waits with me for my train to arrive. As my train comes in, she wishes me a safe journey home. She gives me a hug along with a farewell kiss. The memory of the pretty German girl waving me off from the platform at Paddington is now a treasured one.

6

Memories of a Female Flak Helper

By August of 1944, there were approximately 450,000 German females serving within the German Luftwaffe. The females, usually drawn from the ranks of the BDM, served in many varied roles within the Luftwaffe. Many of the girls were enrolled into the auxiliary anti-aircraft defence. Before their enrolment was possible, they officially had to join the *Wehrmacht* (German Army). The official line was that it was forbidden for young girls of the BDM to be seen as performing any armed duties. Germany's ever-deteriorating military situation meant that every single resource had to be exploited. As the Second World War reached its inevitable climax, more girls were brought into the anti-aircraft defences, where they were trained to operate light flak (anti-aircraft) guns. This was a role that was not for the fainthearted. It often meant that females would be right in the thick of any action, therefore selection was, even by late war standards, very thorough.

Katrina Duvaal volunteered in November of 1944 for the Luftwaffe flak arm. She recalls her time:

> I desperately wanted to assist in the defence of our nation. The problem was that in some areas there was still the idea that girls could not perform their tasks as good as the boys. The situation in late 1944 became so desperate, that the authorities were prepared to change the rules if it meant winning the war. Where males had exclusively operated anti-aircraft weapons females were brought in to free them up for other more important defensive roles. Little was ever put into writing, so there was no incriminating evidence to be left.
>
> As a BDM, girl I was taught to do many things over the years since joining. I had immense practical experience at so many things. It was a joy to know that you had mastered many things, from child care, cooking, home care, advanced first-aid techniques, assisting firefighting

teams, to feeding bombed-out families in the cities. The list was just endless and there was nothing we could not do. If we were set a task we would not stop until we had accomplished it. That was our attitude, and if we could not achieve as individuals, then we worked as a team. We were closer than sisters, and in the anti-aircraft defence they picked you and your closest friends to work with you. That method was for us the best way, as we knew each other well and could thus work together more effectively than if we were placed with total strangers. Of course, the men were in control of administration, direction and training, but once trained and operational, we were as effective as any of the males in anti-aircraft defence.

As a team, we were trained to use the 20mm *Flakvierling* 38 gun. This weapon had four barrels, which were fired using two foot-controlled pedals. Each pedal fired two diagonally opposed barrels in a semi or fully automatic firing cycle. The rate of fire in combat situations depended largely on the competency of the gun's crew. Eight-hundred shots per minute was the usual rate of fire [The cyclic rate of fire of the *Flakvierling* was 1,800 rounds/min.] If you fired the weapon continuously, there was the danger that the gun barrels would overheat, leading to a failure. Ideally, you worked to fire in short, well-aimed, controlled bursts to conserve ammunition and prevent any technical failures occurring.

The *Flakvierling* 38 had four ammunition containers. Each one held twenty rounds of high-explosive and armour-piercing shells. The ammunition containers had to be loaded manually, so you would have a girl either side responsible for feeding two of the four barrels. Speed and good coordination was essential for this task, as it could often be performed in the dark. The tracker was in charge of traversing and elevating the direction of fire. This was controlled by two manually operated hand wheels. The whole gun system was mounted on a carriage that could be towed by a vehicle.

It was rare that you remained in one position for long, so we frequently relocated in case Allied aircraft had spotted us and noted our position. The 38 had a vertical range of some 2,406yd, which equates to 2,200 metres. Ground targets could be engaged at a range of up to 5,230 yards or 5,783m. The ammunition used had a muzzle velocity of 2,953 feet per second, which was quite considerable.

The idea was to spot the enemy and lay your fire, so that the ammunition was fired into the aircraft's flightpath. If you aimed at the centre of the aircraft, by the time your rounds reached that point, the aircraft would have flown past that point. The gunsight fitted to the weapon aided the prediction process, giving calculations. Once you had locked onto an enemy, and he was within range, more often than not a kill was guaranteed.

Training on the weapon was not that difficult. There was just a case of familiarizing yourself with your particular task and learning the techniques. We were always taught by experienced flak crew, and we absorbed the information and practised what we were taught. The technical side of things took more attention as it could be complex. But most of us could repair vehicle engines in trucks and cars, so a gun was not intimidating to us at all. If a barrel stopped firing, you would have to assess very quickly what had caused the problem, then fix it as fast as you could. The main cause of a barrel failing to fire was normally when a cartridge case from a fired round had jammed in the breech. If a cartridge case was knocked, or was slightly deformed, when fired it may jam. There was a special tool used to extract jammed casings from a gun's breech. If in action a barrel failed to fire, the loader would have to make the rest of the crew aware of the problem by shouting 'stoppage top left' or 'stoppage bottom left', and vice versa for the other side. Firing would cease while the problem was dealt with. It was really not that difficult at all, but it was very dangerous work.

We often operated in the thick of the bombing attacks. Our targets were the low-flying aircraft, while the heavier guns engaged the medium to high-altitude targets. For these roles, we used 37mm, 88mm and 128mm weapons.

As we were trained as a crew, we quickly grasped the rudiments of prediction, gun-laying and controlled fire. It was easy to become nervous and start firing too soon. This was something you had to instil in yourself not to do. Our discipline as German maidens was exemplary and we were superbly trained.

Our first operations began at Juterbog aerodrome. This airfield often came under attack from Russian aircraft.

One afternoon, a large flight of Shturmoviks [Ilyushin Il-2, heavily armoured and armed Russian ground-attack aircraft] came into view. Immediately, we leapt onto the gun and my tracker began to traverse the barrels towards them. Checking my sights, I waited for them to be within range. I remembered these Shturmoviks were extremely well-protected and carried heavy-calibre guns. We could not take too many liberties with these beasts as their 23mm cannons could easily penetrate the thin metal shield of our Flakvierling 38. The shield was our only protection from flying splinters and cannon shells, but it was nowhere thick enough.

The Shturmoviks came into range and I depressed the pedals firing the gun. Firing in bursts, I saw hits on three of the lead Russians. One peeled off to the right, appearing to be turning back for home. The other two continued as shells began to explode around them. I fired in short bursts as we had learned in training. Bernadette, our tracker, operated perfectly, and the girls loading the barrels performed without any problems. Our shells found their mark as the propeller blade was shot clean off one of the two Russian aircraft. The Russian plane rolled over onto its back and I saw one of its two-man crew falling out of the plane. His 'chute did not deploy and he fell to his death. I think he was already dead, though. The second fired his cannons at us, the 23mm shells striking a building to our rear, well off the mark. I depressed both pedals, firing the guns again, and as he passed, Bernadette had him tracked. He was so close, we could have almost touched him. There was an explosion as the Russian aircraft fell from the sky, ploughing a long furrow into the ground as it went in.

By this time, our aircraft had joined in the fight. The sky was soon full of Focke-Wulfs and Russian aircraft in a dance of death in the skies above. We stopped firing as we did not want to risk hitting our own boys, so we watched the spectacle.

The Russians lost six of their aircraft on that day, of which we had claimed two. Our work was congratulated by the commanding officer, who asked us into the mess that evening for celebratory drinks. We were treated not only to glasses of red wine, but dinner too. We had a memorable evening and felt quite elated at it all.

The next day, rain stopped play. There was thick fog also, so we guessed we would see no action so long as the bad weather hung around. We decided to go and see the remains of the aircraft we had shot down the previous day. The closest one we shot down had left a long furrow in the brown earth, which seemed to go on for hundreds of yards. It led directly to the mangled remains of the Shturmovik. The one crewman was still strapped inside. I asked our escort why they had not removed the body from the wreck. 'Ah, no leave the fucker there as a warning to the others', he replied.

We looked around the wreckage and picked up various pieces to examine them. I found lots of ammunition under the remains of the wings. There was a 23mm cannon lying on the ground that had been torn out of its mounting during the crash. The salvage boys would soon be along to remove anything of use. The wreck of the Shturmovik remained where it was right up until we moved out of the airfield. I never found out if they buried that Russian pilot or not. I hope he received a burial, as I was not that full of hatred that I would have denied any enemy a proper burial.

As dawn broke, on what would be a clear day, we were roused from our bunks. It was cold, and we shivered as we made our way out of our hut to the canteen to get a hot drink. We sat down to drink the hot coffee, which Bernadette said 'tasted like shit.' We laughed to ourselves about her remark, but it warmed our bodies. As individuals, we all took time to wake up properly. Some of us would be quiet, while others would be as bright as the sun.

Around mid-morning, our Russian friends returned yet again. The drill was the same: we would jump up onto the gun and prepare to fire. Bernadette would traverse and aim the barrels at the oncoming wave of attackers. I would wait patiently until the enemy were in range before opening fire. I saw rockets streak overhead from the planes, but they exploded well aft of their intended targets of the airfield huts. I muttered to myself 'right you bastards have this', before depressing the pedals, the guns blazing away at the enemy. The enemy planes returned fire and you could see the flashes from their wings. There was a loud crescendo of metal on metal. Bernadette screamed as she was blown backwards by the force of bullets thudding into her body. Giselle immediately took over both tracking and loading the left-hand guns. We could not stop, so we carried on firing.

I watched the enemy plane dive sharply to our right. It vanished behind some trees, followed by a loud bang as it hit the ground. Another enemy plane flew directly overhead. At maximum elevation, we tracked it, firing directly into its belly. It exploded and crashed into the ground a short distance away.

It seemed, that with each attack, there were fewer of our Luftwaffe planes to meet the attackers. The attackers had bombed the airfield, shooting it up with rockets and cannon fire. We had accounted for three of them in all. One that we had damaged was caught by one of our aircraft and shot down. As the attackers turned away for home, we jumped down to help Bernadette. For the first time, we were in a kind of panic. Bullets had ripped through her body in mid-thorax. We tore open her coat, jacket and shirt to see how much damage had been done. There was so much blood. She was alive, but her colour was rapidly changing from pale to a sickly blue. We could see the extent of the damage. The wounds were terrible. We just cried over her lifeless form as the German Red Cross van arrived to take her away.

We had to remain on stand too as it was reported that another Russian attack was on its way. This attack did not come, as they veered away to attack some of our trucks they had spotted on a nearby road. By the time we were able to stand down, it was getting dark and the cold was increasing by the minute. We desperately wanted to go to see if Bernadette was alright. Surely our excellent medical people could help her and she might be okay. It is funny how you know that someone is badly hurt and that they will probably not survive, yet your brain tries to convince you otherwise.

Our commanding officer told us to go over to the canteen and get some food and hot drinks. He would join us shortly. When he arrived, he dismissed the other people from the canteen. He took off his hat and sat down. His words were solemn:

I'm so sorry to have to be the bearer of such terrible news, but your comrade died on the way to the hospital. They could do nothing to save her as her injuries were just too severe. If there is anything I can do, please do not hesitate to come and see me. I know these things happen in war – I have lost friends too. I will arrange a wreath to be sent to her family over the next few days. I will grant all of you leave to attend her funeral if you wish to go, which I am sure you will.

The CO stood up, saluted us, then put on his hat and walked out of the canteen. We sat there in stunned silence, occasionally looking into one another's faces. That night we could barely eat, and sleep was impossible. We huddled around the small fire in our hut. We just sat, absorbed in our own thoughts as the red flames flickered away. We felt as if our world had ended. We had lost not just a dear friend, but also a sister. We were all sisters in our eyes, and we loved, respected and looked after each other as best we could.

The next day, a young girl arrived to take Bernadette's place as tracker. I asked her, 'What's your name and how old are you?'

She replied, 'I am Stephanie and I am 16 years old.'

This young girl was two years younger than the rest of us – she was just a kid. I had reservations as to whether she would be able to do the job properly. The next morning, we were all stiff from sitting around the fire trying to sleep in our chairs. Stephanie was in her bunk. I walked over and looked at the sleeping girl, but I had to turn away as I began to cry. I couldn't see any more of my sisters die. I felt we had to try and make this kid feel a part of us, one of our sisters.

I recovered my composure and, wiping the tears away, I gave Stephanie a gentle shake to wake her up. She rubbed her eyes then got up and dressed, before following us over to the canteen. We sat down with our hot coffees as we always had done. It was not quite daybreak outside. Stephanie sipped the coffee, when, to our amazement, she pulled a funny face, saying, 'Err, this stuff takes like shit.'

We looked at each other and roared with laughter. Stephanie sat with her mouth open, then asked, 'What? What did I do?'

I told her, 'Never mind. It's a long story and we will tell you later. Now get ready.'

We were still sniggering to ourselves as we made the walk out to our gun position, which had been moved during the night to the western periphery of the airfield. When we arrived at the gun position, I noticed straightaway the damage to the gun made by the bullets that hit Bernadette. There were deep gouges in the metal base and chips of metal missing here and there. Most notable were the holes in the metal shield, which was meant to protect us. We agreed that they should have given us another gun, rather than make us use this one after what had happened.

Giselle wanted to be tracker but I insisted Stephanie be given the chance to prove herself, as it was what she had been trained to do. Giselle agreed and smiled. There was no squabbling amongst us as we respected each other too much. We each had a steel helmet of the standard type to wear. Stephanie's was a little too big for her, which made us smile too. I think she knew what we were smiling about, but it was comical seeing her little face and the helmet covering her eyes, so she had to keep pushing it up.

An attack warning came through as American P-47 aircraft were spotted heading our way. We hoped the warning was a false alarm as the P-47s were excellent tank-busting aircraft that could take heavy punishment from ground fire and still fly home. We were very tense and at readiness for attack.

'Enemy from the south-west', boomed a loudspeaker.

In an instant Stephanie had the weapons trained perfectly, elevating the guns towards the direction of the attack. I saw them appear in my gunsight, willing them to come on so that I could start shooting.

They began to climb and I saw several bombs falling from the P-47's wings. The bombs exploded in front of us, several hundred yards away. The bombs were carried forward by the momentum of the oncoming planes, which had now turned away. They were not close enough for me to get a shot, yet we tracked them as they banked back around. They dropped down to very low level. Stephanie adjusted the barrels, precisely following them round in their turn.

At last they were in range. I depressed both pedals and the guns blazed into life. The tracer rounds help me shoot at them with good deflection. Suddenly our fire converged on the American plane. It began to trail thick, black smoke, pulling up as if trying to escape from us. We continued firing into it, when we saw a small black speck come away from the plane. This was the pilot baling out of his stricken aircraft. His plane stalled out during its climb, before beginning its fall to earth. I looked up and thought that thing could fall on us. We were preparing to run away when it veered away, before crashing into some woods about a mile away.

The pilot of the P-47 drifted down to earth in his parachute. When he landed, our forces were there to greet him. He was unhurt and was taken into the commanding officer's hut, where he was given a drink and checked over for any injuries. He was very frightened about what would happen next, but the CO reassured him that he would be fine and that he would be taken away to a prisoner-of-war camp. Here he would be with other airmen shot down over the Reich territory. He was reassured that the German Red Cross would inform the British Red Cross that he was safe. Arrangements would be made for letters to be written to his family.

The CO was a good man and we liked him very much. As we stood down, I walked over to Stephanie and gave her a big hug and kissed her on the cheek. I told her that she had done an amazing job, and that it was down to her that we had claimed another enemy aircraft. She looked as proud as punch as we all hugged, before moving off to get a light dinner and to have a drink before settling down for bed. It had been an exhausting few days and we were on standby from dawn until dusk. At night, another shift would take over our position. It used to piss me off, as those on night duty always seemed to have a quieter time of it, compared to us on daytime duty.

The day of Bernadette's funeral came and arrangements were made for us to make the short journey to her home town where her parents lived. The journey was a quiet one, as we were not looking forward to seeing our sister buried. When we arrived, we helped lay out the wreaths inside the church. There were many people there, which did not surprise us at all. Bernadette was a lovely girl, always cheerful and always joking when away from her duties. Stephanie had asked if she could attend the funeral with us. We agreed that she could. We lined up outside the church and awaited Bernadette's parents. When they arrived, and began their solemn walk into the church, we removed our caps, bowing our heads. The service was much the same as any funeral. There were readings from Bernadette's brothers and sisters. Some of their readings made us smile as we reflected upon our memories of her.

After the service, there was the internment. Afterwards, we had the chance to speak with Bernadette's family. They were eager to talk to us as we were with her the day she lost her life. They wanted to know all the ins and outs of what happened as the authorities had been vague in their report. So, we sat them down and answered their questions as honestly as we could. We were all feeling emotional and there were many tears. Even little Stephanie was in tears and we comforted one another through it all. As we bade our farewells to Bernadette's family, it felt like we were leaving a part of ourselves there in the ground with her. The journey back to the airfield felt like an eternity in the back of a cold truck. When we arrived back at the airfield we went straight to our hut and did not even undress for bed. We just got under the covers, exhausted by the day's events, and slept.

We had the next day off and we all went into the nearby town. We posed for photographs and just had some fun. Some boys stopped us to talk as we were wearing our uniforms. Photographs were taken with them and one of them asked for Stephanie's address. I told the one that 'she is too young for you boy.' But he would not take no for an answer, so she obliged.

Over the next few days, she received *Feldpost* [German military mail] from him. We would ask her to share with us what was in the letters, but she would say 'nooo.'

We would tease her all the time about the saucy letters her admirer was sending her. With our day-off over, we returned to the airfield and our hut. The air outside was now very cold, and the hut, even with the fire going, was cold. It would condensate in the winter months and droplets of water would drop down on you in the night.

The next morning, we awoke to frozen window panes and snow on the ground outside. We did not relish the prospect of being on duty in the freezing weather. We had our thick winter coats on over our uniforms, and we were issued with gloves to keep our hands warm. The gloves were a bit awkward for Stephanie, as she found that they made her job more difficult. We hoped the bad weather would keep the enemy planes away. That day, there was little air activity and, although we heard engines in the distance, they did not enter our sector. We had a day hanging around in the cold. An orderly made sure that hot coffee was brought out to us, but this made you want to pee all the time. It was a comical sight watching one of us run to the ablutions hut. Stephanie was the worst, as she would come back and twenty minutes or so later she would need to pee again.

Two days passed. We saw no action and wondered what was going on. In the distance, we heard thuds and rumbling noises, but did not really think too much into it. Another two days passed and the noises became more distinct – it was the sound of artillery. But whose artillery was it? We just did not know. We were called for a meeting with the CO, who explained that we were being stood down with a view to transfer. We understood by this that we were being stood down ready to be sent home. We were wrong, as we were given orders to move east with a convoy from the nearby German army barracks. We were to act as reinforcements to our forces engaging the Russians. I had misgivings about this move to the east, giving rise to a growing sense of unease.

The weather began to compound the problems. Heavy snow made the journey slow going. Several times the truck became bogged down, so we had to jump out and help push the damn thing. The wheels would just spin on the rapidly forming ice – it was horrendous.

It felt like we had been travelling all day, but we had not really got very far. We were told to prepare to camp for the night, so a fire was made on the edge of a wood. Several more fires were started along the convoy route so people could have warmth and be able to heat water for food and drinks. We got out of the truck, but it felt warmer in the back of the truck than out by the fire. We were given blankets and we huddled up together for the night, which we knew would be a sleepless one. The sound of artillery could clearly be heard, continuing throughout the night and into the early hours, when we were roused from our sleep. We did not want to move as we were quite comfy huddled up in our blankets in the back of the truck. Wearily we climbed out into the cold air and snow, and walked over towards the light of the fire where hot drinks were being handed out. We cupped them with our hands and stamped our feet to stay warm. It was an hour or so away from daybreak. The flashes from artillery fire could now be clearly seen as well as heard. We were given the order to move out about thirty minutes later, and so the journey continued.

We arrived at our destination after what seemed hours. But it wasn't hours, it was just the fact that the poor weather meant we moved at a crawl through the countryside. We were ordered to set up our gun at the edge of a wood and then dig a trench, which would be deep enough for us all to lie down in. We cursed at the thought and wondered what we were in for. We helped set up the gun and checked it all over, before cleaning some of the parts so it would be ready. We then set about the task of digging the trench as instructed.

We had just about finished digging out the trench, when a group of young men in Luftwaffe uniform, and wearing heavy coats, came across to us. They were fresh-faced boys from the Hitler Youth. I'm sure one of them was barely 15 years of age. He did not look old enough to be out here. Then we were told by another officer, 'Get your things together as you are to report back to Anti-Aircraft Defence at Berlin.'

Stephanie said, 'Are they fucking about with us, or something?'

I told her not to swear, because if officers heard us swearing we could get into trouble. Swearing was not considered lady-like at all. We did swear among ourselves, but not in the company of the men or officers.

We had to throw our things back into another transport and climb in for yet another torturous journey by road in the freezing cold and snow. We were getting really fed up by this time, until the truck left the road and drove up through a small wood and parked up.

'Okay, come on, out you get, your flight is waiting,' the driver shouted at us.

'What do you mean flight?' I asked him.

'The one over the ridge, there, through the trees', he replied, pointing.

We grabbed our things and headed through the trees over the ridge. There was a specially prepared clearing where a [Junkers] Ju 52 aircraft was waiting. We could see others going inside, so we began to run, thinking that there would be no room in there if we didn't hurry up. We were ordered to show our identity papers before climbing up into the aircraft and settling down inside. I had never been in an aeroplane before, so this was very exciting indeed. The grass runway did not look long enough to me. The engines were started and we were soon bumping and lurching up the field, until that sense you were airborne came and all was quite smooth. We were all tired, but the excitement of the flight meant we could not sleep.

We landed at Tempelhof airport where we reported to the city anti-aircraft command post for further orders. We were told to report to the Berlin garrison as they would have some work for us there. We were given directions and were making our way there just as the air-raid sirens began to sound. We headed for the nearest shelter and settled down inside with civilians, women and children, and old men. Fifteen minutes later the rumble of bombers overhead could he heard. Then there came the whistle and explosions of bombs that shook the ground. It made you want to run, but as bad as it sounded, it was far safer in the shelter than up there above ground.

The bombing lasted for over an hour. There was a pause, then the all clear sounded. We made our way up the stone stairway out of the shelter and continued to garrison headquarters. When we arrived at the HQ, we were instructed to report to Tempelhof, as defences were being prepared there. Tempelhof was formally a civil airfield, but during the Second World War, it was used by fighter aircraft for emergency landings. It was also used for the supply of parts and the assembly of military aeroplanes. We were assigned again to a Flak 38 battery, so you could say we knew the ropes. There were few young women here, so the men tended to look at us funny. Their staring soon stopped when we began to strip the guns down to check, grease and oil them as required. Then each barrel was cleaned thoroughly with a brush and pull-through. Stephanie then checked all of the magazines for any malformation or corrosion. Magazines with deformed lips might not feed properly and could cause jamming of the rounds. After checking each magazine, she then cleaned them all and began to load them with 20mm shells. She loaded a mixture of high-explosive incendiary tracer and armour-piercing shells. I admired her, as for such a young girl, she was better with weapons than what most men were. Whoever had taught her, taught the kid very well.

We were now on night operations and we didn't really relish the prospect of being on duty in the wet and cold winter nights. Trying to get sleep in the daytime was often a waste of time. After a few days, you slept through the exhaustion. None of us ever felt fresh on night ops, and we began to hate it.

Initially, we didn't see much action, as the bombing raids at night were far too high altitude for our 20mm guns to engage. The one evening, RAF Mosquito aircraft were reported heading into our sector. We were already pointing our Flak 38 in their direction. We heard their distinctive engine sounds, and on their approach, they began to fire, tracers streaking low over us. I knew they were not yet in range, but I pushed down the pedals and the guns burst into life. Our fire was like water coming out of a garden hose. Stephanie elevated the guns and the rounds were now finding their mark. She then had to drop the barrels, frantically spinning the elevation wheel anti-clockwise. I saw flashes on at least two of the RAF planes, but one now had a dull yellow glow behind its cockpit. It roared overhead and, as it did, Stephanie tracked it perfectly. I resumed firing throughout. The enemy plane was now a fireball and losing altitude rapidly. It disappeared over the rooftops and out of view. We claimed one damaged and one possible destroyed.

We tried to verify the claims the next day, but no enemy aircraft had been reported as having crashed. It is possible they crashed out of our sector, but knowing the men, they probably wanted to steal our glory.

We remained at Tempelhof, and were there when the Russians attacked. We were instructed to fire at the Russians on the ground and to use our Flak 38 in a ground role. Against soldiers, the flak guns were deadly. Sometimes, you could even knock their tanks out with them. If our armour-piercing rounds failed to penetrate the turret armour, they would often tear the tracks and wheels, to the point where the tank could not drive anymore. When their crews jumped out, we opened fire on them. There was not much left of them afterwards.

The Russian attack was not stalling. Instead, it seemed to be gathering momentum. Hitler Youths with *panzerfaust* and *panzerschreck* anti-tank weapons began to arrive. The *Volkssturm* had been mobilized and things were becoming more chaotic by the day.

It must have been 25 April 1945, when we were ordered to leave Tempelhof. The order came directly from Commander Bottger, who did not want any women falling into enemy hands or taking part in military activity. He personally disagreed with the situation at Tempelhof, and was not happy with having Hitler Youth boys and girls and *Volkssturm* around. He said he did not wish to be responsible for their pointless deaths. A short while later, he defied orders to destroy the buildings at Tempelhof, then took his own life.

The seven of us had to make a decision as to what we were going to do next. We were told to go. Others said that they wanted to try to get back to their homes near Juterbog. We wished them luck and there were many tears at this farewell. Would we ever see them again? I took Stephanie's hand and told her, 'You're coming with me kid.' In the darkness, we made our way through the nightmare ruins that were under constant bombardment. We took cover when we had to, but it was imperative that we get away as quickly as possible. Our aim was to get to one of the big air-raid shelters in the Tiergarten district of Berlin.

After what seemed an eternity, we made it there. I told Stephanie to throw away her coat with the Luftwaffe insignia on it, and make sure she had nothing on her that could give the enemy any information about her. I did the same, and we went into the shelter, which was by now crammed with civilians. The smell inside was awful: cigarette smoke, cordite fumes, damp air, sweat and fear, all mixed up. People had been too scared to go outside, so they urinated and defecated inside the shelter. I held onto Stephanie and did not let her go. We could hear the guns firing on the roof and the fighting outside. There were several very loud booms and the ground trembled slightly, while the lights inside blinked.

Then, gradually, the noise seemed to stop. People began to leave the shelter in small groups, so we followed. I held onto Stephanie's hand as we just walked out into the darkness, into the unknown before us.

'The Russians are here,' she whispered.

I told her to say nothing. Don't look them in the eyes and keep walking with the others. We saw some women being pulled out of the line of civilians. We all knew what was going to happen to these poor women. We kept our heads down and hurried on. We were placed in a kind of prisoner of war camp and no harm, as such, came to us. We told the Russians in charge that we were sisters, which they put down in their documentation. It was ironic really, as Stephanie discovered that her family had been killed.

I made arrangements for her to come and live with me and my family after the war. She did so, and ever since, we have remained like family, like sisters. We have had a special bond all the way through our lives. I still nickname her 'the kid', even now [she laughs].

Both girls later went on dates with two brothers whom they went on to marry. They settled down, had children of their own, and now live quietly in their retirement.

7

Berlin: The Violation of a City

April of 1945, with Hitler dead, and the Red Army firmly in control of Berlin, it was the view of many Germans that they had exchanged one dictatorship for another. What happened to the citizens, particularly young girls and women, during that exclusive period of Soviet occupation has been the subject of strong controversy ever since.

It is certainly true that the western Allies had the manpower, coupled with the resources, to have taken Berlin without Russian involvement. This issue has been reiterated many times over the years by former Allied commanders, including General Patton, who have argued the case. Many were of the opinion at the time that, had the western Allies been given the opportunity to take Berlin, the defenders, having less to fear, may have put up far less resistance than what they had against the Russians. This was also made quite clear by senior German officers within the besieged city.

It was feasible that at the time, Berlin could have surrendered to the western Allies without a fight, thus preventing many thousands of civilian deaths. Both the western Allies and the Germans were well aware of what was going to happen when the Russians entered Berlin by the sickening events that had been taking place in the newly recaptured former German colonies in the east.

The Prussian village of Nemmersdorf was the first German settlement to fall to the Soviets. In that village, every single man, woman, baby and child were brutally murdered. Near the east Prussian city of Konigsberg, the bodies of dead, often mutilated, women littered the roads. In Gross Heydekrug, a woman was found crucified upon the altar of a local church, with two German men strung up in the same fashion either side of her body. These were acts of savagery on a level incomprehensible to many.

As the German forces retreated from the Russian advance along with thousands of civilian refugees, stories of mass rape, butchery and murder spread. Photographs of the victims of Russian barbarity began to appear in the German press and on propaganda leaflets being distributed around Berlin. The photographs were very graphic, some showing the bodies of young girls who had been stripped, beaten, raped, then shot.

The people had been terrified of the prospect of a Russian invasion. In many respects, they were faced with little choice but to fight to the death to protect their women, children and families. It would appear at this time, that Berlin, once the capital of Adolf Hitler's Third Reich, would be abandoned to its fate. The Supreme Allied Command may have felt obliged to allow the Russians to take Berlin, as the Russians numerical superiority largely negated the impact of their heavy losses. There was also the issue of revenge for the atrocities perpetrated in the east by elements of the German military. Of course, these arguments have some foundation, as any military historian will be aware. Argument aside, it has to be said that the victors also had a moral responsibility not to allow barbaric behaviour in the name of the destruction of Nazism. The threat of Russian reprisal instilled such terror, that mothers and fathers were prepared to commit filicide on their children. Nineteen-year-old Berliner, Bertha Sohne, watched in horror and disbelief as her 23-year-old neighbour led her two little girls to the banks of the River Spree.

> She was beside herself with grief and fear. I asked her, 'What are you doing?'
>
> She just looked at me vacantly and replied, 'I am taking my two girls with me and we will all die together in this river, rather than at the hands of those beasts.'
>
> I pleaded with her not to do this, but she held her two girls' hands as I watched them jump into the water. I saw them disappear beneath the water. I thought I can't let this happen and jumped in after them. I was too late. By the time, I was able to find them, the little ones had drowned.

Of all the interviews given to me during my research for volume one of this project, without doubt, one of the most harrowing was that given by American nurse Carly Hendryks. In *Hitler's Girls*, it was not possible to include a full transcript of her interview, but this is the full account:

> After the fighting, our role was a non-discriminatory one. We entered Berlin to help and treat anyone in need of

medical attention: German, Russian, American, whatever. As a nurse, I understood that, and I was prepared for it. I was ready to do what I would have to do.

What changed my overall view, however, was the fact that almost every girl or woman I treated, had been the victims of brutal rapes. Treating victims of rape was nothing new to me. I had treated rape victims back home in the US, but the injuries I had seen inflicted on girls and women in Berlin was far beyond anything I had experienced before. The one young victim became a kind of spectre that would haunt me to this day.

She was 10 years old when her mother brought her in to me. I had an interpreter with me. I asked the girl's mother what had happened. She began to cry, saying, 'The soldiers took her.'

'What soldiers? 'I asked, and the mother replied, 'Russians.'

The child stood there. She was pale and expressionless. We tried to offer her some chocolate, but she would not take it. It was then that I noticed the dry congealed blood on the insides of her thighs. The blood had run all the way down to her ankles. I explained to the mother that I would need to clean the blood away and examine her daughter so as to ascertain if she had sustained any injuries.

Already in my mind, I was dreading this examination. I carefully laid the child down on the examination table. I was already fighting back the tears, which were welling up in my eyes. There was silence as I removed the girl's tattered dress, then revulsion at what I saw next. Carefully cleaning away the dried blood, and trying to console the now sobbing child, I could see teeth marks in her skin around her neck, shoulders and on her torso. Some of the teeth marks had broken the skin, drawing blood. There were multiple bruises and some cuts and grazes on her knees, conducive with being dragged along the ground.

I carefully washed her and could clearly see from damage around her vaginal area that she had been subjected to a brutal and sustained sexual attack, probably involving more than one attacker.

I stopped the examination to write down some notes, before telling the interpreter to inform the mother that an anaesthetic and some suturing would be necessary to treat a tearing wound around the vaginal entrance.

We prepared her for this procedure, giving her gas to render her unconscious. The wound was treated within a few minutes. The girl was then transferred to another unit and then on to a nearby makeshift hospital to recover.

After the procedure was complete, I had to go outside, where I was sick on the floor. I began to cry myself. I lit a cigarette and just tried to gather my thoughts and restore my composure. As I mentioned to you before, I no longer felt safe in Berlin. I did not want to be near Russian soldiers – at that point, I wanted to go back home.

Shaking with both anger and emotion, I complained to my seniors, and indeed anyone who would listen. However, I was told in as many words, 'Look, let's not make a fuss. Do your job and let's not upset our Russian friends'.

I even wrote a letter to the Supreme Allied Commander [General Dwight Eisenhower] himself, but I don't know if he ever received it. In fact, I never received a reply.

I have not been able to get the image of that girl out of my head, and it's been over fifty-five years now. I wonder if she recovered enough to lead a normal life, and if she had a happy life afterwards? I hope she did.

The girl is like a ghost, and I brought that ghost back home with me to the US. Maybe if I could meet her before I die, I would give her a hug and ask her about these things, then I might find some peace – I don't know.

As for the events that followed – the falling out of bed with Stalin and the Berlin Wall going up – was I surprised? No, I was not surprised at all, but just fearful that we would go to war with them and end up suffering the same fate many Germans had in April of 1945. I did talk to other medics, nurses and surgeons, some of whom telling me in confidence that German girls, some as young as 7 and 8, had been raped. The higher powers, however, said nothing to the Russians, for fear of compromising relations between our two countries.

'Oh, we must not upset the Russians. They are our ally and we owe them a debt of gratitude.'

Inge Strauss and her family suffered a nightmare ordeal in April 1945, when the 'devils from the east' came. The following account that Inge gave to me was again typical of the wave of murder, rape and mayhem that occurred everywhere the Red Army had appeared. Inge found it incredibly difficult during our short interview to convey her story. Visibly shaking, she recalled:

> They came in the night, and we didn't even hear them approaching our home. Me, my two older sisters, and grandmother were upstairs, asleep in bed, when they just burst in. They battered down the door and barged in. They immediately began to beat my mother and father who were sitting downstairs. Me and my sisters were woken by the commotion and ran down the stairs to see what was happening. My father shouted for us to run. We froze in terror on the stairs. Before we were grabbed, I saw them smash a rifle butt against my father's head. I knew they had killed him as they hit him several more times. While this was happening, other Russians were coming in. They proceeded to rip my mother's clothes off, raping her there and then on the floor in front of us. Me and my sisters were dragged down the stairs and thrown onto the floor, where they began shouting at us, and kicking and slapping us around the face. They dragged my grandmother along the floor and began to tear at her clothes. They raped her too. My mother and grandmother were raped over and over again over the next few hours: ten, twenty, thirty times – maybe more. I don't know.
>
> Once one group had their 'fun' with us, others would come in their place. I was just an 8-year-old child at the time, but they took off my nightclothes and they tried to rape me. I felt excruciating pain as they tried to force themselves into me, but they could not penetrate fully. So, they stopped and made me perform other sex acts on them, while threatening me with a pistol held against my head.
>
> My two older sisters, who were 13 and 15, were not spared. Both were beaten and raped several times. When they finally left, we were covered in blood. Both our parents and grandmother were lying dead in front of us.

Elsa Lantz, whom I had interviewed briefly when writing *Hitler's Girls*, gave a harrowing account of how she lost her parents during the Russian assault on Berlin in April 1945. Elsa was only 10 years of age at the time of losing both parents in a shell attack. Suffering the pain and humiliation of being raped was something that would blight her life for many years afterwards. After the rape, the soldiers let her go. She ran off, trying to find somewhere to hide away from the Russians. She was called into a cellar by a group of German civilians, so she joined them, thinking she would be safer with them.

We were safer down in the cellar below the building, as shells were landing all around – the noise was quite intense. The Russians were using heavy guns to clear a path for their tanks and infantry. We could hear tanks coming. They made a kind of rumbling sound when you are down under the ground. One of the women in the cellar took hold of me and held me tight against her. She noticed I was partially naked and was bleeding. She did not have to ask me what had happened. She already knew, but she held me tightly against her as the rumbling noise grew louder. Dust began to fall from the ceiling and the rumbling sounded right above our heads. Then it stopped. It was deathly quiet for some seconds. We looked at each other, wondering what was going to happen next. Then the outside door was kicked in, and five or six Russians burst in with flashlights, shining them in our faces.

The one shouted at us in German, 'Boys, are there boys in here?'

No one answered him, so he just barged in and pushed us over onto the floor. He found two young boys who had been hiding behind their mothers. The boys were dragged out by the scruffs of their necks and the soldiers shouted at us, *Aus! Aus!*' [Out! Out!].

So we came out of the cellar and were pushed down into a side street. The boys were thrown onto the ground and the German-speaking Russian told them to remove their trousers and kneel down. The boys began to cry. Their mothers tried to rush forward to stop this from happening, but they were pushed back, with guns pointing at their faces. The two boys were sodomized before the eyes of their mothers. They cried out, '*Mutter! Mutter!*' [Mother! Mother!], but the poor women could do nothing to help them.

I closed my eyes, not wanting to see this happening, but I could still hear it all – terrible screams, agonized crying. A woman broke free from one of the soldiers holding her, but in the blink of an eye she was shot dead. She fell to the floor and bled out.

Then they shouted for us to come forward. I knew I was going to be attacked all over again. We were made to kneel down on all fours. I saw one of the women being sodomized, like the boys had been. One of the soldiers tried to enter me. I felt him against me, trying to push inside, but he couldn't. In frustration, he slapped me hard on the back of my head, which spun me around onto my back. He then lay on top of me, forcing my legs apart. I tried to push him off, but he held me down by my wrists and tried again to penetrate me. All I felt was pain as, this time, I could feel him inside me. I screamed out, but screaming was hopeless as no one could stop it happening. I knew when he had finished with me as he let out a loud groan. He got up off me, left me there on the floor and walked away.

I could smell the soldiers. They reeked of sweat, urine, alcohol and shit. They were all unshaven. Their eyes were wild and angry all the time. Another one was about to rape me when he was stopped. This attack only stopped when one of their officers, whatever he was, shouted for them to move on. We were left in the side street while they, along with the tank, moved off. We got to our feet, but we did not know where to go. So we went back down into the cellar and waited. The women and the boys were crying loudly. I remember how the one boy was holding his backside – he was maybe 12 or 13, I don't know.

A second group of soldiers came through, as we could hear them shouting to one another. We were petrified as we thought we would be attacked again, but they burst in with flashlights and told us to go outside. They looked at us, and, after speaking among themselves, one of them gestured at us to follow him. We thought this would be it; we would be attacked again. I could not take this anymore. I just wanted to die, or find a way to kill myself. We were, however, taken away from the fighting and put with other German civilians. We were given some water and later some food. These Russian soldiers seemed to be different from the ones we had encountered first. They came and asked us what had happened to us. We told them. One of them said, after I told him I had been raped, and he said this in German, 'I would like to find and shoot the fucking pig that did this; this is not what we should do in war'.

Halcyon Days in Hitler's 'New Germany' before the nightmare of total war. *(Courtesy of D. Smith)*

A typical wartime portrait photo of a girl in her BDM uniform.
(Courtesy of D. Smith)

Monica Vanessa Kieler Dorsche prepares for one of her first glider flights in the 1930s. *(Courtesy of M. Dorsche)*

Anna Dann's brothers, Franz (left) and Josef (middle), who attempted to escape Berlin by stealing a Luftwaffe truck. *(Courtesy of A. Dann)*

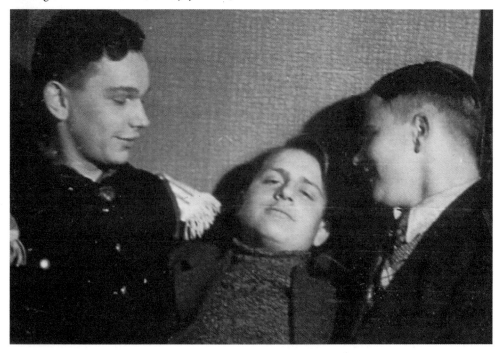

Weiner Katte, aged fourteen in the BDM. Weiner is seated front row, second from the left. *(Courtesy of W. Katte)*

Dora Brunninghausen with friends before the war. *(Courtesy of D. Brunninghausen)*

Vaida Raab pictured with friends of the BDM during skiing on the Salzburg. Vaida is on the right in the photo. *(Courtesy of V. Raab)*

Vaida Raab in a
studio portrait taken
on her birthday,
prior to her joining
the BDM.
(Courtesy of V. Raab)

Ilsa Hirsch in the BDM. *(Courtesy of Bundesarchiv)*

Theresa Moelle's husband-to-be, Raif, running in a Hitler Youth sporting event. Raif is on the far right in this picture. *(Courtesy of T. Moelle)*

Theresa Moelle relaxing in 1944.
(Courtesy of T. Moelle)

Theresa Moelle with her daughter by the seaside, date unknown.
(Courtesy of T. Moelle)

The Moelle farm in operation, post Second World War. *(Courtesy of T. Moelle)*

Walter Moelle post-Second World War. *(Courtesy of T. Moelle)*

Gangs of German women on rubble clearing duty in post-war Berlin.
(Courtesy of D. Smith)

A little girl playing with discarded weapons after the fall of Berlin.
(Source unknown)

A German girl
photographed in
the Ardennes by an
American soldier.
(Courtesy of Keith Costa)

Inge Strauss
exercising, post
Second World War.
(Courtesy of I. Strauss)

Eleonore Kirschener and Earl C. James photographed on their wedding day. *(Courtesy of E. Kirschener)*

Kristel Bernd, post Second World War. *(Courtesy of K. Bernd)*

Two medals awarded to BDM girl Wiener Katte, following the Battle for Aachen in 1944. On the left is the Iron Cross 2nd Class, and on the right a War Merit Cross 2nd Class. *(Author's collection)*

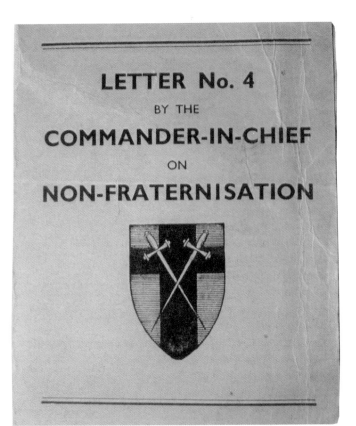

LETTER No. 4

BY THE

COMMANDER-IN-CHIEF

ON

NON-FRATERNISATION

Non-fraternisation leaflet No. 4, 25 September 1945. *(Author's collection)*

Non-fraternisation leaflect No. 4, contents. *(Author's collection)*

TO ALL MEMBERS OF THE BRITISH FORCES IN GERMANY

1. The Allied Control Council has decided that the time has come to abolish all separate zonal orders on the subject of non-fraternisation with the German people, and to adopt a universal policy which will ensure uniform treatment of Germany

2. All present orders about non-fraternisation are now cancelled.

3. The following orders will remain in force:-

(a) No members of the armed forces will be billeted with German families.

(b) Members of the armed forces will not be permitted to marry Germans.

4. I rely on all members of the armed forces to conduct themselves with dignity, and to use their common sense, when dealing with the Germans: twice our enemies in war during the last 30 years.

B. L. Montgomery

Field Marshal,
Commander-in-Chief,
British Army of the Rhine.

25 Sep 45

Monica Vanessa
Kieler Dorsche.
(Courtesy of K. Dorsche)

3. SABOTAGE INSTRUCTIONS ISSUED TO THE HJ

R (1st March 1945):-

On the 1st March 1945, the HJ - Moselland (12) - Recruiting staff for the SS Pz Div "Hitler Jugend" sent out pamphlets on sabotage for distribution to HJ Führer or their authorised deputies. After pointing out the immense damage that can be caused to the enemy by sabotage in his rear and citing famous exponents of this type of warfare, the pamphlet enumerates the following basic rules for petty sabotage:-

1. Sugar in gasoline
   Pistons get stuck, the motor becomes unserviceable
2. Sand in gasoline
   Fuel lines and valves become clogged, the motor temporarily unserviceable
3. Tar in grease in-take valves on motors and wheels (in case of railway cars)
   Bearings burn out, vehicles get out of control, and become unserviceable
4. Placing of metal spikes at road curves during the night
   Tyres of vehicles blow out, vehicles get out of control and become unserviceable
5. Stretching piano wire across the road in the dark (in this case consider the colouring of the wires)
   Vehicles, especially motorcycle couriers, are put out of action
6. Laying boards with nails at road curves
   Result same as in 4
7. Placing rocks into switches
   Switches cannot be set, trains will derail or collide, the enemy suffers heavy losses
8. Laying drag-shoes on open track stretches
   Trains derail
9. Destroy wire mechanism for controlling semaphore signals
   Trains go past signals, derail or collide
10. Connecting power and telephone lines by throwing wires over both lines
    At all exchanges connected with that line the apparatus will burn out
11. Piercing membrane in telephone receivers by means of a pointed pencil
    One party can hear, but the other one cannot
12. Tearing down enemy telephone cables
    Interruption of enemy communications and command systems
13. Steal from the enemy whatever you can
    Weapons, ammunition, equipment, parts of uniform, food, gasoline; in fact everything that belongs to the enemy and that he can utilise destroy in any out of the way place, so that he cannot find anything on you if you are searched.

Memo listing the various sabotage instructions that were issued to the Hitler Youth on 1 March 1945, including laying boards with nails at road curves and putting sand in gasoline. *(Courtesy of the Public Record Office, Streifendienstder Hitler Jugend, April 1945, W0208/3146)*

Vaida Raab, who was 16 years old during the fall of Berlin, vividly recalled the horrors of the last few days of fighting in the city. We met in a small café in Oxford in 2005, when she was accompanied by her son, Theobald. It was chilling, as the old lady sat opposite me, and closed her eyes, preparing to recite events that had occurred so long ago.

> During April 1945, we, as *Bund Deutscher Mädel* girls, were doing so much work to help. We helped the civilians by setting up kitchens, which provided meals. We were competent enough with first aid to be able to help those hurt in the bombing raids, and later on those wounded in the actual fighting as the Russians came. We also assisted with firefighting and, indeed, any other tasks that we were asked to do. It was not a case of 'oh, I can't do that or I can't do this.' If we didn't know how to do a particular task, then we learned it without any questions. That is how it was. We wanted to help as much as we could, as it helped relieve the pressure on the other authorities. We were all so tired and exhausted, that when I managed to get some time to myself, I would sit down, rest my head on my arms, and be fast asleep in less than a minute.
>
> The soldiers gave us tablets, though we had no idea what they were. The soldiers told us that these would help make us feel better and that they were good for us. After taking those tablets, you would not feel tired or fatigued. They made you feel like you could work all day and all night. I later discovered that the drugs we were being given were called Pervitin. They were among some of the drugs that Hitler had been prescribed by his doctor.
>
> Before the Russians arrived, they attacked with heavy artillery. This bombardment was indiscriminate, and many innocent civilians, including children and babies, were killed as a result. The first time you see the remains of the victims of a bomb or shell attack, it makes you feel sick, but I saw many, many such victims, to the point where it became normal. We lived with death all around us for so long that it did not scare me anymore.
>
> When the shelling stopped, we knew they [the Russians] were coming. Their tanks came first, the soldiers following behind them with their rifles at the ready. German soldiers who had been trying to defend the city were now being shot. Some were killed instantly, while

others would die later from their wounds. The German soldiers we were with would not allow us to fight or use any weapons. They told us that if we wanted to help, then we could help with the wounded that were coming in, in ever greater numbers.

I was asked to comfort this young German soldier who had been shot in the head. His head had been heavily bandaged, mainly to hold his head together. The blood was seeping through the bandaging. I sat down on the ground and I cradled him in my arms. I just tried to smile at him. His eyes were open and he seemed to understand what was happening around him, though he could barely even moan or call out. He uttered the words 'maiden, beautiful.' All I could do was smile down at him. What can you say to a dying boy? There are no words, are there?

An officer came over to me and he said, 'Comfort that boy, as your face will be the last one he will ever see in this world.'

There was no morphine to give the boy, so he must have been in great pain. His eyes then just went dull and glazed over. I pressed my face against his mouth to see if he was still breathing. He wasn't. He had gone. I suddenly realized I was crying, but was I not immediately aware of it.

I got up and covered him with his blanket. I could see I was wet with his blood. When the Russians appeared, we were still helping to treat injured German soldiers. Some of these Russians behaved like monsters. We were pulled away from the men we were treating, only to see them being machine-gunned to death as they lay on the ground. Once the injured German soldiers had been shot, the soldiers just ran off. Some Russians came after them, and as they passed through, they stabbed the bodies of the dead Germans with their bayonets, or kicked their heads.

I remember one Russian soldier stopping to examine one of the dead Germans. He took out a knife and sliced off one of the fingers to remove a gold ring. He just cut off the dead man's finger, took the gold ring, and threw the finger aside. He then searched through the pockets for other valuables. They were also abusive towards us. I was kicked more than once for no reason other than being a German. It was horrible and it will live with me until I die. When I spoke with a friend about this sometime later, she also confided in me that she had seen several bodies laid out in a line. Each had its throat cut and had been mutilated in other ways: eyes gouged out, breasts and genitals cut off. She said the bodies were German civilian men and women, and that the Russians had been doing these things all over the city.

It would be unfair at this stage to not include at least some explanation by former Red Army soldiers who were involved in the assault on Berlin in April 1945.

Anastas Sogiyiev, who served with the Russian Eighth Guards Army, recalled the following during an online interview with me.

The criminal element of our Red Army was not entirely representative of us. There were many good soldiers within the Red Army who did not choose to take and rape German women or take them as spoils of war, myself included. The problem, you see, was that Stalin had made a pact with criminals in the Gulags back home, that if they chose to serve their country and fight the Germans, they would, in return, earn their freedom, providing that they survived. The only criminals exempt from this pact were political prisoners.

So here you have men who were not sound of mind and quite dangerous being offered their freedom, or a pardon, in exchange for military service. Many of these individuals were murderers, rapists, thieves and drunks. In many ways, it was the hope that many of these men would be killed and therefore unable to enjoy the bargain into which they had entered.

They would fight desperately against the Germans. We were sure of this, that in many cases they were sent in first, as cannon fodder, as you call it. It was hoped that we, following behind, would then, in turn, encounter far less resistance. It was purely a tactical decision on our part.

Such methods were not unique to the Red Army. Many other countries have used similar tactics over the past centuries. We viewed these men from the Gulag as undesirables. We did not talk to them much, other than to issue them with orders. They were given the worst tasks, such as cleaning up our mess, digging latrines, burying the dead, and helping to cook, etc. We were aware that some of these men were what you might call crazy. We caught one of them having sex with animals on more than one occasion. We let him get on with it, as we were sure he would not survive for long – he didn't. Besides these Gulag men, there were many uneducated peasant types within the ranks. These men just wanted revenge for their homes and their land destroyed by the German incursions into the eastern territories from 1941.

Another former Red Army soldier, who had also served with the Eighth Guards, remarked to me, 'I intervened and stopped the rape of German girls, women and boys on more than one occasion. It was easy, I would just point my rifle at the soldier attempting the rape, and tell him if he did not stop, I would shoot him.'

I asked if he had ever carried out his threat. He calmly replied, 'Yes, in one instance I did.'

There were many other Red Army veterans who have claimed that they took measures to try to prevent the rape of girls and women. In many cases, these were genuine concerted efforts. Evidence does suggest, however, that the vast majority of Red Army soldiers were not so forgiving, as many had lost family or friends. Many had experienced or seen suffering on an epic scale, all the result of the German invasion in the east. Many wanted to exact their revenge either by killing, looting or raping.

Another Red Army Berlin veteran, who did not wish to be named, recalled:

Do I regret my actions of that time in Berlin in 1945? No, I have no regrets at all. Our people suffered when the Germans began their invasion back in 1941. They murdered thousands of our men, women and children, destroying their homes as well as their lives. They subjected us to appalling cruelty, so why should we not do the same back to them?

Yes, I took German girls and women when I was in Berlin. If they did not volunteer then I would take them by force, even if I had to beat them first. I enjoyed raping them. They would plead, 'oh no, please don't do this,' to which I would say back, 'a few months ago, you were still cheering for Hitler and you were still actively supporting the regime. No, no, no. I am going to do this, and if you try to stop me, I will kill you without hesitation.' I also helped myself to things from their homes, things like jewellery and other possessions. Whatever I wanted, I took from them, as I had nothing but contempt for them, you have to understand.

Heidi Koch has vivid recollections of the aftermath of the battle of Berlin:

> The world was proclaiming 'Victory. War is Over', but the war wasn't over, was it? Our forces had been beaten. Hitler was dead. We had ceased resisting the Russians, but there they were, looting, raping and executing, doing whatever they pleased, while the Allies stood watching it all. What the Russians were doing was committing war crimes in what should have been peace. I know of several girls who committed suicide in the weeks after the Russians came. I know of two who killed themselves by taking poison. At least one of them had discovered that she had been made pregnant by her Russian rapist. Another discovered she was pregnant. She jumped from a high building, killing herself.
>
> These girls had been destroyed by the rapes. The shame they had felt was just too much. In some cases, with no family or home, they felt that death was easier than living, especially in a Germany under Russian rule. Many girls who had been made pregnant by being raped received no real support from their parents. All they felt was shame. Thousands of abortions were carried out, in which some girls died as the procedure was not carried out by people with a proper clinical knowledge or background. In England, you call them 'backstreet abortions'. There was much money to be made by the butchers who carried out these abortions. One father shouted at his wife, 'I will have no daughter of mine give birth to any Russian. I will kill it with my bare hands first.'
>
> So, what choice did many of the rape victims have in the matter? Talking about this makes me so angry. God, it is painful, but if these words are left unsaid, no one will hear them. They will then say that it never happened or it was a lie. So long as I am alive, I will not give them that privilege. The Russians also raped thousands of their own women, which is a little-known fact, but it is true. Why do that I just don't understand it?'

A female telephone operator with the Red Army recalled:

> When we took a German town, we had three days in which we could do as we pleased. Our men could rape, beat and even kill German girls and women if they wanted to.

This was unofficial of course, and after three days it had to stop, or one could be court martialled. I remember one raped German girl lying naked with a hand grenade between her legs. Only now do I feel shame, but back then I did not. It was not easy to forgive the Germans. We hated seeing their undamaged white houses with roses growing in their gardens. I wanted them to suffer. I wanted to see their tears. It is only recently that I can now feel pity for them.

Another Russian soldier wrote in his diary:

We entered a house in Germany, inside which there was a woman on the floor. She was wailing and moaning. Beside her on the floor was a dirty, filthy mattress, and on this mattress, there was this child, a girl of maybe 10 years young. The girl was quite dead and we discussed this how many men had been on this girl [raped her], maybe two or three, maybe a whole platoon, we didn't know. We left the house, and as we walked away, the sounds of the woman wailing and moaning became distant again. It must have been awful, as the woman was the girl's mother. It is now a haunting vision now I am older.

Russian female soldiers who had arrived in the shattered city were brutal or somewhat unpredictable, as Kirsten Eckermann discovered:

I was with my mother one morning, just walking around, when two Russian women in uniforms with rifles approached us. We tried to move out of their way, but they would then step in front of us, blocking our path. I recall people standing around, but they did not intervene. One of the Russian women then slapped me across the face for no reason. My mother tried to shield me behind her and she was struck across the face hard too.

'Why do you do this?' We tried to reason with them, to which they said something like, 'Because we can and because we hate you, that's why, and we want to drink your tears'.

We stood on the spot, waiting to be struck again, when they decided to move on. As they walked on they were laughing like little girls would laugh after doing something they shouldn't have done. The German people still just stood watching and did nothing. My mother grabbed my hand and said, 'Come on, we are getting out of here.'

Accounts of Red Army barbarity could continue to fill an entire volume. I believe what is presented here should suffice. However, during the years since *Hitler's Girls* was written, more information has come to light regarding the issue of Allied war crimes. This volume would not be complete without some analysis of this controversial subject.

US soldiers were reported to have committed 11,000 rapes in Germany. Most were gang rapes of girls or women at gunpoint. It has been stated that some offenders were identified, court martialled and duly punished.

The Army legal branch recorded that, for brutal or perverted sexual offences against German females, some soldiers had been shot. Yet research would suggest that, while white US soldiers were excused the death penalty for their sex crimes, coloured US soldiers were executed, which is no surprise when one understands that segregation was a large part of American society at the time.

A high rate of violence against the German and Austrian populations lasted well into the first half of 1946, with five cases of German women being found dead in American barracks in May and June 1946 alone. It is something of a curiosity that, in many cases where German girls or women were raped by American soldiers, gifts of food were normally left behind for the victim, as if the act were not that of rape, but of prostitution.

Where British soldiers were concerned, it is difficult to ascertain how many rapes were committed as no reliable record exists on this issue. What is understood, however, is that many British soldiers raped German girls or women while under the effects of alcohol or suffering from post-traumatic stress disorder.

There was the attempted rape of two young women at gunpoint in the village of Oyle near Nienburg, which ended in the death of one of the women when, intentionally or not, one of the British soldiers discharged his weapon, the bullet striking the woman in the neck. There is also an account of three German girls being raped by British soldiers in the town of Neustadt am Rubenberge. A senior British army chaplain, following the advancing British troops, reported that 'there was a good deal of rape going on'. He then hastened to add that 'those who suffer rape have probably deserved it.'

With French troops, it is recorded that they were responsible for the rape of 385 women in the Constance area, 600 in Bruchsal and 500 in Freudenstadt. It was also reported that French troops went on an orgy of rape in the Hofingen district near Leonberg. French Moroccan troops, in particular, were considered as brutal, sadistic and sexually violent as those of the Red Army.

To summarize, female deaths in connection with the rapes in Germany overall, are estimated at 240,000. New information suggests that a figure in excess of 2,000,000 German girls and women were the victims of rape. This was undoubtedly one of the most shameful episodes to have taken place. The rape and abuse of German girls and women continued well into the winter of 1947–48.

Many Russian soldiers took German girls and women as sex slaves, sometimes offering food and a degree of protection in exchange. Things only improved when the Russian occupation authorities finally confined Russian troops to strictly guarded posts and camps, thus separating them from the residential population in the Soviet zone of Germany.

Anita von Schoener, who suffered her own horrific rape ordeal, told me this when I was preparing work for this particular chapter:

> Was being raped our absolution? Was rape a fair trade against our lives being taken?
>
> I often asked myself these questions afterwards, and thought, would it have been better to resist and face being shot instead? Had I not had my son Anton, who was only a toddler, then maybe I would have defied them. I am quite sure, had I fought with them to try and stop them from having forced intercourse with me, then they would have killed Anton. These were not the kind of men that you could have bargained with. They cared not that I had a child with me, using the child instead to get what they wanted. When a gang of soldiers are holding your child with guns against his head, do you then say, 'No, I will not comply with you.' They know that they have an advantage over you, and that they have the power. I made the conscious decision to let them do what they wanted with me and not resist them. Maybe then I could walk away from it with my baby still alive.

8
Anita von Schoener: My Rapist's Baby

Anita von Schoener's rape ordeal at the hands of Russian soldiers after her capture in Berlin in April 1945, was graphically recounted in *Hitler's Girls*. It is therefore not necessary to again recount the details here.

It was not long afterwards that Anita discovered she was pregnant. The torment of being made pregnant through being raped, was extremely stressful. In Hitler's Third Reich, abortion among German 'Aryan' girls and women was made illegal. Such an act was classed as a capital offence. The only exception was if the foetus was found to be deformed or disabled, in which case, abortion was permitted by the state as a necessary course of action. Even after 1945, abortion remained illegal throughout west and east Germany. These laws forced many girls and women to seek help with what can only be described as 'backstreet abortionists'. These were people initially denied work within medical practices due to their unsuitability or limited aptitude, but who possessed enough medical knowledge to be able to profit from performing these illegal and potentially dangerous procedures.

The techniques used by these illegal operators varied. They included the patient having to drink methylated sprits or turpentine, consuming preparations made from ergot, a fungus said to be especially effective at terminating pregnancies, consuming tansy oil, which was found to rot internal organs, knitting needles used in a probe fashion, or the infamous coat hanger. Large doses of Vitamin C were also said to have been effective methods of termination.

All of the above methods had their own dangers, including gangrene, haemorrhaging, sterility, psychosis and permanent injury. Even if the procedure was carried out successfully, it was essential that all foetal tissues be extracted, or it could decay within, with potentially fatal results.

Many women who were able, travelled to the Netherlands where abortion was not illegal. The abortion laws in Germany would not be relaxed until well into the 1970s. The situation must have been something of a personal hell for any of the German girls made pregnant through their wartime rape. The only real hope for those desperately seeking terminations was a sympathetic doctor who was prepared to risk prosecution and jail. For those who decided to go through with their pregnancies, like Anita von Schoener, even harder decisions lay ahead. Anita bravely recalls:

> If the ordeal itself wasn't bad enough, I had also contracted a sexual disease, which I certainly did not have prior to the rape. When I sought treatment in the weeks afterwards, the sexual disease was cleared up. I therefore thought that I could finally start to get over it all, when I discovered that I was pregnant. I had not had any sexual intercourse with anyone before or after the rape, so I knew the child growing in my belly was that of one of the Russians who had raped me.
>
> Involving my mother and father was necessary, yet they didn't seem to understand, or want to be directly helpful. Father would sit in his chair staring at the floor, not wanting to look me in the eyes. My mother did the same. I don't think they really knew what to do or what to say.
>
> It was my father who said the one evening, 'Abortion is the only possible way.'
>
> Mother agreed, saying that 'it was for the best that I get rid of the child as soon as possible.'
>
> To be honest, at that stage I was still in shock over the whole thing. They kept going on about how they knew someone who could carry out the abortion for me. In the end, I shouted at them, 'For Christ's sake, why don't you two shut up.'
>
> I was so angry at them, and it was then that I told them, 'Yes, I am going to go through with the full term of the pregnancy and I am going to give birth to the child. Then I am going to give the child up as soon as it is born.'
>
> Mother snapped, 'Well, that is your decision then, and so be it.'
>
> I couldn't understand how things had come to this as we had always got on very well. I guess, in one sense, that this was their way of trying to deal with the situation and support me. The war had changed everything. We felt like strangers to one another at that point in time and we argued a lot.

To make matters worse, I received a simple letter from the German Red Cross, stating that my husband, Bruno, who had been serving with the Waffen SS, had initially been listed as missing during operations in the east. The letter then went on to state that the relevant authority could now confirm him as having been killed and that he is in an unmarked grave. It had been difficult to identify his remains, but what was left of his *ausweiss* (I.D. card) had been discovered and his identity confirmed. We had virtually no time with one another. We had married more out of duty than love, but the news was still heartbreaking. I was now in a situation where I was a widow with a young child and pregnant through rape. Together with all the problems with my parents, I just felt so alone and desolate – it was the worst time of my life.

When I began to show, things were even worse. My father once complained to me, 'How the hell can you walk around with that thing inside your belly. You should kill it.' I had made the choice early on against abortion, even when my father arranged for a doctor with whom he was friendly to carry out the procedure for free. The thought of someone doing that to me was every bit as bad as the rape itself. I therefore made the choice to go through with the pregnancy, have the child and then give it up straight away. Had I kept the child, it would have grown up being hated, and I did not want that to happen. I wanted, if nothing else, for it to have a better life than I had.

The birth of the child was long and painful, but I gave birth to a little boy who weighed 7lb 12oz. He was perfectly healthy. The midwife, who had been with me at our home throughout the birth, asked me if I wanted to see the child. I told her, 'no.'

I told her that I wanted the child gone. 'Take him away, now please.' I was very tired and felt utterly miserable and dejected. I just wanted to get over this now.

My parents cared for Anton as I recuperated, but I came down with a fever and was quite ill for two weeks afterwards. It seemed that the dark hovel of a bedroom in my parent's house had become like a prison. I did not leave that room very much over the two weeks. I was ill, so it was with some relief when I began to feel well enough to just go outside into the warm sunshine.

When I looked at myself in the mirror, I thought I looked like death, I was pale and had black underneath my eyes and my hair was a mess. My mother was able to heat some hot water for me to wash in, and afterwards I felt so much better.

I then began to think of the future and what I was going to do now. I wanted to support myself and Anton independently of my parents, but I knew how hard this would be as a single woman with a child and no work, having to live with my parents again. Despite all of these problems, I felt no remorse and no regret, but just the instinct to survive. This is what the *Bund Deutscher Mädel* meant when lecturing us on being emotionless, hard, resistant and ruthless in our lives and endeavours for the state. The BDM made us hard. Some of us couldn't feel emotion, could never cry, could never feel regret.

Gertrud Scholtz Klink once said to us during a presentation she gave at our school, 'The weakling will never reside at the breasts of the pure German woman. The weakling will perish in the way that nature selects all weakness to perish, including the weaker races of our world. You have this personal duty to your Fuhrer, Adolf Hitler, and the German Reich. There is no love, only duty, and in your duty, you must learn to not only despise weakness, but also to destroy it.'

Heinrich Himmler, the head of the SS, had a near pathological interest in race, biology and eugenics. The idea of experimenting on humans to discover particular traits, such as hereditary diseases, deformity and mental illness fascinated him. The Slavic races were particularly hated by the Nazis. Anything that came from the east was viewed as this sub-human culture. Its origins would have been more than obvious to many had I kept the child that resulted from the rape. It would not have been fair to either of us to have to live a lie.

I was not the only one. I knew of girls who had babies, not just from Russians, but from sleeping with American or French soldiers. They would have the child, then just go and leave it somewhere where it would be found and taken away. There would be no responsibility and no further burden to themselves.

9

Ilse Hirsch and the Assassination of Franz Oppenhoff

The name Ilse Hirsch is a name that is unrecognizable to many. Yet her name is associated with what has to be perhaps one of the most daring assassinations of the Second World War. Although the victim was a relatively minor figure within German society, the mission was one not out of place within the realms of a James Bond film script.

Operation Carnival (*Unternehem Karneval*), as it was known, was an operation launched by members of the Werewolves. Their target was 41-year-old Franz Oppenhoff, a lawyer who had agreed to become mayor of Aachen under American supervision as of 31 October 1944. Oppenhoff's appointment as *burgermeister* was subject to much secrecy as, apart from the obvious dangers he would have to face, he had family still living in German-occupied territory. Measures were taken to try to prevent news of his appointment reaching the Nazi hierarchy, as the safety of his family could be compromised.

Despite the secrecy, the news of Oppenhoff's 'treachery' soon reached the ears of SS chief, Heinrich Himmler. Himmler instructed SS *Obergruppenfuhrer* Hans Adolf Prutzmann to eliminate Oppenhoff. Prutzmann quickly formulated a plan, assembling four of his most reliable SS troopers and two members specially chosen from the Hitler Youth. One of the Hitler Youths chosen to assist the assassination team was 23-year-old Ilsa Hirsch.

Ilse Hirsch was a captain (*hauptgruppenfuhrerin*) in the BDM, or League of German Maidens.

Born in the industrial town of Hamm in 1922, she had joined the BDM at the age of 16. Hirsch excelled in the BDM, becoming one of its principal organizers in the town of Monschau. She was a favourite of the Nazi propaganda photographers. Her image was used countless times in various periodicals or propaganda material. She was a very good-looking girl, with blonde hair and striking blue eyes. Her natural beauty, non-threatening appearance and commitment, would no doubt have played a part in her selection for Operation Carnival. Hirsch considered her selection for Operation Carnival as an honour. She trained at Hulcrath Castle for her part in the operation.

SS *Obergruppenfuhrer* Prutzmann was absent from the actual mission, acting as coordinator from Berlin. The assassination team consisted of the following members SS *Untersturmfuhrer* [lieutenant] Herbert Wenzel, *Unterscharfuhrer* [sergeant] Josef 'Sepp' Leitgeb, Karl Heinz Hennemann, Georg Heidorn, Werewolf trainee Erich Morgenschweiss and Ilsa Hirsch. Wenzel was placed in charge and would lead the operation, while Leitgeb was appointed his second-in-command. These two were the assassins. Hennemann and Heidorn, having a sound knowledge of the target area, would act as guides for the team, while Hirsch and the 16-year-old Morgenschweiss would help the team to procure supplies in the area. The idea would be that Hirsch and Morgenschweiss would pose as refugees and, whilst seeking food, would also gather information. Both were familiar with Aachen. Hirsch, in particular, had many connections in the city through her activities with the BDM.

The team underwent intensive training in early 1945. The team would have already been competent with concealment, and escape and evasion tactics, along with basic survival and first-aid techniques. In fact, the only skill that Hirsch and Morgenschweiss would have to master was that of parachuting. Hirsch appeared to be a natural during her intensive parachute-training course, which she passed without any problems at all.

The team finally took off for their mission on 20 March 1945, in a captured American Boeing B-17 bomber named 'Wulf Hund'. The use of the captured B-17 was to help avoid any unwelcome attention from the Allied anti-aircraft guns and fighters.

The team parachuted into a Belgian forest to the west of Aachen, which would allow the team to approach from the direction of the Allied advance. This was a clever move to further ensure that the team appeared non-threatening, blending in with the local population. The team jumped out of the B-17, disappearing into the night sky. Hirsch became separated from the others, but she landed safely and proceeded to hide her parachute as instructed, before making an assessment of the situation. She decided to continue on pushing on to Aachen alone.

In the meantime, the others had also landed safely. Fearing being compromised, they had to kill a Belgian border guard at the frontier. The guard's body was dragged into the woods, where it was hidden beneath some foliage. The group then set up a camp near to Oppenhoff's residence.

Hirsch made her way into Aachen, calling on a friend from the BDM. The two women talked well into the night, during which Hirsch's friend was able to confirm the location of Mayor Oppenhoff's residence as 251 Eupener Strasse.

Hirsch met up with the rest of the assassination team on 25 March. It was then decided that it was time to confront Oppenhoff on the doorstep of his home. When the team arrived, they found Oppenhoff was at a party at his neighbour's house. Oppenhoff was quickly summoned to come to speak to the strangers at his front door. The team was able to convince Oppenhoff that they were lost German pilots looking for the German lines. Oppenhoff was completely oblivious, cheerfully trying to convince the team that surrender was the best solution.

At this crucial point, Wenzel hesitated, while Leitgeb stepped forward, shouted 'Heil Hitler,' and raised his pistol to Oppenhoff's head. He squeezed the trigger, a shot rang out, and Mayor Oppenhoff fell backwards into the hall of his home. A pool of blood quickly formed around the body. The assassins scattered just before a US patrol arrived to check why the phone lines were not in operation at Oppenhoff's residence. Wenzel had cut the phone line prior to the assassination team confronting Oppenhoff.

The team, led by Hirsch, fled from the city. It was during their attempt to escape that Hirsch caught her foot on a tripwire attached to a landmine. The mine exploded, bowling them over and killing Leitgeb and badly injuring Hirsch. Her injuries meant a lengthy stay in hospital, but she eventually returned home to Euskirchen.

After the war, the surviving members of the Oppenhoff assassination team, with the exception of Wenzel, were tracked down and arrested. They were sent for trial in Aachen in October 1949, at what became known as the 'Aachen Werewolf Trial.' Subsequently, all were found guilty and sentenced to between one and four years in prison. Hirsch, however, was released. One could most definitely argue that the sentences handed out were unduly lenient, considering that they had shot a man dead in front of his wife and three children on the doorstep of their own home.

In the post-war years, Hirsch settled back down to life in relative normality near Aachen, not far from the scene of the crime. Hirsch always argued that she only acted as a guide and lookout on the operation. She insisted that she was on lookout duty when the shot that killed Franz Oppenhoff rang out. Again, Hirsch cannot be excused from guilt. If nothing else, she was guilty by association alone. She was aware of what the result of her endeavours would be on Operation Carnival. She also spared no thought to Oppenhoff's wife or their three young daughters. Hirsch left a woman a widow, and three young girls without their father, in what was a pointless murder.

One can analyse Operation Carnival, agreeing in many ways that it was a remarkably meticulous operation. Yet what did it achieve? It achieved nothing whatsoever for the German war effort. At this stage, the war was already lost. However, it did prove that well-trained, motivated individuals within such groups as the Werewolves, Hitler Youth or *Volkssturm*, could still prove to be a considerable nuisance to the occupying Allied forces in Germany.

In the post-war years, Ilse Hirsch has lived a peaceful existence, marrying and having two sons. It seems strange that Franz Oppenhoff had premonitions of his own murder some time before the event. He told his wife prior to the assassination, 'Somewhere the parachute jumper is ready to kill me.'

Over the years, the surviving members of Operation Carnival have expressed no remorse for Oppenhoff's murder. Ilse Hirsch has agreed to be interviewed on very few occasions. In one such interview with Hannes Heer at her apartment in Voreifel, she declined to show her face, only agreeing to talk with her back turned to the interviewer. Heer described her demeanour as 'cold, repulsive, without remorse.' A former friend of Hirsch recalls her in the BDM:

> Ilse excelled very rapidly within the organization. She had a knack of being able to learn things very quickly and to remember an enormous amount of information. Girls like Ilse were soon chosen to lead BDM girls as they had that natural ability. She was a very pretty girl and she had such beautiful blue eyes. She was chosen by photographers on many occasions, her picture appearing on or in many Nazi publications. As a BDM leader, she was strict, expecting all the girls to follow her principles by the book. If you got on her wrong side, then you were in big trouble. It did not surprise me at all when I heard that she was involved in the killing of Franz Oppenhoff. In a sense, she was perfect for the job, having all the prerequisites to succeed. She was not afraid of taking on any challenge asked of her. I doubted if she would ever kill anyone, but I'm sure if she had to do it, then she would not have hesitated in the task.

I did see her a few times after the war, where she showed me the scars on her legs from the landmine that almost killed her. She did not really talk much about the Oppenhoff killing, other than saying, 'he had been a traitor and as such deserving to die' and 'how many girls do you know that could have parachuted into enemy territory at night to assassinate a traitor.'

I reminded her that Oppenhoff had a wife and children. What about them? She became angry and agitated, the look in her eyes scaring me. She had no regret at her part in the killing, that was obvious. She saw it as just another duty to be performed for her country. There was an awkward silence for a few minutes. We stared at each other like two angry cats preparing to fight over territory.

She placed her cup of tea down on the table and said, 'Maybe it's best you leave now.'

I was quite taken aback by her sudden hostility towards me as we had been friends a good while. As she escorted me out of her front door, I turned to her to kiss her on her cheek. She pulled away, standing there with her arms folded, still looking angry with me. I just said 'goodbye Ilse' and I never went to visit her again. I did write to her but received no reply and that was it really. Our friendship ended at that point.

Hannes Heer also noted that, at the trial of the Operation Carnival assassins, 95 per cent of the jurors were former Nazi party members. This was certainly something that would serve as a saboteur to justice. This case does, however, exemplify the fact that Third Reich Germany was not just primarily focussed upon its leader Adolf Hitler. Third Reich German society was also a fanatical national community. To the end, there was an unbroken confidence in Hitler and those in his circle of power. Even the disloyal were forced into being loyal servants of the Reich. Operation Carnival, however irrelevant it may appear in the vast sphere of the Second World War history, serves as a measure of the toxicity that existed in German society at the time – even when the war was clearly lost and murder no longer served any useful purpose.

10
Don't Talk to the Germans

Allied authority was imposed over all of the territory of the former Third Reich west of the Oder–Neisse line. Supreme Allied Commander in Europe, US General Dwight D. Eisenhower, drafted a strict non-fraternization policy to be observed by all commands of the Allied occupation army in Germany. The policy was implemented almost immediately after the German surrender. American, British, French, Commonwealth, and indeed all Allied troops, were expected to comply with the policy. It would not have taken a genius to recognize that such a policy was totally unenforceable. As such it was largely ignored by Allied troops.

As time went by, things became more relaxed, until Eisenhower finally called a halt to the entire effort to enforce a non-fraternization policy among the Allied troops in Germany.

In total contrast, by January 1946, US authorities began to permit marriages between US soldiers and German women. Consequently, many German girls would leave Germany with their soldier husbands to start new lives in America. For those lucky girls who did meet and fall in love with an American or British soldier, such an outcome, though never easy, was seen as something of a salvation from the general hardships of living in a country with virtually no infrastructure. There are stories of true love and devotion, which will warm the coldest of hearts, and some stories of love that sadly were never to be.

The story of Eleonore Kirschener is typical of many:

> Initially, I think the British and Americans were so suspicious of us Germans, that they thought in some ways we were monsters. Over time, though, things became more comfortable and the suspicion in which we were once held began to wane. No one seemed to care anymore who was doing what, and against my parents' wishes, I began to see a young American soldier.
>
> He was 21 while I was 19. I had seen him one or two times when he finally came up to me and asked

me my name. His German was awful, but we could communicate. He told me that his name was Earl Caderton James and that he came from New Jersey. He wanted to take me out on a picnic. I agreed, and our romance began to flourish very rapidly from that point. He would come to my house in his car, but my parents did not want to meet him. So, I would go out to him and we would drive to the countryside where we would enjoy many hours together. I fell very much in love with this young man and I knew he felt the same way about me. At the time, I was not worried about what my parents thought. I just wanted to live my life to the full now after all the years under Hitler and the Nazis and the destruction brought about by the war.

We would drive out of the city and find a quiet spot to just talk – and kiss of course. Earl was fascinated by the stories I told him about things that had happened during the war, while I would ask him about his country and what it was like. If we had not been in Germany, we would have been just another normal young couple in love. Earl was the first proper boyfriend I had ever had and I learned a lot from him. He wasn't just using me for sex, as there were probably much prettier girls who would have given him sex in exchange for a bit of food, or whatever.

My last outing with Earl was not a memorable one, for unhappy reasons. He turned up as usual, but was visibly upset. We drove out of the city as we had done normally in the past and sat down on the bank of the river beneath a tree. He looked at me and said, 'Look Eleonore, I adore you and love you, but my folks have written me a letter saying they are not happy that I am seeing a German girl. They want me to break things off with you.'

I know Earl had written to his parents and told them of us. I felt uneasy about what they had said, but basically, they threatened to disown him if he continued seeing what they called 'one of the enemy'. It was ridiculous and broke my heart. We spoke little on the drive back into the city. We arrived at my home and I got out of the car. I leaned over to Earl and I gave him a kiss on the cheek. I said 'goodbye,' and started crying as I turned away to walk through the front door of my home. I did not look back.

I closed the front door and heard him drive off. My parents were sitting in the living room. I think they knew from my tears that all was not well. I went up to my room, but they did not follow to ask what was wrong, or anything. It was a big blow to fall in love with someone like that and for it to fall apart just because someone else did not like it. With time, the pain in my heart went away and I began to think less of the young man from New Jersey with whom I had spent so many wonderful warm sunny days.

I would go on to have a few relationships, but I would never let myself fall for any of them, which caused problems and they would end it. I started working at a coffee shop when, one morning a year later, I heard a car driving up behind me as I was walking to work from my parents' house. The car drove past and the driver was looking back at me. I'm thinking, 'Don't look at me you moron, look where you are going.' The car pulled up ahead and the young man behind the wheel shouted, 'Eleonore! Eleonore!'

I stood there for a few moments wondering who this was, when suddenly I see its Earl! He jumped out the car and ran to me. I asked him, 'What are you doing back here?'

He held both my hands and began to babble to the point where I have to tell him to stop, take a deep breath, and talk to me slowly, as I couldn't understand him. 'I've come back for you, Eleonore, if you will have me. I will do anything you want. I have left the Army now, and if you would like to come and live with me in America, then we can do that. Or we can stay here or go somewhere else.'

I asked him about his parents. He explained that they got so sick of him moping around and being upset, that they discussed things and felt they should let him make his own choices. I didn't know quite how to react or what to say. I didn't go to work that day. I went back home and talked to my parents about it all. I don't think they were too happy at first, but once they had met Earl and talked with him, they began to change. They could see he adored me, and the fact that he had come back for me meant a lot. My parents knew that there was not much of a future for girls and young women in Germany at that time, and, after a while, they were happy to let me go to America with Earl.

We came back to Germany to get married so that my family could be there. We then returned to America.

We went on to have four children: three boys and a girl. Some American people were not that nice to me, with me being a German, but most were understanding and were fine once they got to know me. Earl promised me that he would bring me flowers every single day. He kept to his word.

In all, I have lived a good life, apart from my youth under Hitler. I am thankful that I had many good years afterwards. You have to be thankful for everything you have in life, as there were thousands who did not live to see the end of the war to enjoy a life living in peace.

Anita von Schoener's life was about to change in the months after the end of the Second World War. She had lost her husband in the fighting in the east, and had suffered being raped by Russian soldiers in Berlin. She had had her own small child to consider and had gone through with the pregnancy caused by the rape. All of this against the backdrop of a ruined city, with no adequate food or water supplies, and an uncertain future where an undercurrent of anarchy quickly began to spread.

If you were lucky, you could go and live with another family in or around the city, or stay with friends if you still had any left. My parents had been pretty well off before the war started to go the wrong way. I know my father had allocated various funds to overseas banks, so he seemed to be able to influence people and get what he needed. As I have mentioned, my relationship with my parents had begun to deteriorate. We had begun to constantly argue over things. My parents were not happy with living in what was effectively a ruined house in Berlin. They were not used to the hardships of having no food or water, and no amenities such as a toilet and things. Many of these basics, or their structures, had been destroyed in the Allied bombings.

The Russians were a constant nuisance to us, grabbing at any woman who took their fancy out on the street. It made you just want to leave and go anywhere to get away from it all. When the Americans and British arrived, things began to change a little. There was, however, still so much hate. People hated the Allies and the Russians. They hated each other, and old scores were easily settled in a city without law and order.

I know of Germans who went out and murdered other Germans just for food, clothes or a pair of shoes. I also heard one story of a young German man killing a drunken Russian and taking his personal effects. The Russians body was never found as it was thrown down a sewer.

The first Americans I encountered looked at me with suspicion. You know, they stared at you with no discernible expression, so you did not know what they were thinking about you. I could speak English, as this was one of the many privileges of my upbringing, so I volunteered to help with translation duties. At first I was told bluntly to 'fuck off.'

I replied that there was no reason to be so horrible, was there? This Yank shouted, 'Oh, isn't there? Go and say that to the inmates of Sachsenhausen.'

Sachsenhausen was around 22 miles away from Berlin. I soon discovered that it was where 30,000 people had been murdered. Even medical experiments had been carried out there. In the BDM, you were told that political prisoners, Jews, and enemies of the Reich had to be relocated and re-educated. Other information as to what happened afterwards was vague. We had heard rumours of the death camps, but we saw none of them personally; not until after the war.

The Americans rounded up thousands of Berliners who had owned businesses or had positions of wealth in the city under the Nazis. They then took them to the camps to see for themselves what had been going on there. The Americans called us out of our home one morning and told us to 'get in', pointing to a truck full of other Berliners. My father asked where we were being taken and what this was all about. He was sternly told that he would see when we got there.

We were taken along with a convoy of other trucks to the camp at Sachsenhausen. Some people said they could smell rotten flesh before we even got there, but I couldn't. The smell of death was something I had lived with for so long, that I had become almost immune to it. The soldiers used to tell me the same. They could no longer smell it as they had lived with it for so long.

When we arrived, we were made to stand in lines. We were ordered to walk through the site. But what was there to see that I had not already seen? Just more death? Rotting corpses?

It was not quite the same, as there were bodies of women and children lying in heaps on the ground. Swarms of flies crawled over the bodies, which had a huge impact on me. Most of the victims had been starved to death. Now I knew the truth. I had seen it for myself and I just thought 'oh my God, no.'

The truck ride back to Berlin was quiet. Everyone was absorbed in their own thoughts of what they had seen. It was a sobering time in many ways, and now there could be no more denial of the truth as we had seen it with our own eyes.

Things did change slowly. Instead of the Americans saying 'don't talk to Germans', they began to take German girls as girlfriends, and so did the British. I know some German girls gave their bodies to American and British soldiers in exchange for food or goods that we could never have obtained in any other way. It was a form of prostitution and sexually transmitted diseases became rife in the city as a result of this practice.

I for one did not go with any men of the occupying forces, as I had too many of my own problems to contend with. I became friendly with a group of Americans over a period of time. They gave me food and things for my young son Anton, and as I had offered to help with translating a few months earlier, I asked them again. I told them I was competent with first aid and childcare, so they gave me a little job helping them with these tasks. It gave me something to occupy my time and on which to focus. I liked helping people no matter where they were from.

There was one American, a young man, who introduced himself to me as Henry McMillan. We got talking and I told him my story: where I had come from, my son's father, and everything that had happened. He politely asked if he could draw a portrait of me. I agreed, but asked him why he wished to do so. He explained that he liked to draw using pencils, so he drew a really good picture of me. He said that it was 'for my folks back home in Illinois.' I asked him about America and what it had been like there for girls and women, and if they lived the same as we did. He told me things that amazed me, like how people in the USA enjoyed great freedom, apart from African Americans, for whom segregation and other rules were in place. Henry said he didn't agree with black people being told they could not go to certain places, or do certain things. I interrupted and said, 'It sounds like what the Nazis were doing with us, yet we followed when, really, we should not have.'

Henry smiled and just said, 'It isn't quite as easy as that, but that's how it is.'

I met Henry a number of times afterwards and we would go for walks. I would bring Anton with me. Henry was really good with him and I began to feel happy for the first time in years. He sat me down and asked me what I would do if ever anyone showed any interest in me, and could I love again after all that I had been through? I just told him I would not know until that actually happened. He didn't push things and left it at that, but I understood what he meant as I could see it in his eyes – they seemed to sparkle.

We would meet up anytime we could and just go walking. He would always bring things that I could take home for my parents. My parents asked who it was that I was going walking with. I was honest with them and told them. I was quite surprised that they did not react with anger. I think both my parents understood that we were now going to have to get used to living in a very different Germany. We were fortunate to be living in one of the Allied occupation zones. These later became West Germany, though it was no better than the eastern Soviet zone for a long time.

After nearly four months of meeting with Henry, I plucked up the courage to take him to meet my parents. I warned him that our home was still in a state of disrepair, and not to expect much. However, he said he had no problem with that at all. When I brought him into my parents' home, he removed his hat, offered his hand to my father and said 'pleased to meet you, sir,' a typically American way of greeting. My father took his hand and shook it. My father's English was not as good as mine, so I had to translate for them.

I was totally shocked when Henry told me to ask Father, 'Would you mind if I asked your daughter to marry me, sir. I promise you I will always look after her and Anton and love them both unconditionally. I know she might not want to marry me, as she has told me all that has happened. But if I ask and I am told no, then I can eventually go back home knowing I did ask both Anita and yourself, sir.'

I didn't know what to say. I think Mother and Father were too shocked to reply, but I was at an age where I could decide for myself. My father asked Henry for a few minutes to talk alone with me and Mother.

Mother and Father just said, 'If you wish to marry this boy, then we give you our blessing. There is nothing much for you here, is there?'

Father asked if I wanted to be with this boy, but I told him that I didn't know, as I was worried what they might think.

Father said, 'He seems like a nice young man. If he is prepared to care for you and our grandson, then that is settled.'

At that I went and brought Henry back in. He shook hands with Mother and Father again and said he would see them again soon.

Henry said to me before he left, 'I can't wait to see you next, as I will have something to ask you. Do you know I love you as you are the most beautiful girl I have seen? I want to be with you more than anything else in the world, and if it means I come to live in Germany with you, then so be it.'

For the first time, he leaned towards me and kissed me on the cheek, gently, then he jumped into his car and roared off down the road. I waved him goodbye. I felt strange. I had never felt this feeling before, not even with Bruno, the father of my son. This is that feeling they called 'love' and I was experiencing it for the very first time in my life – God it felt wonderful.

I met with Henry two weeks later and we went for a walk. It was this time that he asked me if I would marry him. My reply was 'yes' and we shared our first proper kiss. He was due to leave Germany to go back to the USA and he promised that he would write me letters. He would return after his demobilization was complete, and then we could leave to start a new life in America if I wanted. Henry kept his promise. He wrote me letters and told me how much he was missing me. He had told his family that he had fallen in love with a beautiful German girl.

His family were Christians, and as such they could bear no grudges or hatred, but they expressed some concern at me having a child with no father. Henry explained that my son's father had been killed in the war, but he made no mention that he was SS.

During our period of separation, I had a visit from some Americans who told me that they were US Army Intelligence. They asked me questions about Bruno, but I did not know anything other than that he had been serving in the east with the SS *Totenkopf* [death's head division] and that he had been a corporal. They asked me if I had any letters from him, and in all honesty, I did not. I did give them the letter stating that Bruno was confirmed dead/killed in action. They even asked me if I had any associations with the SS, which was ridiculous. I gave them the ID papers I had been issued under the National Socialist government, which they took away. I never received those papers back, and it's a mystery as to where they ended up.

After four months, Henry turned up in civilian clothes. We could not wait to get out of Germany. We went to Switzerland, where we stayed in a hotel for two weeks, just enjoying the crisp, clear air and the beautiful countryside. We came back to Berlin to wish my parents farewell. We told them that we would write to them every week and visit once we were settled in America.

After spending some time with my parents, we went back to Switzerland. From there we travelled to Ireland. Henry had relatives living in Ireland, where we stayed for a few days before leaving for America on a ship.

Henry's family were lovely people. They made me feel welcome, though I was nervous about what things would be like in America. Would people hate me when they discovered I was German, and things like that? When we arrived, I found that America is a vast place. It swallows you up, and, for a German girl with a German accent, it was a little scary. I had never been much beyond Berlin before, so this was a huge adventure for me. The things I would experience in America were amazing.

Henry's family were, I think, a bit wary of me at first, but after a while, they could see how happy me and Henry were. I worked hard to fit in with the family. I found work at a small café, where I discovered that the owner's father had been born in Germany. He understood what the National Socialists had done to Germany, and how it had brainwashed the youth and then sacrificed them in a pointless war.

There were, of course, some problems when it came to us making love. I know Henry desperately wanted to make love to me. He never once put pressure on me. The problem was we would get so far, and then at the critical point I would have flashbacks of the rape. Whenever Henry would get on top of me, I would feel suffocated and would begin to panic and fight for breath, which frightened him. We would have to stop and pleasure each other in other ways.

Back then, there was no counselling for these kinds of problems. The manual *How to be the Perfect Housewife* did not cover such things either. It was a young nurse I talked with, who suggested certain methods we could try. She explained that if you feel suffocated every time your man tries to make love to you in the missionary position, then try other positions, for example where you are on top or he is behind you. It was embarrassing having to discuss these things, but she was very good and I wanted to sort out this problem. I wanted Henry and I to be able to enjoy a normal, loving relationship, and maybe have children of our own. We tried the nurse's advice and it seemed to work. After much patience, we were able to make love like any normal healthy young couple would. Henry and I only had one child together, a daughter, so Anton had a younger sister to look after.

We had our problems over the years, but then so does everyone. I read in the newspapers about what was happening back in Germany, especially when the Soviets began the blockade and then the troubles leading to the Berlin Wall being erected. This did not surprise me at all. I am amazed we did not end up going to war with them when the Cold War began. When the Berlin Wall was finally torn down, I breathed a sigh of relief. Maybe now Germany could finally be at peace with itself.

I consider myself very lucky, as I have seen a lot of the world and have experienced many cultures and learned so much more. My son and daughter grew up free to find their own destinies in a free society. They now both live in New York and have excellent careers – we are both so proud of them both. When my daughter left home for New York, I felt so afraid for her, as I have been so protective of her after what happened to me when I was young. Henry reassured me that we have to let her go and that she would be fine as she was strong like her mother.

Do I regret having had any association with the *Jüngmädel Bund* and the *Bund Deutscher Mädel*, the Hitler Youth organisations for girls? Yes, in some ways I do, but in others I don't. They did raise us to be strong, fearless and determined even if in the wrong context of things. The pain of those years is still there, though they are easier to live with today. There is now more understanding of what life was like under the Third Reich and how it worked to control everyday life and society in general. I wish I had been stronger and had resisted completely. If my story is a lesson or a warning to the youth of the future, then all that happened to me was not in vain.

The last time I was in contact with Anita, both she and Henry were well. Anita told me of a trip they had made to Berlin in 2004, as Anita put it, to put a few ghosts to rest. She went back to look at and walk up the street where she had been raped by the Russian soldiers. It took some time to find the right place, but it was still there, although new buildings now stand where the old ones once stood as silent witness.

> It was unsettling coming back to the exact spot where I had been attacked back in 1945. It was a breezy day, and the wind moaned like a ghost as it swirled around the buildings. I just stood at the spot for a few minutes, reflecting on things. I then closed my eyes, said a prayer, and then said to myself, 'They wanted to destroy me. They hoped they would tear my soul away. But no, they didn't destroy me. I lived, I loved, and I am still here.' It was the closing of a chapter.

Anita and Henry went to see Anita's old home, followed by a visit to her parents' grave, where she laid some flowers, whispering to the grey slab of stone, 'Sleep well, Mother and Father, we love you.'

Kirsten Eckermann, who had survived the war along with her parents, was also relieved when Allied forces began to arrive in Berlin.

We were gratified to see the Americans and British, but at first it was a case of 'don't speak to Germans'. We understood that these were orders dictated by their military, and in a way, we understood. Many of the Allied soldiers probably hated us. In fact, I know that some of them did. When they first appeared, we were happy. We felt that their presence might help stop the Russians from raping women and beating up men and boys, which they continued to do right up until they were confined to barracks away from the civilian populace of the city.

For weeks there was this kind of 'don't talk to Germans' stand-off, but we knew, that at some point, we would have to talk to each other and work with each other, otherwise how could we progress the peace? I was still wearing my small diamond-shaped Hitler Youth badge on my jacket when this British soldier noticed it. He just grabbed me and removed the badge. He didn't hurt me, but he looked angry as he pulled the badge off, throwing it away muttering as he did. They had the authority to search our clothing, which they did, but they found nothing at all. We had nothing, and we looked a mess with dirty faces and torn clothing.

As time passed, they would offer us some food, chocolate bars and cups of hot tea. The tea was something else!! I vividly remember how good that hot cup of tea tasted that was given to me by a kindly British 'Tommy'. I looked up at him and said '*danke*,' which is thank you in German.

The Americans gave us chocolate bars, but I ate so much that it made me sick. What we really needed was some proper food. Makeshift kitchens were eventually set up by the occupying forces, where vegetable stew was boiled up. We were given a bowl full with some bread. It did not take much of this food to fill me up, as it felt as if my stomach had shrunk though a lack of food.

I recall this little girl in Berlin. She had a piece of coal that she was chewing on, she was that hungry. I went over to her and took the piece of coal off her telling her it would make her sick. I then gave her the last half of a bar of chocolate that had been given to me by one of the Americans. The little girl shoved the entire piece into her mouth until her cheeks were bulging out like a hamster, before turning and running off.

I also recall leaflets being distributed among the population, stating that any jewels, badges, banners or pictures bearing the Swastika or Adolf Hitler, or indeed any form of Nazi iconography, was now illegal and subject to strict de-Nazification laws. There were all manner of flags and discarded Swastika emblems that had once adorned buildings now lying in the streets. These were piled up and burned by the occupation forces.

Weapons lay everywhere, and as a result there were frequent accidents. There were some deaths due to children playing with live discarded weapons such as grenades, pistols, rifles and ammunition. I heard a story about a child who had picked up a grenade, then pulled the ring out, unaware of the danger. The grenade blew up in her hands, killing her instantly and injuring several other children that were playing nearby. There were hundreds of unexploded bombs lying around too. I recall children playing near these things as if they were nothing.

Many young girls turned to prostitution in exchange for everyday goods that were in short supply, though this was happening more in many of the big cities. Sexually transmitted diseases soon became a problem, especially what they called 'VD', and as a result, the occupying forces brought millions of condoms with them. It is funny really, when you think that condoms became more essential than food and medical supplies.

As former BDM girls, we could help women look after their children. We would help clean and dress wounds, then began to help with everything, including the removal of rubble and the digging of makeshift vegetable patches. Any food that could be grown was encouraged to help relieve the severe food shortages that we all faced. Rationing of food had to be observed for some time after the end of the war, so if you could grow potatoes, cabbage, carrots, onions, and anything else, you did. The problem was, that you would grow vegetables, and just when they were ready for harvesting, under the cover of darkness someone would steal them – that's how it had become.

I heard that one time a German man had shot dead another for trying to steal some potatoes. People were prepared to kill for food. That was scary, but we all knew that this would go on for a long time yet. As they say today, things would get worse before they get better.

Dana Henschelle remembers her first encounters with the British and American forces, recalling how, at first, relations were very cold.

I was personally not too concerned about them, as I had witnessed what the Red Army were like, and no army could be any worse than what they were. The main difficulty was the language barrier. Although they had translators with them, there never seemed to be enough of them around. The first British soldier I was able to talk with, through an interpreter, told me he was an officer. He asked me all sorts of things, such as if my parents were Nazi supporters and had I taken up arms during the siege of the city? I answered them truthfully, as I had then, and still have now, in my opinion, nothing to hide or to be ashamed of.

We were up against an army of rapists and murderers, and we were told that if we did not fight, we would be raped and murdered. Of course, this was not entirely true, as I did not suffer rape, but I know many who did. I told the British officer what I had witnessed. He listened intently to me, while scribbling down the information in a small notebook. When he had finished, he stood up and said something to one of his men. The other men were shaking their heads, as if in disbelief. I told the officer that if he wanted to see the bodies of German women who had been raped and shot, I could take him to the place to see for himself, as the corpses were probably still lying there. The translator said to me, 'It's okay, we will investigate in due course. Thank you for your information.'

I wonder what happened to the information I gave, as nothing seemed to get done about it all, which made me angry. I fully understood the hatred that some British and American soldiers felt towards us, as many had seen what German forces had done to innocent people, and, of course, six million Jewish people had been murdered in the death camps.

In time, we talked more and became friendlier, to the point where we would discuss what the future of Germany would now be. The truth was, at the time, we did not know what the future held. The young had to be de-Nazified and re-educated, while we had to pick up the pieces of our lives and carry on. We, as the Hitler Youth generation, would also carry the burden for the Third Reich until our deaths. We were there and we followed, and we were thus partly to blame. We were, however, used by the Nazi state. We were exploited. When the time of reckoning came, all of the people like Goebbels, Hitler, Bormann, Göring, Axmann, von Schirach and Scholtz Klink went into hiding in bunkers. They were cowards, and they left women and children to fight their war.

Heidi Koch recalled in our last interview:

I remember a sign put up not far from our home. This was after the Americans came into the city. The sign was paper, pasted up onto a board. The poster said something like 'Germans are not your friends – remember, do not fraternize.'

My father saw it and said, 'This is good, isn't it. We have lost the war and the Nazis have gone, yet this is the kind of shit Hitler would have been proud of.'

Early on, he was not happy about the 'don't talk to Germans' thing. It didn't last long though, and pretty soon the American and British boys were asking us if we had any souvenirs, Hitler autographs, Nazi awards, flags, bullets and other things. A number of times I was asked if I had Hitler's autograph. I just laughed at them and said no. I gave one an RADw [Reich Labour Service] pin badge, with which he seemed very pleased. I gave another my father's *Volkssturm* armband. They also wanted us to pose for photographs. They loved taking photos of us girls and would tell us to do model poses and things. One even asked me if I still had my Hitler Youth BDM uniform. He was very disappointed when I told him no, it had been burned.

Not all JM or BDM girls wore a uniform. You see, once accepted into these organizations, your parents had to buy the uniform for you. Some parents couldn't afford to buy these uniforms, so their girls went without them. Another one asked me if I had a swimsuit I could put on for a photograph.

So, all the fuss over being friendly with us was short lived and pointless, wasn't it? I know one girl who even offered to take her clothes off for a photograph, and yes, she stripped off and started doing all these poses.

These young American boys were going frantic with their cameras, click, clicking away until all the film was gone. It stopped when she heard her mother shouting to her, '*Komen sie hier*, Hilde.' [Come here, Hilde]. The girl quickly grabbed her clothes and put them on before running off in a panic without even collecting her fee. It was quite funny when I think back, but I could never have done anything like that.

Sophia Kortge, who had joined in the fighting and had given her account of shooting a Russian soldier dead during the fall of Berlin in *Hitler's Girls*, was happy the war was over, but vividly remembers the anti-German sentiment that many, Berliners in particular, were subject to.

The Russians hated and despised us, and they took great pleasure in telling us that. It was a mutual hatred between two opposing ideologies and cultures. We had always viewed these Russians as the sub-humans that we were taught under our National Socialist schooling and the *Jüngmädel Bund* and *Bund Deutscher Mädel*.

I was kicked and punched many times by Russians, purely because they knew I had been fighting against them, and had been captured in the rubble of Berlin. I can remember each day praying that either the British or Americans would come, and maybe then the brutal treatment would stop. We were not resisting anymore. The war was supposedly over, so why did they keep being like this towards us?

Our home was gone, my parents and I were herded into a makeshift camp where homeless Berliners would be billeted for months. Many chose to stay in their ruined homes rather than go into those horrible temporary camps, some of which were moved to fields on the outskirts of the city.

Notices about non-fraternization with Germans appeared before the arrival of American and British soldiers. The laws were at first obeyed by more or less everyone. The problem was we could not ignore one another as we had to work together. We young girls and women were formed into working gangs to start removing the piles of rubble from bombed buildings. Soon we had young Allied soldiers either working with us or directing clear-up operations, thus we had to speak to one another. German girls began to see some of the soldiers and would meet up with them in secret. I know of a few who sneaked off to have romance time with English or American soldiers, which I found quite amusing really. Here we all are working together, removing piles of rubble, when just a short time ago we were trying to kill each other.

I was surprised at just how many of the Allies could speak German, which was good, as they were much nicer people and we felt that they were easier to talk to than the Russians, who we still did not like. We talked about all sorts of things: where we had lived before the war and what we hoped the future might bring. I was interested to learn about England and America and what life was like there. Many of the young soldiers were homesick and missing their parents, brothers and sisters. The soldiers would show us photographs of their wives and children. Some had photographs of their girlfriends. They would talk about how they just wanted to go home now.

One of the English soldiers was particularly kind to me and before he left he said, 'You German girls, you're not bad, not like they say you are.'

Working in gangs removing rubble was very hard work indeed, but we had these conveyor-belt machines that we could drop the rubble onto to save us walking back and forth. But our hands soon became very sore, and would get cut and bleed. The good thing was the Allied boys always had good first-aid kits and lots of bandages with them. One of them wrapped my hands up to protect them from further damage. No, the non-fraternization thing did not last. In reality, how could it?

German girls and Allied soldiers were soon having sex all over the place. It was not uncommon to walk around a corner and find one of your friends having sex up against a wall with an American or British soldier. I once went into a bombed-out shop looking around for something to eat, when I heard moaning noises coming from one of the rooms. When I looked in the room where the noise was coming from, I had a shock. I saw a girl I knew, who was only about 15, naked and knelt down on all fours, while this man was having sex with her. They both looked up at me, but were so engrossed in what they were doing, that they just carried on. I turned away and walked out of the shop. I just thought that was so wrong as the man must have been in his thirties or thereabouts. She was just a child, probably letting him do it for some kind of reward.

Some girls even married and left Germany to live new lives in England, Ireland, Canada or America. I had not even had a proper boyfriend at that point, but that never bothered me. My father always used to say, 'Young men – they are nothing but scoundrels, girl, and you must wait until the right one comes along.'

So yes, the 'don't speak to Germans' signs that did appear, soon deteriorated, and when they did, they were never replaced.

As for the Russians, we didn't like them at all. They were swine, rapists and killers. They took many girls and women as their personal sex slaves, which went on for a long time. They enslaved women under the threat of execution. Some of the women accepted this and adapted their lives around it, using it to get food and clothing and for protection. This in my opinion was wrong. But, in desperate situations, you do desperate things, I guess. Who am I to criticize someone just for trying to survive?

11

Green Potato Mash and Rats

Karin Hertz and her two younger sisters and brother had been sent to live with their grandparents who lived in Kopenick, a town to the south-east of Berlin. Their parents had begun to question the safety of their children long before the threat of Russian and Allied invasion came. The family had a few near misses during the air raids on Berlin. As the daylight bombing attacks steadily increased in ferocity, Karin's parents arranged for them to live out the remainder of the war with their grandparents, where it was hoped that they would be safer. Kopenick itself is a beautiful location, comparable to the English Lake District.

Karin's family were what many would describe as high-middle class. They never went without anything, enjoying an above average lifestyle. Karin takes up the story:

> My father was a member of the Nazi party. He had been there from the beginning, and yes, as a supporter he believed in everything. I know he joined the NSDAP. He had a small company that worked as a sub-contractor to a furniture maker. His company manufactured small metal components, and cast fittings for chairs, sofas, cupboards and all sorts. Even with our relative wealth and my father's influence, everyday essential items started to become very scarce. We were sent to Kopenick more for safety reasons than economic ones. When the Americans began bombing Berlin, it steadily became increasingly intense.
>
> I had been a BDM girl from 1943. My mother and father insisted I join. They bought my uniform for me and that was it. I also recall them giving me a special copy of Hitler's *Mein Kampf* book for Christmas that year. I wasn't eagerly political, as understanding politics was much like learning a new language. I understood and grasped the basics to not be embarrassed in class at school when asked about certain things. If you were asked to stand up in front of the class, and the teacher asked you things, like

when was our Fuhrer's mother born and you could not answer, then God help you.

The incentive to learn was through fear and from the influence of our parents. As the war drew nearer, our Hitler Youth activities were interrupted. The talking and holidays were over. We went out into the streets as a troop, where we set up mobile kitchens, serving watery soup to the people who had been bombed out and those who had nothing. We organized clothes and helped with babies and young children. I enjoyed that side of it, as we were helping to maintain the morale of our people.

After one or two frightening incidents, my father made arrangements for us to be taken to Kopenick. My younger sister had been fired on by Allied fighter planes and we had nearly all been killed in the bombing. Soon bombs were falling all the time, day and night. My father arranged for a car to collect us early one evening. I remember it well, as it was pouring with rain. Father knew the chances of bombers attacking that night would be less than if it were clear. I had already said my goodbyes to my friends with whom I had grown up and been with in the BDM. I was very sad to have to leave them. I wanted to stay, but arguing with my parents was not a good idea.

By late 1944, my father's workshop was employed in making small components for ammunition for the military. In this context, he was an active member of the Nazi party, involved in production towards the war effort. When we got into the car that came to pick us up, he just told us, 'You be good. Look after each other, and we will see you soon.'

There were no scenes of emotion, no hugs or kisses. Mother and Father viewed such things as being weak to us children. We were to be strong-minded, strong-willed and tough. That is how we were raised.

When we arrived at Kopenick, Grandmother greeted us and brought us in out of the rain. Grandfather was sat beside the bare fireplace, smoking his pipe. We ran up to him one by one and greeted him, then Grandmother prepared our beds for the night. We were tired and excitement soon gave way to a blissful sleep.

In the morning, we were woken by Grandmother at 7.00 am, when we would help her with her chores. It was an early start, but then we were used to that, not like children today. There was washing and housework to do, then we would have to help prepare food. There were apple trees nearby, and whenever there was fruit on them, we would pick them and put them in storage in straw in a shed next to the coal house, as my grandparents called it. There was a wash house next to that where all the washing was done. They had a small vegetable patch out the back, which was used for growing things to eat. Meat and sugar was becoming quite hard to procure, as was flour for making bread. Grandfather had a shotgun which he would take to go out after rabbits or squirrels, which were fairly prevalent. Sometimes he was lucky, but I don't think he was a particularly good hunter. He would come back grumbling and cursing, and Grandmother would say, 'not in front of the children.'

The nearby lake was also a source of food where, if you were lucky, you could catch a fish. None of us was a particularly good fisherman, but we did try with our improvised rods made from tree branches. We were taught to use a tiny bit of rabbit or squirrel entrails for bait. Grandfather would make the hooks himself. Fishing was not something I liked, as I was an impatient girl and found the endless sitting around at the edge of the lake boring.

My grandmother would make soups or stew, as these were the easiest things to make, though there was never much. She would make bread when she had flour, but supplies were becoming hard to get. You grew or made anything you could, trying to make it last for as long as you could.

We had neighbours and we all chipped in to help each other out. We did play with the other children and soon made friends in the area. I became friendly with a girl named Frieda Altmann. Her father, she said, was a rat catcher. Most mornings, he would leave the house with a small dog at his side, pack on his back, and with a shovel over his shoulder. I would go around to their house with Frieda, where I recall him sat in his chair by a wireless with a cigarette balancing on his lip. He would listen intently to the daily broadcasts on the progress of the war. There was talk of some new wonder weapons, which would change the course of the war. We did not know what they were and had never seen any of them, but believed in them.

We would often see Messerschmitts and Focke-Wulf 190s in the skies. We could recognize them from their engine sounds and, of course, their silhouettes. I had learned from the Hitler Youth boys all about our aircraft and the different types. So, I knew them quite well, and it was great watching them in the sky. We once saw a fight between a group of our aircraft and the enemy, but I could not tell the nationality of the ones they were fighting. We saw one of the enemy planes falling from the sky, trailing smoke. Seconds later, there was a muffled explosion as it hit the ground. It looked close, but it was some miles away. I know some locals went to have a look at the crash, but our military would not let them get close or touch anything.

Some of the local boys would come back with bullet casings that they had picked up. They would then barter or exchange these things for other items they needed. We were not permitted to go far from our grandparents and the neighbours, or the Altmanns, as we knew they were our boundary. Our grandparent's house was nestled in the trees, with four other houses next to each other.

By late 1944, with the onset of winter, things became steadily worse. Food was becoming a problem, even in our rural areas. Grandfather would continue his rabbit-hunting forays. He would go out with other men into the forest to try to shoot some for us. He might come back with two, if we were lucky. He would then skin them and use as much of the carcass and innards of the animal as possible. Kidneys, heart and liver were all food for the pot, as he and Grandmother would tell us. We would watch fascinated as he skinned the rabbits, our hands over our faces. The smell was unpleasant, especially when the guts was removed. It was a kind of cheesy smell that reminded me of dirty socks. Grandmother would use every last piece of meat from the animal and cook it in a pot. The bones would be kept to flavour 'soup', as she called it. The soup was no more than boiled water with a few vegetables in it. If we had bread, we could say this was a feast.

It was while we were at the Altmanns' house that the phrase 'green potato mash and rats came about.' Mr Altmann would arrive home and pull out these thin strips of meat from his bag and hand them to his wife. His wife would boil some water and place the strips of meat in the pot, where they would be cooked slowly. She would add anything she could find to the bubbling broth, which would serve as a kind of evening meal and a lunch for the next day.

While out playing one afternoon, I said to the boys that Mr Altmann always comes home with these strips of meat, but never says what they are? One of the boys quipped 'rats, that's what they are. Mr Altmann is the rat catcher and any he catches and kills he brings home for food.'

I recall the rather horrible looking green potatoes that Mrs Altmann would mash then serve with the meat broth. I was a little concerned, as I had enjoyed some of the broth while at their house with my friend Frieda. Oh my God, I thought to myself, have I eaten green potato mash and rats? While out playing, I began to sing the words out loud 'green potato mash and rats, green potato mash, green potato mash and rats, green potato mash and rats is good.' The other children out playing joined in, singing the words. Frieda stopped with a puzzled look on her face and said, 'Are you talking about Mother and Father, as it sounds like it.'

I didn't know what to say to her and felt slightly embarrassed. I just stood there and said 'sorry Frieda,' feeling really upset with myself. In response, she burst out into hysterical laughter and began singing my little rhyme again. The chorus was interrupted by Frieda's mother's voice calling her in. Every time I went around to Frieda's after that, we would start laughing to ourselves, and the adults would say things like 'what has gotten into you girls? What do you have to be so joyful about?'

As winter passed into spring, we saw fewer of our aircraft in the skies, and more and more enemy ones. My grandparents began to dig out the floor of the coal shed. The younger children could not understand the reason for this, but I knew what they were doing. They were digging a bomb shelter and I helped them do it. Grandfather packed earth and planks of wood from the garden fence around it to reinforce it.

I said to grandfather one morning, 'The war is not going well, is it?'

He had received word from our parents in Berlin and I don't think the news was good. I was 16 by that time and I was not stupid. We went inside and Grandfather explained that our father had closed his workshop under orders and was told to report to the military authority in Berlin Central.

'Does that mean Papa has been called for service?' I enquired. Grandfather nodded his head, looking upset.

'What of dear Mother,' I then asked.

Grandfather just said, 'Your mother will be fine. She is with others and they are in a big shelter where they will be safe from the bombs.'

'What if the enemy come to the city? 'I asked.

Grandfather then became agitated: 'Look, these are things, which are of no concern to you, will be alright, they have to be alright. You should concern yourself with helping your two sisters and brother. They are missing their mother and father too you know. It's harder for them to understand, so don't go upsetting them with any of your stories. We will win this war, be sure of that my girl. Now go and help your grandmother.'

That night I did not sleep very well, and the drone of aircraft above did not help. The noise of bombs falling could be heard most nights and through the day. We never thought much of it, and because much of the view was obscured by trees, we were, in a sense, detached from it all. My two sisters and brother were oblivious and slept through the noise. In the morning, they were woken as usual.

They did not miss out on schooling as a local lady would come each morning of the week, and gather all the young children to give them lessons at a house a short distance away. After a few hours, she would bring them all back, dropping them off at their homes. One morning, the woman did not arrive as usual. We thought nothing of it at first. We thought maybe she was ill or something. Around mid-morning, a stream of people began making their way through Kopenick heading west. They had prams, carts, bags and all manner of things. We were told to stay inside, while my grandparents went outside and began talking to the people. The people looked frightened and had dirty, haggard-looking faces. The children looked no better. They were pointing their arms in the direction from which they had come, but I had no idea what they were saying.

When our grandparents came back in we were told
to pack as much clothing as we could carry as we had
to leave. The younger children did not seem to be too
worried, but I was very worried.

'Where are we going?' I asked my grandparents, but
they just said again, 'Get your clothes and don't ask
questions – just hurry up and do as you have been told.'

I went upstairs and gathered as many clothes for us
as I could carry. My grandparents bundled clothes and
things into a sheet and tied it at one end into a kind of
sack. Any food items we could take with us, we took. We
the left the house and joined the column of people.

As we walked, I asked a family what was going on and
where are we going. The woman solemnly replied, 'The
Russians are close, so we are leaving our homes. If we stay,
they will kill us. Where are we going? I can't tell you where
we are going, as I don't know myself. Somebody told us
the Americans are in the west and we should go west, so
we are going west.'

My grandparents were not as old or infirm as many
grandparents, so we were lucky. We trudged through the
night, occasionally meeting bands of our soldiers. They
were obviously told of the situation, so they did not try
to stop us or turn us back. Besides, there were too many
of us. We were refugees now, just like they soon would be
too. My grandparents said we will go to Hanover to the
north where we had relatives from both my mother and
father's side.

The column of refugees slowly thinned out as people
began to fan out and go in different directions. Hanover
was a journey that would take around three or more
days on foot. We had to think about where we would
stay overnight and where we would find food. So many
horrible things were on our minds. We begged help from
the villages on our way.

We began to encounter American troops, most of
whom just looked at us. Some took photographs of us as
they drove by in tanks and trucks. People took us in for
the night, after which one kindly old gentleman gave us a
ride on his cart a little of the way.

With Hanover in sight, we bid farewell and walked into
captivity. We were soon found by an American patrol that
picked us up as refugees. They told us that 90 per cent of

the city was in ruins and it was not safe to go there. We gave them addresses of where we needed to go, explaining who we were going to. They looked on their maps and, after questioning and searching us for weapons, they were satisfied with our explanation. They made notes of our names and former address.

In the event, we went to my mother's sister's home. Their house was not near the city centre, but more in the outer suburbs. There was terrible bomb damage, even in these areas, and we came across people leaving Hanover. We met more Americans, so we were stopped and asked questions more frequently. Every time we were stopped we were searched. We were held in suspicion as there had been forced labour camps in Hanover, so all Germans were stopped and interrogated. Our now slightly wretched state was obvious though.

We reached our destination to much consternation and fuss about the state we were in. We had to sleep on the floor of a tiny living room and share meagre food rations provided by the German Red Cross. They did a wonderful job and helped prevent many starving to death. The food was not much, but it would keep you from dying. The shortage of adequate food supplies was a major problem during the closing stages of the Second World War. It would be some time before we would eat properly again.

My thoughts turned to my mother and father and I wondered if they were still alive. My sisters and brothers were now the main concern, and I often took less of the meagre food rations so that they could eat more. The love I began to feel for them was something which I can't describe to you. It was like I had to become their mother and father, which, in a sense, I did. Our grandparents were very good, but I knew that if the worst had happened and our mother and father had died, I would have to be like a guardian to them. Having been a BDM girl I was quite capable of looking after my younger siblings.

Teenage girls these days would be horrified at some of the responsibilities we had to carry on our shoulders. Nothing really intimidated me – I was a German maiden. My spirit had been wrought from the struggle of our ancestors. At that time, I was proud to be a German girl, even though the war, as we discovered, had been a catastrophe for us.

It was nearly five months later when we received news that mother and father were alive. My father had been arrested and charged with being a war profiteer and a member of the Nazi party. My mother had been released and was in a refugee camp under the Russians. My father had all of his assets and business confiscated, not that this mattered anymore. If I remember correctly, we would not see Mother and Father again for another six months. When we were reunited, they had changed beyond belief. They weren't the same people anymore. They never spoke about what had happened to them in Berlin. All talk about it was forbidden. They took whatever had happened to them to their graves. I learned of some of the things that had happened to German girls and women in Berlin. Had my mother suffered rape? I don't know, as she would not discuss any of it. All I know is that after the war, things were unbearably hard for them both. My father had taken to drinking, maybe as a way of dealing with his problems. He would drink until he fell asleep, then wake up and vomit. This became his daily routine, while my mother went out and worked as an office junior. She had to leave the job after two weeks, however, as her employer was not happy with father's background. It would tarnish the name of his company, so he told her: 'We can't have anyone with a Nazi party affiliation here. It's bad for business.'

I only found out what they had said to her after I went to see the owner of the place and he told me. Mother would not tell me anything and she would become angry if I asked too many questions. Looking back, she must have been under immense strain.

I also went out to work, finding a job in a small clothes shop. The wage was not much, but it helped to a degree to keep us all fed. Father continued his drinking and we started to have rows over money. He would ask me for more money so that he could go out and buy black market alcohol. I refused and he actually called me a '*hundin*', or bitch in English.

I shouted back, 'And what are you? Look at yourself, you old drunkard. You sit around feeling sorry for yourself, all day every day. You're a German, aren't you? Why don't you act like one?'

I walked out of the house to calm down and just kept walking. I started to cry, not because of what I said, but out of frustration. When I returned, my father had gone. I did not care at that moment, but I became a little concerned when, even after two hours had passed, he had not come back home. I prepared an evening meal for my sisters, brother and mother, then went out to look for father. I searched everywhere I could think of, but could not find him. I began knocking on the doors of his friends, but he was not there.

The next day, I woke early as usual for work and made sure that my sisters and brother went off to school. Mother was frantic with worry and I did my best to keep her calm. Shortly before I left for work, there was a knock at the door. It was a local representative of the *burgermeister*. He asked if he could come in and talk, as he had some sad news for my mother. He sat us down and told us that a man believed to be my mother's husband had been found.

'Well, where is he?' I asked impatiently, 'Why isn't he with you? Is he drunk again somewhere?'

The man replied, 'I'm sorry to have to tell you, but we believe that he had taken his own life. We found him, and it appears that he had hanged himself from a tree.'

The shock of the news was numbing, but mother didn't cry. I think she was in shock. We had to go and identify the body, which was not pleasant. As we were shown the body at the local mortuary, we could see it was my father. We both broke down and cried and returned home in silence. I had to tell my sisters and brother what had happened. This was probably one of the hardest things I have ever had to do in my life. As time passed, things became a little easier, but Mother began to blame me for Father's death.

I continued to live at home until my sisters and brother were old enough to choose their own way in life. I had occasional boyfriends, but nothing serious. I never seemed to have time for romance, as my life focused around my family. I was in my mid-twenties by the time I left home and went travelling with a friend. We travelled to Switzerland and France, and then went on to Ireland. We did casual work, doing anything we were given. We had some great times. We even visited England in the 1960s, albeit very briefly.

We returned to Germany and began working in offices and shops, in fact anywhere we could earn money, which we then saved up for travelling. While back in Germany,

I wrote to Frieda Altmann, with whom I had made some good memories. I just hoped that she and her family were okay because, after we left Kopenick, I never saw or heard anything from her again. Would she still be there? Was she still alive?

The wait was almost unbearable, but I had a letter a few weeks later from her. She was at a new address, but she was no longer in Berlin. Her family had left the old home shortly after the war. We arranged to meet and I travelled up to Hamburg where she was now living with her husband and her first baby. It was amazing to see her again after all this time. She had changed so little. She had her husband and her little girl with her and she took me back to their apartment in the city. Her home was lovely and we knew we had so much to catch up on. I told her everything and we stayed up quite late into the night talking.

Frieda insisted that I stay with them one more day and have dinner with them. So, the next day, as we were all sat at the dinner table and are about to start eating, when Frieda starts singing, 'green potato mash and rats, green potato mash, green potato mash and rats, green potato mash.'

We laughed hysterically and I said to her, 'How did you remember that, Frieda? That is so long ago now.'

She explained that the rhyme had since become a long-standing joke in her family after she had told her father what I had said.

I replied, 'Oh no, you didn't tell your father, did you? He must hate me for that.'

Frieda replied, 'On the contrary, not at all. He found it quite amusing.'

Then I asked her, 'Well, what *was* that meat he used to bring home after work some evenings after he had spent the day catching rats?'

Frieda explained, 'It certainly wasn't rats. Father used to set traps in the woods on his way to work. On his way home, he would check them. Sometimes there were birds caught in the traps, but mostly it would be a squirrel or two. He would just remove the legs and head and bring back the meat.'

I left Frieda's home with a smile on my face and feeling warm inside. We continued to write to each other and I visited frequently.

I wanted a life of freedom, so I decided that a life of marriage and children was not what I wanted. I love children. I now have nieces and nephews and they fill the gap for me. I have had good jobs and have lived independently. I am still close to my sisters and brother, who visit regularly as I do them.

Mother passed away long ago now. I was with her when she took her last breath in this world. Before she died she said, 'I'm so proud of you.'

I told her that I was sorry about Father.

'Don't you worry about your father,' she said. 'I will soon be having words with him when I get hold of him.'

At that I told her I loved her. I held her hand and said to her, 'I love you Mother, now go to the angels, go to Father, and tell him I love him too.'

A few seconds later she was gone. I cried holding her hand. My sisters and brother were with us. They kissed Mother on the forehead and that is how we remember her now.

Life is something we can never predict, but those of us who were born and raised under the Third Reich have an obligation to ensure that it never happens again. History should never repeat itself if we learn from it. I was extremely lucky, as I was more fortunate than most. Yes, I had some unhappy times, but then we all do, don't we? What is funny, is that whenever I prepare potatoes for a meal, I always think of that rhyme and sometimes sing it to myself. Green potato mash and rats. My nephews and nieces used to ask, 'What are you singing, Aunty?'

'Oh, nothing,' I would reply.

Then, if they were there, either my sisters or brother would relate the story.

12
East Berlin and the Grey Edifice of Communism

It is not possible to chart the entire social geo-political event that followed Germany's defeat in the Second World War, as these were just too extensive to record in detail here. We can examine certain aspects that affected some of the contributors to this book.

In brief, the victorious powers decided that Germany must be stripped of all of her territorial gains made during the war. In addition, a portion of her industrial infrastructure would be removed as compensation. To compound things, ten million German-speaking refugees poured into the devastated country from central and eastern Europe. Many German prisoners of war, captured by the Russians during the fighting, were transported to the east, where they would literally be worked to death. Many would never return home to Germany.

At the Potsdam Conference of 17 July–2 August 1945, the Allies agreed that Germany should be divided into four separate military occupation zones. France in the south-west, Britain in the north-west, the United States in the south, and the Soviet Union in the east. It was also agreed among the Allied powers that the Russians would occupy an area that included the Potsdam-agreed final Russian zone, along with all of the 1937 German territory east of the Oder–Neisse line. The northerly part of eastern Prussia was placed under Russian administration under the Potsdam Agreement. The agreement sanctioned administrative assignment of various former eastern German territories to Poland, while Russia shifted the borders westwards to what had been Germany before the war.

Approximately fifteen million ethnic Germans suffered intolerable hardships from 1944 to 1947 as a result of the flight and expulsion from the eastern German territories, and what had been Nazi occupied Poland and Czechoslovakia, especially the Sudetenland.

The Allies also decided that Germany's armed forces should be abolished, and munitions and armaments factories dismantled, plus any civilian concerns that could support them. Civilian industrial concerns that possessed military potential were placed under severe restrictions. It was hoped that much of Germany's post-war industry would be geared towards agriculture, rather than that of war, notwithstanding the growing tensions between the Allies and Russia at the time, the necessary changes were implemented.

With the advent of the Cold War, (the political stand-off between the West and the Soviet Union), it was soon realized that West German industry would need to be brought back on line, not only to assist with the restoration of the whole European economy, but also for the strengthening of West Germany as an ally against possible Soviet aggression.

Life for many Germans in the west was still incredibly difficult, particularly the harsh winters that followed 1945. Yet life in West Germany, as hard as it was, was nothing compared to that of those Germans in eastern Germany under Soviet rule.

Where housing was concerned, such was the destruction inflicted on German cities during the Allied bombing campaign of the war, that many residents were resigned to living in hastily erected camps. The camps existed in both the east and west. The prevailing conditions differed greatly with each camp. Those families whose homes were at least partially habitable, in that they were not in any danger of collapse, chose to remain in them, making do as best they could.

Food and basic essentials became so scarce that a thriving black market began. Many German women refused to prostitute themselves in order to obtain food and everyday goods, but soon had no option but to sell themselves. Again, exploitation and abuse raised its ugly head, particularly in East Berlin. Gertrud Kretzl, who was 18 years old, recalls the situation:

> The Soviets took full advantage as they held all the cards. The Russian soldiers never seemed to have to go without food. If I went out, I was often subject to their taunting. They would show you items of food, like a small bag of potatoes, or would hold up a dead chicken, and they would say to me, 'You can have this if we can have you.'
>
> They made me feel sick. Even though I was really hungry and my parents and siblings were hungry, I would not let them pleasure themselves on me for food.

Of course, a lot of German girls and women became so desperate that they did become sex slaves for the Russian soldiers. In exchange for sexual favours, they were given food regularly and the soldiers would look after them. I can't say I was not tempted to let them have sex with me for some food, but there are always choices. Then there are those two little voices in your head: one that says 'go on, do it, don't be silly,' while the other says 'no, don't do this, it is wrong.'

That said, it did not matter either way if the Russians wanted to take you by force. They would simply do so. They forced many girls into sex slavery. They then felt compelled to feed them afterwards, maybe to make themselves feel better about what they were doing. I don't know.'

In May 1949, Britain, France and America united their occupation zones into a new country, West Germany. On 20 June 1948, they introduced a new currency, the Deutsche Mark, to stabilize the country's post-war economy, which, at the time, was being dominated by a powerful black market. In anticipation of the introduction of the new currency, on 18 June, Soviet dictator Josef Stalin ordered that all rail and road traffic from West Germany be banned, effectively starting what would become known as the Berlin Blockade.

The West saw the blockade as a blatant attempt to cripple west Berlin economically by halting industrial production and the transport of Allied war materiel. Stalin, wanted the Allies out of what he believed was his city, and he was prepared to starve the city into capitulation. So, it was decided that West Berlin would be supplied from the air. The subsequent blockade of Berlin by the Russians lasted for 323 days, during which 278,000 sorties were flown, transporting 2.3 million tons of supplies, of which 1.5 million tons alone was coal. An aircraft landed every three minutes at Berlin's Tempelhof aerodrome. This was a remarkable logistical accomplishment, and one that former Luftwaffe chief, Hermann Göring, might have been proud of.

On 12 May 1949, Stalin ordered an end to the blockade. His decision was certainly not done because of any humanitarian concerns. Stalin was not interested in how many German citizens might die from hunger or cold. The contempt he had for his own people was proof enough of this. Either way, west and Soviet relations would become increasingly strained from this point.

In 1952, Stalin's grey edifice began to emerge from the ruins of East Berlin, as construction began to create what would be the first of East Germany's socialist streets. The resulting apartment blocks were in typical 'gingerbread style' of the Stalinist Soviet era, hastily built from prefabricated concrete panels that were uniformly grim. These apartment tower blocks could only now be described as eyesores, but they could be built rapidly, fulfilling a demand for rapid housing development. The waiting lists for an apartment in one of these blocks was long, yet the conditions within were of a surprisingly high standard to what most Germans had been used to before the Second World War. Dana Schmidt recalls:

> We had been in one of the camps. They were horrendous places, where there was no real escape from the elements such as wind, rain and biting cold in winter. Sanitation was poor. My parents had applied for housing, and we were relatively lucky to be given an apartment in one of the newly built blocks in East Berlin. Our apartment had a kitchen, dining area, a toilet and bathroom, and bedrooms. The block did not look that nice from the outside, especially when compared to Berlin's older buildings, but they were thought of as modern at the time, and had been built rapidly to deal with the housing problem. They were very cold in winter, but anything was considered better than living in tents or improvised camps. So, we were given our apartment, but we would soon learn what an error we had made by choosing to live in the eastern sector. We were desperate at the time, and did not think that east and west would soon be divided and that we would effectively be trapped there.

The divide that Dana Schmidt mentions, which many Germans had feared, was that of the Berlin Wall. The Berlin Wall was to become the greatest symbol of communist oppression in Europe. It would be universally despised by East and West Germans alike. Construction began on the wall on 13 August 1961. The wall completely cut off (by land) West Berlin from surrounding East Germany and from East Berlin. Guard towers were placed along the large concrete wall, with anti-vehicle trenches and other defences to reinforce the security of the concrete structure. The Russians referred to the wall as anti-fascist, insinuating that West Germany, under the North Atlantic Treaty Organization, NATO, a military alliance incorporating many countries, including Britain,

France, America and West Germany, was equal to the fascists. The
hated Berlin Wall would remain, another of Stalinist Russia's grey
edifices, until 1989.

With the wall in place, Ingrid Herschteller recalls when she was
a child:

> We could no longer visit friends or family in the west.
> I remember early on the panic setting in, and people
> trying to make last-ditch attempts at escaping from East
> Germany. I remember one family could see their relatives
> from their home. They tried throwing a rope between the
> two buildings. There was a commotion and shots were
> fired in the air, and the four people trying to escape to the
> west by this rope, abandoned their attempt.
>
> Soon the wall was reinforced with barbed wire. It
> became too dangerous to attempt escape, as the Russians
> guarding the thing would shoot you if they had to. Most
> of us felt like rats trapped in a barrel. We didn't want to be
> isolated with the communists. Once they put that wall up,
> it was just as bad as being under the Nazis again. In fact,
> in some ways it was worse.
>
> Under Communist Russia, I knew that I would never
> be able to take A-level examinations, or study as I wanted
> to or to take up a career. In fact, they did not want
> independent thinkers. Any child whose parents were not
> members of the Socialist Unity Party of Germany, or loyal
> followers of the regime, were denied the chance to study.
> Many German parents therefore decided to teach their
> children at home where they stood a better a chance, but
> the communist system ensured that anyone described as
> an independent thinker, such as a home-educated child,
> would not be able to rise to any great position in life. The
> communist schools were much like those of the Nazis.
> You had to give a military-style salute to the teacher upon
> entering the classroom.
>
> Paranoia began to permeate every part of society
> and people began to tell on one another for the most
> irrelevant of things. The state secret police, Stasi, were as
> ruthless as the Gestapo, the Nazi secret police. They were
> everywhere. They wore civilian clothes, so you didn't
> know who was Stasi and who was not. They watched
> your every move, especially if you defied the system and
> your parents insisted that you were educated at home.

They would come to our home at night and question my parents, then search our apartment, tipping up paperwork from drawers and throwing books onto the floor. They once left with a pile of my books, telling me that they were being confiscated as being 'too democratic'. The books were about history, geography and wildlife, and they took them off me. They left our apartment in a mess, and as soon as they were gone, Mother and Father would pick everything up and put it all away again. The problem was that we knew they would keep coming back until I agreed to attend their local 'socialist school'. My parents were absolutely against this idea and they would say, 'The Nazis have gone, but now we are under the control of another bunch of Nazis. We did not resist then, but this time we will resist as much as we can.' My parents wanted me to grow up as an educated child who had a chance of a future, so it must have been horrible for them.

The winters were the worst time of all. The dark overcast skies set against the dull grey concrete buildings, the cold and the rain, it all made East Germany a depressing environment to have to exist in. There were many suicides. I heard of one young man who had been separated from his family who were in the West. He applied to the authorities to let him join them in the West, but they declined his application every time. He could not take it and the one morning he hanged himself from a tree. I also heard of whole families committing suicide: a mother and father taking the lives of their children then killing themselves. These people were like us. We had survived the Nazis and the Second World War, and now here we were, again facing a far worse future than before. For us, victory had not brought about an end to war – it was merely an extension of it.

In 1963, my father suffered a severe accident and the authorities classed him as disabled and thus a drain on socialist resources. My parents applied three times for a permit to leave East Germany and go to the West where we planned to live with relatives. The authorities only agreed on the fourth occasion, when my mother and father could give them money, jewellery and other things from our home in what was a bribe. We were effectively expelled from the East and told we could never return there again. We were happy with this arrangement, as we did not ever wish to go back to that hell hole.

When we arrived back in West Berlin, we were interviewed by the authorities there. We were initially under suspicion of being Soviet spies, which was ridiculous, but that is what it was like – the paranoia was everywhere.

We stayed with relatives and I began to attend school again, which of course was completely different from the communist schools and education system. The class teacher would ask me to stand up and give talks about what life was like under the communists, and I told them on more than one occasion that it was worse than life under Hitler. This would cause some amusement to the kids in the class, until the teacher shouted 'quiet' and wielded his cane in the air. One lad continued to giggle and he was frogmarched up in front of us and given the stick across his arse. I recall his face twisted with pain as the stick hit his arse. I have to say that, after that thrashing, he was not giggling anymore.

Back in the West, things were slow to change in terms of housing and help for those in great need, but the changes were happening and we were free, unlike those in the East. I took my examinations and I did very well. We were eventually given an apartment in a ground floor block. My mother had to work to help support us, and when I was old enough, I took a job at a clothes store. This was good, because the owners were lovely people. I could buy clothes from there and I was given a discount. I had desires of becoming a doctor and, although I studied hard for this, I did not quite reach the accepted level, so decided to go into nursing instead. I was encouraged to try again and after some persuasion, I began studying again to become a doctor. After much hard work, I was successful.

I worked in Germany for a year, before going on an assignment in Africa, where I was attached to a charity organization. I spent two years in Africa, where I met a young man who soon became my boyfriend. We spent so many hours working together, that a relationship just evolved from it. He was from Germany too. He had wealthy parents who had fled to Switzerland before the Nazis came to power in 1933. I reminded him how he had missed all of the 'excitement'.

During the warm African evenings, we would sit on the veranda of our lodge and talk, and if we were not working the next day, we would sit and watch the sun rise.

It was a beautiful place and there was so much that you could study besides carrying out medical work with the local people. We began making plans of what we would do when we returned to Germany. We decided that we would save all of our money and build our own house. We had a good family friend who owned some land. He said that he would give us a nice plot overlooking a lake, and all we would have to do, was arrange for something to be built there. At this stage, we had not even slept together as this was not permitted by our superiors, but we began discussing marriage. We decided that we should get married in Switzerland. My boyfriend could ski and I wanted to learn. He used to say that the skiing in Switzerland was the best in the world.

One evening, we stayed up and watched the sun begin to rise. We kissed and after a few minutes, we just thought to hell with it and we went inside the lodge and spent the next wonderful few hours making love on a fur rug inside. It was my first time and, although we were both very nervous, it was an enjoyable experience for us both. Afterwards we got dressed and, before leaving for our separate accommodations, I said, 'We did not use any birth control.'

We agreed to discuss it later and turned in to get some sleep.

Two hours later, my boyfriend was roused from his bed by colleagues who needed him to go with them on a short trek to a nearby village to examine a child with some strange symptoms. I was fast asleep as they left and didn't even hear them drive off. It was around four hours later and I was still asleep as it was my day off, when I was awoken by one of the local doctors who told me there had been an accident involving my colleagues. None of them knew about our relationship and initially I pretended not to be too concerned, until my boyfriend's name was mentioned. The vehicle he was riding in had hit a rut in the dirt track and turned over, throwing some of those in the vehicle out. They said there had been fatalities, and when I asked who had been killed, my boyfriend's name was among those of the dead. I just fell apart and broke down and had to be given a sedative. Later on, and while my colleagues comforted me, I told them that we had been having a relationship and planned to marry upon the completion of our duties.

During the following week, I began the journey home back to West Germany. I had written to my mother and father and told them a little of what had happened, adding that I would discuss it further with them once I arrived home. They were waiting for me when I arrived at the airport, and once home, I told them everything. Naturally my parents asked if we had 'done anything', and if we had 'been sensible' (meaning had we used birth control) as having children out of wedlock was considered a sin, even after everything that had happened in Germany. I had to tell them there had just been the once and we had not used any birth control. Mother just said, 'You silly child, God forbid you are not pregnant.'

Fortunately for me, the weeks went by and I was happy not to be pregnant. I was, however, unhappy about what had happened, as we had made plans to spend our future together. Once I was able to, I travelled to Switzerland where I visited my late boyfriend's parents. They made me welcome and we talked about a lot of things. The family took me skiing for the first time, where I learned to ski.

I returned to my work as a doctor back in West Germany with a local practice. I did find love again. I settled down in the city I knew as my home and went on to marry and have children. I now have grandchildren too. It is with great pride that I can say that my grandchildren have all graduated from university and can determine their own futures. I think of it all and I can say to myself, 'Not bad for a girl from East Germany.

Dora Brunninghausen and her family were also among those who had no choice but to be resettled in eastern Germany under the Soviets. She recalls her life living there:

I don't know, it was weird. It felt like everything was grey, damp and cold, like a corpse. It was a truly depressing place, but I soon discovered that some of my friends from the BDM had moved here too. We found comfort in chatting and meeting at one another's homes whenever we could.

Simple things like this soon became complicated, as I noticed, on many occasions, that I was being followed by cars as I visited my friends' homes. The communists were suspicious of us. Once they burst through the door of my friend's home, demanding to know what we are meeting for? Are we planning activities or propaganda against the state? They trashed the place looking for paperwork or propaganda, which of course was not there. We were just friends meeting up and it was entirely innocent, but you could not get this through to them.

The paranoia was unbelievable in that place. You felt as if everyone was watching and informing on you. The Stasi were everywhere. We had more than one visit from these people, for the first few years, they just would not leave us alone. Schooling under the communists was comparable to that of the Nazis. Even though the two considered themselves opposing ideologies, both politically and socially, they were much the same. In the East, the people were forced into being the property of the state. Choices and freedom were not allowed, while conformity to the mass ideal was the goal in life. We just had to live as best we could under the circumstances facing us.

I settled down as best I could and took a menial job in a small plastics factory. We all took what work we could, but even though we worked very hard, we never had much to show for it. You could say we were nearly always hungry. Everywhere you went, trying to get on with daily life, we were reminded of where we were. The communists had these banners and posters everywhere. Most had Stalin's image on them. The hammer and sickle was everywhere. Politics was everywhere. Informants were everywhere.

You would see a queue of people outside a shop. They would be waiting to spend a month's pay on barely edible stale bread and, if lucky, a few green potatoes. To dare to speak out against the communists meant certain death. They were totally ruthless people. Many Germans vanished, no one knowing what had happened to them. The fear of them coming in the night and taking you away, never to be seen again, was always there. Any sudden noises in the night made you jump out of bed. Your heart would pound as you would think it was the dreaded Stasi coming to arrest you for something. There was despair and fear in the eyes of all around. It felt like one was being swallowed by this huge grey edifice.

13

Illicit Liaisons

The preconception of girls of the BDM being totally obedient to their male peers is somewhat a misguided one. In many of the images of the girls of the BDM, they appear beautiful, but unapproachable, pure and chaste. In some respects, this was the ideal the Nazis expected them to live by. They should remain beautiful maidens, only to be deflowered in the interests of their biological duty. Within the BDM, there were many illicit relationships: girls sneaking off to meet young males, some with the same sex. Very few would divulge such personal information, even today. It is with immense credit that Lilla Kallenberg reveals a relationship that blossomed from her early youth in the Third Reich.

I joined the *Jüngmädel Bund* along with a friend named Helene. We had known each other more or less from when we were infants. Our parents were friends too. As a result, we spent much time together as children. We helped each other out when we joined the Hitler Youth for girls, both at the age of 10. As 10-year-olds, our friendship was purely platonic, yet we always felt comfortable with one another, no matter what the situation was. As teenagers in the BDM, we continued to be with one another a lot of the time, as we both attended the same local school and would meet up afterwards.

When we were about 15 years old, we began to realize that we were closer than what our society might permit us to be. We were around girls all the time and saw many girls of our troop naked. We never had any interest in any of the others, just ourselves. I looked at Helene the one day and thought how pretty she was, but I was terrified to say anything.

There were one or two occasions when we were alone when neither of us said anything. We would just smile at each other, as words weren't necessary. Other times we would be in our tent and we would just lie down and talk about things. The one time we did this, Helene just took my hand and held it. I turned around to face her, just cuddling and stroking one another. It was all perfectly innocent, though I felt things I had never felt before. Helene said she felt the same way, as if her tummy was rolling around.

We were not stupid and realized we had to be very careful about what we did and avoid anyone finding out. If our leader or any of the other girls discovered what we were doing, it could have meant one or even both of us being expelled from our troop. Our parents would be informed, and we would most certainly have had a beating. We might have faced ridicule on the streets when the news reached our town. There were all kinds of fears back then.

The good thing with the BDM on camping trips, was that at night it was sometimes chilly. We girls in our tents were encouraged to huddle up to help keep warm in the evenings. Helene and I would have the perfect chance to cuddle up and I would wrap my arms around her. On one occasion, we were alone in our tent, and we kissed and both enjoyed it. It was a secret between the two of us, and as we grew older, we had to work very hard to keep it that way.

We were not the only ones. I heard of some other girls doing the same, though this was after the war. We were able to snatch brief moments alone when we were home, or on BDM camps by the lakes. As we got older, we became more daring and sneaked off once to find somewhere quiet. It was the first sexual experience for us both. It was instinctive. We undressed and explored each other's bodies in the same way any couple would. I enjoyed the feeling of her hands on my body and learning the ways we could pleasure each other. Afterwards we knew we could never be apart.

By the time we were 24 years old, people thought us strange for not having boyfriends or being married. After what had happened during the war, I just felt I could never trust men again. I didn't hate men. I did not feel that I could form relationships with them or love a man, that is all. Helene felt exactly the same way and we would spend much time alone, talking about things. The one time, she said to me, 'People are starting to talk about us being lovers.'

I replied, 'Well, I don't care what they think. Fuck them, and yes, if they say we are lovers, I don't care.'

She looked startled for a few seconds before smiling and said, 'Look, how do we deal with this? What about our parents? We know how we feel, but it's hard for us.'

So, we decided that we would have to keep this to ourselves, probably forever, which we both knew would take immense discipline and patience. So, we became partners, having to keep everything secret. It was not good not being able to go out and hold your lover's hand like men and women could. We had to do this indoors and out of sight. We could not go out and spend time making love in the fields like heterosexual couples could.

Apart from the Nazi attitude to gays and lesbians, post-war society was universal in being against both gays and lesbians. Both the Nazis and the Soviets treated it as a kind of psychotic disorder. Helene and I continued our relationship, which had blossomed within the Hitler Youth. We were both very much in love with each other.

Eventually, we moved into an apartment together. We convinced our parents that we were doing this to share the costs of living. In our bedroom, we had two single beds instead of a double, so that visitors would not think it odd. We would just push the two beds together at night to create a double one.

It was not easy in post-war Germany, but we had survived the war and were together. We would sit up late on weekends listening to music on the radio. We would try on different make-up and paint each other's nails. We were totally forbidden to wear any beauty products under Hitler, so make-up and nail paint was a real luxury. It's true, we couldn't keep our hands off each other, but we were young people and had every right to be happy. They were hard but wonderful times in a way. Of course, there were former BDM friends who would see us out together and they would shout unpleasant things at us. They just guessed we were lovers, but we ignored them. Who has the right to judge you like that? Tell you that you are a lesser human being than what they are? Things did get a little easier over time, but we often kept ourselves to ourselves.

The 1960s were good years, as society seemed to change in the West. It did not change the way me and Helene behaved though. The hippy generation and flower power offered some liberation for the oppressed. The hippies didn't really care who slept with whom. It was all about love and peace and smoking Marijuana. Helene and I didn't smoke, so we never tried it.

But one evening Helene came home with this bag. I asked her what was in it, and she told me to have a look and see. When I looked inside the bag, there was this replica penis with a belt attached to it. I was shocked by it and said to her, 'Oh my God, what the hell is that thing for?'

She laughed at me and said, 'It's for us, silly.'

She later demonstrated by putting it on, and after some reassurance that it had never been used before, we tried it out. After much giggling, it became one of our favourite things. I'm not ashamed to talk about it, why should I be? I'm certainly not going to explain it any further, though [she laughs].

When, years later the Berlin Wall started to tumble, we actually got into Helene's car and drove to see it all happening. The streets were packed with people who appeared to be celebrating. It was chaos. People were everywhere, like ants crawling all over the wall, drinking from bottles and singing. Some had West German flags draped around themselves, sat or standing on top of the wall, raising their arms in joy. There was much singing and jubilation from everyone.

Then a large slab fell down and people peered through, sheepishly at first, then stepped across to shake our hands. People were hugging and kissing us. Many were very young people. Helene and I looked at one another and I said to her that if only we had this new freedom back then, it would have been a wonderful life. We were both quite emotional, yet happy at the same time. Russian President Mr Gorbachev helped make this happen. What a wonderful man he was. We were entering a new era, thanks to him really. At that we walked across into East Germany, just to have a look and trying to take it all in. It was a moment I will never forget, as it finally felt that the war was over. For some of us, it took that wall to be pulled down before our war was truly over. We felt a sense of freedom and liberation. We felt we had lived under a shadow of tyranny all of our lives and now we felt free. I felt sad that my parents could not have been here to see this happen.

My best years were gone and I wished I was young again, so I could travel and see so much more of Germany and the world as it is now. Sadly, both me and Helene are just too old now, but we are happy. I still have many of my old friends around and we sometimes get together to have a good moan about everything. Helene and I still have our little apartment, and I love her now as much as I did back then. I adore everything about her. All the years of secrecy means we are still very discreet when out in public. We wouldn't dare hold hands in public. For one thing, we are too old; people would point fingers. I just wish we could go back in time and have our youth again, and enjoy our love as we should have enjoyed it.

This is quite a remarkable revelation, which will hopefully help erase one of the few taboos that has surrounded the BDM over the years. The notion that Hitler's girls were unlike those of other societies in the emotional and sexual sense is nonsense. Another former BDM girl named Kristel Bernd, who joined in 1943, recalled:

Our educators within the Third Reich failed to school us in any aspect of human sexuality. They applied everything to the themes of nature, and nothing was direct as it is today. Any normal feelings of sexuality were regarded as lust. No BDM girl was permitted to harbour any thoughts of a lustful or sexual nature. To feel sexual attraction was to be lustful and impure. Only the lesser races indulged and allowed themselves to be weakened by these emotions. That is basically what we were taught.

'One who is promiscuous is a danger to the Reich!' Gertrud Scholtz Klink once roared at us during a talk she gave at our school. 'The animal that wonders and allows itself to be impregnated by a miscellany will only harbour poison within its womb.'

She also said to us, 'Homosexuality and lesbianism were two of the greatest sins that could be committed in the Reich, other than being a Jew.'

So, we were of course well aware of what was expected of us and how we should feel. When we come of age, we should seek the sanctity of a pure German male, settle down, have children, and maintain the home for a husband. That, we were told, was unequivocally our sworn duty as BDM girls.

The problem is that as young people come of age, they are curious about the ills of humanity, aren't they? But is sex one of those ills? Of course, this depends on the attitudes of your elders and how they perceived it. In Third Reich mentality, sex was referred to as just reproduction towards the future Reich.

It is certainly true that anything that is forbidden, becomes a strong attraction to some. Another girl and I once fell foul of our BDM leader. We were two young girls who had developed feelings for each other. There was an attraction between us and it was hard to explain. As no males were permitted to be in our company, it was only natural in many cases that girls would experiment with one another. Me and the girl in question were friends, but we really did not know one another as some friends do. There was this magnetism between us. I would look at her and somehow felt attracted to her, and she obviously felt the same way. At the time, I thought of the boys as big smelly things that were rough and hard. To me, she was lithe, soft, graceful and gentle. I thought she was funny, as she liked to joke and play around. She was also very good looking. I would feel the urge to go and wrap my arms around her. I really liked her legs – beautiful, slender, well-defined and athletic. Her feet were beautifully manicured. Oh, she was so beautiful. I would watch her as she exercised, stretching her body. She noticed me watching her and she would pull this funny face at me, as if to say 'what are you staring at?' She would then smile, poke her tongue out at me, and continue exercising.

One morning we were left alone, only for a few minutes, and we started larking about in our tent as young people do. I don't know how it happened, but the next thing we were play-fighting. We tumbled over and she ended up on top of me. She had my arms pinned down, her fingers interlocked with mine. It was the most erotic experience of my life. She looked down at me and began to rub her hips up and down against mine. Squeezing between my legs, she smiled, then we started kissing. It was real kissing, with open mouths and very passionate. We were

both breathing very heavily and were completely lost in
the moment, so much so, that we did not see or hear
the BDM leader striding up to the tent we were in. She
peered inside and shouted, 'What the hell do you think
you two are doing? Have you taken leave of your senses,
damn you? Come out of there now!'

We knew we were in serious trouble and had an
anxious wait to see what was going to happen to us. Once
the other girls had returned to camp from washing she
sent them off to collect wood in the forest while we were
kept behind.

The leader said to us, 'I should report this immediately
to our authority and to your parents. You have been
exemplary in most of your work; I don't understand this.
What has gotten into you both? If I report the two of you,
God knows what will happen to you. I should thrash you
both for this outrageous behaviour, but on this occasion,
I will say no more. I will, however, be giving you both lots
of hard duties to perform and you are to have no further
contact with each other. I shall be watching you both very
carefully, so do not ever even think of trying to do what
you were doing again.'

My friend was trying hard not to laugh at her. She was
stood straight like a soldier to attention, pursing her lips
to stifle a smile. A stern 'stop that smirking at once' from
the BDM leader shook her to attention. We both said we
were sorry and that it would not happen again.

The BDM leader glared at us and said, 'I really hope
that you are truly sorry for this outrage – it is disgusting.'

We apologized again for our 'terrible behaviour',
repeating that it would never happen again. The BDM
leader continued to scald us for some minutes. She grabbed
us by our shoulders and shook us violently. Then she began
telling us what horrible jobs she was going to give us as a
punishment for her not taking the matter further.

Later on, when things had calmed down, she took me
aside and talked to me, asking if everything was alright at
home, and was I happy? I told her I was happy and that
I had no problems at home. She asked what made me do
what I was doing when we were caught. I told her I didn't
know. I felt ignorance in this case was better than the truth.

She explained: 'It is sinful to enter into lesbianism.
The German maiden must be for the German male only,

and that is the way of things. There is no other way, as this is what our Fuhrer Adolf Hitler expects of us as his women. Our lives are destined to be difficult, that's how it is. We have to obey the laws of the Reich, and sanctity is something we are all bound to by God and Fuhrer.'

She was going on and on as if I was a full-blown lesbian, which, of course, I wasn't. Me and the girl in question were like so many others. We had led sheltered lives. Through the BDM we were in continuous contact with girls, and it just happened. We were both 17 years old and were experiencing strong desires. It is much the same as men placed within an all-male prison environment. It is only a matter of time before desires take over and men enter into sexual relationships with other men. As BDM girls, we were so close and spent so much time with one another, that it was inevitable that things like this would happen. We were just unlucky enough to get caught.

Before we left the BDM to begin compulsory work placements with the Reich Labour Service, we did meet up at a coffee shop. We talked about what had happened and about how we felt. We needed to know if it was real or was it simply some kind of adolescent experimentation. We both agreed that it was not experimentation as we initially had perceived it to be. When we met up, we both just wanted to go somewhere quiet and do it again. We knew we could not live a lie, but the state and our parents would never tolerate us being in love. If found out, we could end up in a concentration camp. Weighing everything up, we decided that we should just remain friends, as anything other than that would bring us no end of misery.

When I entered the RADw for compulsory labour service, I began writing to a young soldier at the front, as did many girls. We often made gifts for them, which we would then send along with a photograph. I eventually met the young soldier that I had been writing to. He had been wounded on the Russian front, losing the sight of his right eye and injuring his legs, to the extent that he was of no use to the army. We met and eventually married and had five children. I know my friend with whom I had shared that kiss, also married and had children. I often think back to what happened and what we might have done if we had not been caught. Would we have gone further? I cannot say for certain, but I think what we did was not wrong as so many would have had us believe. We remained in contact, but we avoided meeting alone. I suppose in some ways we would always love one another but, our destiny was not for us to choose. Had it been today in our 'free society', then who knows, we could have had a relationship.

Kirsten Eckermann was quite blunt regarding the issue and recalled:

It was hogwash that we were these divine figures of the Reich. Of course, we had an image to maintain for Hitler and his elite, but by God there was some playing around at BDM camps, but the rule was, 'you could do it, but it was a huge big risk so don't get caught doing it'.

I know of many girls who sneaked off to meet boys and to have sex with them. We were as normal as any other girls in the world, so why shouldn't we have? One girl I was friendly with in the BDM sneaked out to have sex with a Hitler Youth boy she had befriended. She told me that they met up in the woods, where they had started kissing and she opened her blouse to let him touch her breasts. They ended up on the ground and he wanted to have full intercourse with her, but she declined, offering him hand-relief instead, which she did and they parted. The boy, having not got what he wanted, went back bragging to his friends telling them he had screwed her. As a result, people began to hear gossip. She got into big trouble and her parents were informed. When she returned home, her father gave her a beating with a strap, while her mother screamed '*hure*' [whore] at her. It was always like that – the girls were not able to do anything, while men got away with everything. We girls were condemned to burn in hell for everything we did wrong, or what was deemed wrong in the eyes of the state. I had my fair share of fun, but there is no way I will tell you about it [she laughs]. I would be far too embarrassed to tell you.

Lise Hirsch recalls meeting a Hitler Youth boy with whom she had become friendly:

I liked boys, and as a normal 17-year-old girl, why should I not have? I met this one boy once and he was very nice.

We tried to spend time together, but it was not possible most of the time. They watched you like hawks to make sure you did not get up to things. To meet boys in private meant having to take risks. My feelings just pushed me over the edge and he felt the same. We arranged to meet after lights-out, which was incredibly risky. They had people appointed as sentries, even on BDM and Hitler Youth camps, to keep an eye on everything. They wanted to make sure there would be no sneaking around.

We managed to get away and went as far as we felt was safe enough for no one to hear us. The sex was somewhat hurried as we were nervous of being compromised. The thrill was wonderful though, and it felt so nice. I realized, stupidly, that he was not using any birth control. I couldn't stop him as we were in the throes of passion.

I had to tell him, 'Don't you dare do it up me – take it out'.

With a loud moan, he pulled out and made rather a mess over me. I couldn't help but giggle afterwards – in fact we both did. Then we had to sneak back into our own camps without being spotted. Funny thing, next morning one of the senior girls, acting as a sentry, said she thought she heard wild boar mating in the woods during the night! I almost exploded with laughter, thinking to myself, 'was that us that she had heard?'

Marguerite Kopfel joined the BDM in 1941 at the age of 15, and recalls how easy it was to become embroiled in accusations of sexual disrepute.

There was a girl in my troop who, when we went on camp, always slept in the tent with me. She cuddled up right next to me, and as I was falling asleep, I remember her just lying there, looking at me with a smile on her face. I think she gained comfort from it, but it would have been easy for others to misconstrue her intentions, so I did not tell anyone about it.

Most nights, she would run her foot up and down my leg. It felt nice and I enjoyed that closeness and the sensations it gave me. She would stroke my stomach with her fingers, but she never touched me inappropriately. She would eventually fall asleep with her legs over mine. To be honest, I did not mind her doing this. It was rather sweet as I too found it comforting. Affection was not something you had a lot of at home, so if we comforted one another in the throes of sleep, then I did not see anything wrong with that. In fact, I kissed her on the face a few times before going to sleep and always smiled back at her. She was lovely, and there were many really lovely girls that I used to know.

I remained in contact with many after the Second World War. After the war we became different people. Even so, we still had a very special and close bond that few are able to understand today. That short space of time, when you are relaxed and in the dark at bedtime, was probably the only privacy we ever got as girls. As girls, we did not have much to look forward to, other than the camaraderie we had among us. The male Third Reich and the Hitler Youth were awash with sexual excesses of every conceivable kind. The men and boys were not innocent by any means. They just found it easier to hide I think.

I heard of boys having sex with other boys and men having sex with other men. Those in charge of us were no better either, from little things we heard. These things will always happen, won't they? They are not unique to any particular society or race.

I also recall that, often when going to sleep, some girls of the *Jüngmädel Bund*, who were only between 10 and 14, would suck their thumbs. I heard of a few *Jüngmädel Bund* leaders peering into our tents, and any girl found to be sucking her thumb, had her hand unceremoniously yanked out of her mouth. Such things were considered as infantile pleasures, which had no place in the *Jüngmädel Bund*. They wanted to rip away our childhood and enforce adulthood upon us as soon, as they could. As SS chief Heinrich Himmler once said of the *Jüngmädel Bund*, 'even the very junior girls of the Hitler Youth have to be honed within the fires of National Socialism into a piece of hard unbreakable steel capable of piercing an enemy's flesh.'

Hard, emotionless, and unfeeling, were all the attributes those in power expected of their female youth. They wanted birth machines, not human beings with feelings or emotions. We were being groomed to be slaves to our men. Many of those males within Hitler's circle had mistresses, which were permitted, as long as they were discreet and did not cause a scandal. We on the other hand, had to be like robots. Cooking, cleaning, pandering to a husband's every whim, and being there for his pleasure whenever he felt like it.

Our parents encouraged us to marry as soon as we came of age. The church hall dances were the places we could go to meet other members of the opposite sex. We were chaperoned all of the time, so there was no real sense of freedom. If you spotted a boy you liked, you would look at him in the hope he would come and ask you to dance. You could not ask him, as that was considered unladylike. If you met someone, you would arrange to meet at your parent's house for tea. In that sterile environment, they expected love to flourish. If you married, then you entered into it knowing very little about the man you married. You only discovered what he was like when you were married and living together.

I knew of girls who married too quickly, just to fulfil their obligations to the German Reich. They found themselves in abusive relationships, with husbands who beat them for not keeping the home tidy enough, or for not keeping the children quiet while he was trying to read his newspaper. One girl told me in confidence that her new husband threw a full plate of his dinner at her for it not being warm enough for him to eat. The plate just missed hitting her on the head. Many just made do, and continued to love men that they should never have married in the first place.

Wiener Katte recalls her first boyfriend experience:

'The boy was hardly my boyfriend, as we were not allowed any real physical contact. I think the most we ever did was hold hands, and then only when there was no one around.

My older brother took an instant dislike to the boy and once told him, 'Keep your hands off my little sister or I will cut off your dick.'

The boy was frightened off by my big brother. So, you see, even had I really liked him, others would have interfered to destroy things'.

This chapter is exceptionally rare by the way that it proves that those in power were wrong. The girls did have all the normal feelings that, as girls, they should have had. It is not surprising that, under the circumstances, they developed such strong feelings for one another at times. They were more or less banished to their all-female community with unsuppressed emotions intact, until their duty as mothers came about.

As Lilla Kallenberg said, 'We didn't love Hitler. Hitler said that he loved us. But the reality was we loved each other more than we loved him.'

14

The Evil We Followed

Everyone is potentially an enemy of the state, which is why you should observe, listen and inform where you have even the slightest of suspicions. Even your own families are not or cannot be exempt from suspicion. It is your duty to your Fuhrer and the Reich to whom you have sworn to serve and obey.

This was just one of the things said to prospective BDM girl leader, Vaida Raab, during one of her meetings with the infamous Gertrud Scholtz Klink. This was a woman who was described by many former BDM girls as being spiteful, sarcastic and generally unpleasant.

Born on 9 February 1902, Gertrud Scholtz Klink became a fervent Nazi party member, soon rising to prominence as leader of the National Socialist Women's League (NS-*Frauenschaft*). She married young at the age of 18, and had six children with her first husband, a factory worker who died shortly after their sixth child was born. When Hitler came to power, he appointed Scholtz Klink head of the Women's Nazi League. Despite her own political ambitions, she spoke out against the idea of women being involved in politics. She also denied endorsing the use of girls and young women within the *Volkssturm* and Werewolf militia units. This is, of course, yet another lie. However sparse it may be, there is evidence that suggests that Scholtz Klink was implicit in the militarization of young girls of the *Jüngmädel Bund* and *Bund Deutscher Mädel*, particularly during the last years of the Third Reich.

Scholtz Klink was a woman arrogant enough to believe that her past would not catch up with her, but thankfully her guilt was recorded privately by many *Jüngmädel* and *Bund Deutscher Mädel* girls. Vaida Raab kept an excellent diary, detailing many of the remarks of leading figures within the Third Reich. Recalling Scholtz Klink, she said:

She was an imposing figure for a woman: cruel, emotionless and sarcastic in many ways. At this time, she was married to SS *Obergruppenfuhrer* August Heissmayer, a high-ranking officer in the SS. She spoke of us as being like machines that must slave for men, revoke all luxury, and bear as many children for the future German Reich as we could. She told us, 'You will not endeavour to study, as your domain will be the home, husband and your children. You will provide for your man's every waking need, while asking for nothing in return. Duty is duty and this is your duty – there can be no other considerations.'

Of course, at that time we all swallowed this rubbish. We would talk among ourselves and believe that this was the right path for us as German girls. Create many children and further the German race and keep ourselves at optimum fitness for this task. It all made sense. Later on though, if we were needed to we could fulfil a military role on the home front or in the munitions factories, as we were young and very fit. We would be able to take over any of the tasks that were formerly those purely of the males in our society.

Scholtz Klink lied when she said that she did not suggest girls and women should be given weapons to help defend the Reich from the Allied forces. After the war, I remember speaking to one girl who told me, 'I was frightened and I told her [Scholtz Klink] that I just wanted to go home to my parents. She glared angrily at me and snapped, "You will do no such thing. You will do exactly as you are told. You are under the Fuhrer's mandate and within the services of the Reich. Now do you understand me?"'

She also lied when she said that only a few dedicated BDM leaders became involved in fighting and sabotage, and that this took place in and around the Warsaw area. Many girls of all ages became involved in the fighting, unless their parents physically prevented them from doing so. Scholtz Klink was quite happy encouraging them to do so and to defy the wishes of their parents. A lot of the girls did exactly what she told them to, because they were intimidated by her and she would convince them that it was their personal duty to the Fuhrer.

She once said, 'If you wish to serve our beloved Fuhrer, delivered to us by providence itself, then you shall follow, and follow to victory whatever task you are asked to do.' Scholtz Klink was overheard on many occasions making somewhat derogatory remarks about the girls of the BDM. One BDM girl caught the end of one of her spats, hearing her remark to a male colleague: 'the idea is simple. We keep their minds small and their legs open wide.'

Dana Henschelle also confirmed Scholtz Klink as a contradictory character:

> The last time she spoke to us in person was to try and raise our morale and to encourage all of us girls to resist the Bolshevik [Russian] enemy. She said to us, 'You shall become wolves among the ruins and in the shadows, you shall kill them with whatever means, and you shall show them no mercy.'
>
> That was the last time I ever saw her, but it made me very angry that, in the post-war years, she denied so many things in her memoirs and got away with everything. She should have been hanged by the neck or locked up for life in prison for what she did. We were lied to, used, and some of us were sacrificed while she was just a liar and a skulking coward.

At the death throes of the Second World War, Gertrud Scholtz Klink and her husband August Heissmayer fled Berlin. In the summer of 1945, she was captured and briefly detained in a Soviet prisoner of war camp near Magdeburg. However, with the assistance of Princess Pauline of Württemberg, she was able to escape from her Soviet internment. With her husband, she went into hiding in Bebenhausen near Tubingen. Scholtz Klink and Heissmayer spent the next three years in hiding, under the aliases Heinrich and Maria Stuckebrock.

On 28 February 1948, the couple were identified and arrested. A French military court subsequently sentenced Scholtz Klink to eighteen months in prison for forging documents. In May 1950, a review of her sentence classified her as one of the 'main culprits'. She was sentenced to a further thirty months' imprisonment. In addition to this, the court imposed a fine, as well as banning her for ten years from any political or trade union activity, journalism or teaching.

Scholtz Klink was released from prison in 1953. She returned to Bebenhausen, where she began to write her memoirs, which were published in 1978, in a book titled *Die Frau im Dritte Reich* (The Woman in the Third Reich).

In an interview with Claudia Koonz in the 1980s, she reiterated her support for National Socialism, defending her former position within Hitler's Third Reich. She was unapologetic, contradictory, and seemingly arrogant right to the end. In reality. she should have been hanged as a war criminal at the war's end.

She died peacefully at her home in Bebenhausen on 24 March 1999. August Heissmayer, who also escaped the noose, went on to become director of the West German Coca Cola bottling plant. He died in January 1979, just a few days after his 82nd birthday.

Vaida Raab comments on them:

> Those two did very well when you think about it. While the lives of many Germans were in ruins, they were in hiding, but went on to live the high life. Scholtz Klink should have been hanged for the part she played in the deaths of *Jüngmädel Bund* and *Bund Deutscher Mädel* girls who, as part of the *Volkssturm* and Werewolves, she insisted must fight for their country. It made me very angry that she, of all people, literally got away with murder.

It has to be noted here that Jutta Rudiger had been appointed as official leader of the BDM. She served in this post from 1937 to 1945. As with all women in the NSDAP, her role was a subordinate one. In her role as leader of the BDM, she did not possess any independent authority. Nazi policy dictated that any decision making or changes to policy within the BDM, would always be implemented by the male leaders. Baldur von Schirach, along with Artur Axmann, always had control of the puppets strings. Rudiger was certainly a more passive figure in the Third Reich.

Evidence would suggest that Scholtz Klink appeared to have had far more influence than she should have had. Jutta Rudiger was certainly a more educated individual than Scholtz Klink. She was an accomplished psychologist with a likeable personality, coming from a stable family background. It is true that she was a fervent Nazi, supporting many of the Nazi ideals. Yet, unlike many of the others, she was not party to making outlandish statements or comments. It is feasible that Scholtz Klink viewed Rudiger as a threat to her own subordinate authority.

At the end of the Second World War, Jutta Rudiger was captured and detained for two years. During her detention, she was not charged with any specific offences, so was not brought to trial. Upon her release, she continued her career as a paediatric psychologist in Dusseldorf. In one of the last interviews she gave, she remarked:

> National Socialism is not repeatable. One can take over only the values which we espoused. Comradeship, a readiness to support one another, bravery, self-discipline and not least, honour and loyalty. Apart from these, each individual young person must find their way alone.

In 2001, Jutta Rudiger died, at Bad Reichenhall in Bavaria, aged 90. Heidi Koch met Jutta Rudiger when she visited her BDM troop in the summer of 1943. Heidi recalls:

> In all honesty, she was an unremarkable figure. She spoke of devotion, obedience and of our role as the embodiment of the Third Reich as future mothers. There was no sarcasm about her personality and she seemed polite and was certainly not what you would call militaristic. She was like your grandmother, no different to that really. I can only comment and present a view based upon instinct, but she seemed quite nice to me. With Scholtz Klink, there was always an air of self-importance that you were below her league, but Rudiger was just normal. She would come to inspect, shake hands, smile, and that was it.

Head of the Waffen SS, Heinrich Himmler, was also a regular speaker at *Jüngmädel Bund* and *Bund Deutscher Mädel* education seminars. He was a popular figure who spoke passionately about his theories on German racial purity and biological obligations to the Reich, reiterating a girl's moral responsibilities as the property of the Reich. Even Himmler let slip to former Waffen SS officer, Herbert Kolinger, the sinister plan to militarize Germany's female youth should the need arise.

> He was talking off the cuff, as they say, and I heard him saying to youth leader Baldur von Schirach, 'I am of the opinion that girls and women in general will fight with more tenacity than the men, because they know what the enemy are going to do to them if they are caught.'
>
> This is what Himmler told von Schirach and it is the truth I remember thinking after they had moved on, 'My God, have they gone mad?' They had this obvious

contempt for women, which seemed to permeate the
higher echelons of the regime. I overheard Martin
Bormann once, referring to his wife, he said, 'I must leave
now as I have an appointment at my home with my cow.'

Quite unbelievable that one should speak of the
mother of your children in that manner.

Vaida Raab remembers when SS chief Heinrich Himmler visited
her school to give one of his racial hygiene seminars to the girls:

It was obvious that this was a subject about which Himmler
was passionate. He had quite a foreboding presence about
him. He was quite sinister, always looking very serious
and rarely smiling. He started a discussion with us about
the basic laws of nature and how the weakling should
be dealt with. He said, 'The ill-formed, the mongol, and
those with psychopathy are an abhorrence. In nature, they
are selected for termination as a natural course of events.'

He said, 'Imagine yourself a lioness and you have
three cubs. Two are perfect in every way, while the third
is sickly, weak, and cannot keep up with you or the other
two cubs. Do you then drain yourself and your other
two cubs to favour the weakling who will only die as a
matter of course anyway? Sometimes the lioness will
euthanize the weakling herself, understanding that its
existence is all but temporary in comparison to her two
strong healthy cubs. The weakling deprives the healthy,
and in order to thrive, we have to be hard and we have
to be cruel, even ruthless. Such principles should be
fully applied to the wellbeing and strength of our Reich.
Should you, as a German mother, give birth to offspring
that is sickly, weak and inept, then you too must do as the
lioness would do.'

At this point in the seminar, one of the girls questioned
Reichsfuhrer Himmler as to the morality of euthanasia
within one's own race, to which he replied, 'Is it violence
or an association with murder? No, I think not. Nations
do not thrive upon the procreation of weakness, and, in
this sense, we have to make an allegiance with violence if
we are to survive.'

After the seminar, Himmler stayed to shake hands
with the girls and sign autographs before taking tea with
the staff at the school.

Josef Goebbels was another senior visitor from the Third Reich hierarchy who gave a talk at the school Vaida Raab had attended. Vaida recalls that for almost an hour he ranted and raged about Jews: 'The filth of Jewry is being eliminated right now as I speak these words. For too many years, they have had it all their own way, but they are no longer laughing, we are sorting them all out.'

Vaida recalled how Goebbels was like a man possessed, shaking his fists in the air as he spoke. He also scolded one of the girls for falling asleep, which only seemed to irritate his bad mood even more. He closed his seminar by saying, 'No Jew shall ever be allowed to grow within the womb of the German woman, and this goes also for the Negro, Slav and the gypsy. You are Germany's future and you are its investment, its survival. Don't ever let us down – be pure, be German. Heil Hitler!'

For the author of such powerful sentiments, Goebbels also met an unremarkable end like *Reichsfuhrer* Himmler: he chose suicide rather than face capture.

With the Red Army closing in on the Fuhrer bunker in April 1945, Josef and Magda Goebbels poisoned all of their six young children before taking their own lives. Helena Vogel recalls how, as a young girl at school, racial purity was considered one of the greatest virtues of the German maiden.

> One afternoon we had a talk given by a man named Fritz Lenz. We were told that the talk was to address the subjects of biology, race, eugenics and euthanasia, and that Mr Lenz was a leading figure in this study of great importance. When Mr Lenz arrived, he was warmly greeted by our teachers, before taking to the stage for his presentation.
>
> He began with an explanation on the law for the prevention of hereditarily diseased offspring. This law was passed in July of 1933, and stated that anyone suffering from a range of genetic, mental or physical disorders would be sterilized under compulsory laws. Any family who attempted to hide family members with any physical or mental disorder, could be subject to imprisonment or sent to the concentration camps. Every child born after 1933 was subject to checks under the genetic and racial-hygiene laws, and any child failing the requirements of this law faced being euthanized under the T-4 programme. I found out all about the T-4 programme after the war during the re-education and de-Nazification programmes implemented by the Allied powers.

The reason for my interest in this is because I once had a friend in the BDM who confided in me that her younger sister had been born with a physical disability. She knew that the new laws would mean that this would soon be discovered. She told me that doctors had her sent away to what they called a clinic. She never saw her again. She was terribly upset about this, but could not openly show her distress out of fear of being ridiculed by other BDM girls. Her family was later sent a letter explaining that the child had died from measles in the clinic, and that the corpse had been incinerated to prevent the risk of spreading infection. What really happened no one knows, because after the war it was not possible to find out, as much of the documentation had been burned to protect the identities of those individuals involved in what was clearly murder. My friend said to me, 'My sister could never have joined the Young Maidens League as she had a physical impairment. She would therefore have been deemed to be of no use to the state. They killed her for that reason alone.'

The man many of the girls wanted to meet was Dr Josef Mengele, as he was the real force behind the issues on racial purity. They all thought of him as this kind doctor and protector of the state. Many thought he was good looking and they would write him letters. This racial purity issue was drummed into us all the time. We believed it all. We believed that we could not exist alongside anyone other than the finest human physical specimens. It is odd though, that a man like Mengele fled to Argentina after the Second World War, where he lived in peace until his death. He even ran a successful pharmaceutical company under his own name there. It's crazy to think that he was not hunted down and executed as a war criminal, which he undoubtedly was.

After the war, the shame I felt about this was so bad, that I vowed I would tell no one about it ever, but maybe now is the right time and you are the right person to hear it.

The man every German girl of the *Jüngmädel Bund* and *Bund Deutscher Mädel* dreamed of meeting was Adolf Hitler himself. Most of the girls were content enough to catch a glimpse of the Fuhrer at one of the many Nazi party rallies, but some were treated to a visit to the Fuhrers house, the Berghof. Gabrielle Haefker was one of those considered as 'the lucky few' to have visited the Berghof, met Adolf Hitler and had tea on the terrace.

I was terribly excited when I was told that I was going to the Berghof with my BDM troop. Such a thing was looked upon as one of the greatest honours our Fuhrer could give. Everyone I knew was so envious. On the day, my mother made sure I looked my best.

When we arrived at the Berghof I was just amazed. I couldn't believe that, here I was at the Fuhrer's home, and I was going to see him close up. We were so eager, that we almost tripped over each other as we made our way up the staircase to the terrace. We lined up and Hitler came out and greeted each of us with a handshake. It was not a crushing handshake, like the ones many give, but gentle. When he smiled, it seemed to radiate through you. I said, 'thank you, my Fuhrer' as he shook my hand, patted me on the left shoulder and smiled. He did this with each one of us in turn. A butler then came out onto the terrace with tea and cakes. We were all told to sit down at the tables, but we did not touch the tea or cakes until we were given permission to do so. It was so surreal. Here I was, I had met Hitler, and now I was drinking his tea and eating his cakes on the terrace of his home. The tea tasted good and the cakes were delicious.

After the tea, he thanked us all for coming to his home, saying he 'was honoured to have entertained the founders of the future German Reich.'

I was walking around on the terrace, admiring the view, when I was aware that someone had walked up to stand beside me. It was Hitler – he just appeared by my side. He said, 'Beautiful, is it not?' referring to the surrounding green hills, forests and streams. I replied, 'Yes, my Fuhrer, it is so beautiful here.'

He then said to me while gazing at the view, 'All of this beauty you see before you was grown and nurtured on the blood of centuries of Germans. German blood has made our land, our forests and our waters flourish. Never forget that Fraulein.'

I told him that I was so honoured to be here with him today, that I will never forget it. He looked down at me and smiled, then said, 'Who shall remember us when victory is paid with death? Will there be monuments erected a thousand years from now? Monuments where people will look up in awe and proclaim that their bloodline stood side by side with mine?'

With his hands behind his back, he walked off. Before we left, we all got out our autograph books and asked Hitler for his signature. He signed one of the pages of my little book for me: 'With warmest greetings, Fraulein Haefker, from Adolf Hitler.'

This was a treasured possession for many years, but I no longer have it. I think my mother and father burned the book after the Second World War. After the war, my parents forbade anything Hitler related in the house as they felt let down by Hitler and the Nazis. They felt that they had been cheated and then left to the Soviets. So, I don't have anything left from that time anymore. I've had neo-Nazis ask me what Hitler was like and telling me that it must have been great to have been around during that time. They don't understand what it was all about. We were raised in a Germany devoid of choices, where you were brought up on all sorts of poison. Looking back, the adults of that generation should have done more to prevent the Nazis and Hitler from gaining power, but they too were swallowed up by empty promises and convinced that everything would be alright.

Anita Skorz has a different view towards the issue of why her parents followed Hitler and supported the Nazi government, which led to her joining the two female Hitler Youth organizations.

Everybody asks the same question: why? Why did you follow that maniac Hitler?

Then take a look at the Treaty of Versailles and what it meant for Germany after the First World War. That treaty brought about years of misery, to the point where people were starving to death. We could not even afford to buy simple things like bread. We were often forced to go begging on the streets, especially in the areas where the wealthy Jews lived. Some would spare you something to eat, while others would shout at you to go away. Germany began to suffer from high unemployment. Hyperinflation set in and people began to riot in the streets. There was no food, and there was so much political rivalry, that rival political groups would fight and beat one another up in the streets.

Germany was collapsing into anarchy when Hitler came along with his Nazi Party, promising to sort Germany's problems out, get German men working, and make those responsible for Germany's problems pay. Hitler once shouted in the street to my father and his friends who were all out of work at the time, 'Comrades, those that have caused this for you, they will pay with their blood!'

So, I think had the Treaty of Versailles not been so severe and people could have worked and fed their families, then the Second World War might not have happened. It's just my personal view and I could be wrong, but that is it.

Melissa Schroeder was another former BDM girl who had the honour of a personal meeting with Hitler. As a young girl, Melissa was perhaps the embodiment of the Aryan female: blonde hair, flawless skin and piercing blue eyes. Such girls seemed to attract the attention of the Fuhrer. He always appeared mesmerized by the blonde-haired, blue-eyed girls of his Hitler Youth.

I never thought much of it at the time. We knew the Fuhrer was going to be at our parade in Berlin, but we did not expect much more than to see him drive past in his car. He actually stopped and flanked by his SS bodyguards, he began to walk among us, asking questions. I looked at him and we made eye contact. He came straight over to me, I raised my right arm, and shouted 'Heil Hitler!' He smiled and stroked the side of my face, grasping my hand in his.

He asked me, 'Where are you from Fraulein? Have you travelled far today to be here?'

It was just normal conversation really, like me and you [the author] talking now. There was nothing openly sinister in the man and he had a warm, inviting kind of smile.

He said to me, 'You are wonderful and a fine example of our German heraldry. Your mother and father should be very proud. I trust you are all working hard.'

He turned to an officer standing next to him and remarked, 'Yes, this is excellent. How can our women not be the best in the world?'

He turned and looked at me again and smiled, nodding his head. He raised his hand slightly and continued a conversation with the officer at his side, but I could not hear what was said as they began to walk off among the other girls. He signed autographs for some of the girls and press photographers who were there. Many other people had begun to congregate, like a movie star being mobbed.

In a few minutes, he was back in his car and gone, his entourage following behind. When I returned home, I told my mother and father all about it. They asked if I got the Fuhrer's autograph, to which I had to explain that I hadn't. I had been so in awe of the experience, that it had slipped my mind to ask him.

It is hard to believe from that moment in time that this was a man that history has since documented as a maniac and a man responsible for mass murder. Of course, he was a mass murderer. He was a maniac who led our nation to destruction.

After the war, many of us had to look back and question. Perhaps the hardest question of all was that of complicity. As followers of Hitler and the Nazi regime, were we partly to blame? Do we also have the blood of millions on our hands? You ask yourself all of these questions and you ask yourself, what about the concentration camps? We knew of their existence and we knew that people were disappearing, but, as a society, our elders permitted it and did not challenge it. In that sense, therefore, we let it happen.

Many historians today talk of Nazi Germany as having been a racist state, when racism had been prevalent in Western societies decades before Third Reich Germany. Look at America and its treatment of African Americans at the time of the Civil Rights movement and the slave trade, and Britain too, with its history with the Scots, Irish and the slave trade. They have all pursued racist policies at some point in their history, so the Third Reich was by no means unique in this sense.

Even today, the world is full of religious and racial intolerance, yet most turn a blind eye to it. If I could turn back time, would I have still followed the Nazi cause? The answer is not that simple. Had we resisted, then bad things would have happened to me and my family. We did not have the means to flee Germany to start a new life elsewhere, besides we were Germans and Germany was our home. For many Germans, things happened so quickly that you were swept along with it. We, as children, were schooled under the Nazis. We knew no other way, just as children today follow the rules of their individual societies, conforming to those rules and principles as being the generally accepted way.

Hitler Youth leader Artur Axmann is another figure worthy of some examination here. He was the one responsible for suggesting to Himmler that a combat division, comprising young men from the Hitler Youth, be formed. The concept was approved by Hitler, who then agreed that all boys born in 1928 would be considered for service within a newly formed SS combat division, the 12th SS Panzer Division *Hitlerjugend*. Every boy I knew aspired to join that elite regiment. However, now we look back to see what they were responsible for. They carried out executions of prisoners of war, murdered civilians. Everywhere they went, they left death, destruction and misery in their wake. They were hardly a good example for our young men, were they?

Axmann was also guilty of encouraging children into the *Volkssturm* in futile defensive strategies in and around the Reich territories at the closing stages of the Second World War. During the last weeks of the war in Europe, Axmann was in command of units of the Hitler Youth that had been incorporated into the *Volkssturm*. In this role, he was certainly more than just guilty by association.

Born on 18 February 1913 in Hagen, Westphalia, the son of an insurance clerk, Artur Axmann was *Reichsjugendfuhrer* of the Hitler Youth from 1940 to the war's end in 1945. Axmann had served on both the western and eastern fronts. It was during his service on the eastern front that he was severely wounded, losing his right arm. Axmann was also one of those present in the Fuhrer bunker during Hitler and Eva Braun's suicide. In fact, Axmann took the pistol used by Hitler in the suicide, stashing it away, in his own words, 'for better days'.

Axmann fled the Fuhrer bunker as part of a breakout group that included Martin Bormann. He avoided capture by Red Army troops, disappearing into the populace. Living for some months under the alias of Eric Siewert, he was arrested in Lubeck in December 1945, when an underground Nazi movement he had been organizing was uncovered by a US army counterintelligence operation. In May 1949, Axmann was sentenced to three years and three months as a major offender by a Nuremberg de-Nazification court. On 19 August 1958, a West Berlin court fined Axmann 35,000 marks (£3,000) after finding him guilty of indoctrinating German youth with National Socialism up until the end of the Third Reich.

Again, Axmann was a war criminal who got off very lightly for his deeds. What was Axmann like? Helga Bassler recalls:

Axmann was most enthusiastic in encouraging both male and female youth to be aggressive and to take up arms. He was responsible for sending thousands of children to their deaths in pointless military actions. He was in charge of indoctrinating us with the Nazi philosophy. He was not just concerned with the boys of the Hitler Youth, his involvement with the *Jüngmädel Bund* and *Bund Deutscher Mädel* is beyond question. I didn't like the man personally. I thought he was a little lecherous. There was just something about the man I did not like. I only saw him on a few occasions, when he would have a smirk on his face; an arrogant smirk proclaiming how *he* had made us all what we are. Others may disagree, but he displayed all the arrogance that had become characteristic of those Nazis who effectively escaped justice, remained unrepentant and lived very well after the Second World War. I remember my father saying when they arrested him that he would hang, but they didn't hang him. It was unbelievable and my father couldn't understand it.

It just makes me cringe now when I think about it and how foolish we all were. The promise of a better Germany, with a better life style and better things, was a strong allure after the hard and troublesome years under the Treaty of Versailles. It's easy to follow when you have little to lose and nothing to hope for. This was the situation that my parents faced after the First World War.

At the end of the Third Reich, we found it difficult to think that Germany could ever survive without Hitler and the Nazis. We had to forget everything we had been taught and learn again, because all that we had ever known was a lie. The transition took time, but with patience and understanding, it evolved. I knew of many girls who refused to accept the de-Nazification, at least privately.

Once Germany was divided into east and west and the Cold War era began, many were saying that war with

Russia would be the next thing, 'now you tell me that we were wrong?'

The real key to negating all the things that Axmann, Schirach, Scholtz Klink and Hitler had instilled in us, was education. The new education system, introduced after the war, opened our minds to the real world, with its real cultures and diversity, where many lived in relative peace with one another.

Axmann's predecessor, Baldur von Schirach, who held the positions of national youth leader and head of the Hitler Youth from 1931 to 1940, was born in Berlin on 9 May 1907. He was the son of theatre director, grand ducal chamberlain and retired captain of the cavalry, Carl Baily Norris von Schirach. He was raised within an opulent lifestyle. Many within the Third Reich described von Schirach as being 'young, effeminate and aristocratic'. However, he became an important component within Hitler's inner circle, which gave him a high degree of protection within the regime.

In 1933, he was appointed head of the Hitler Youth and given the rank of SA *Gruppenfuhrer*. Von Schirach was violently anti-Semitic, being responsible for the implementation of the militaristic tone of the Hitler Youth. During the closing stages of the Second World War, he was also responsible for sending children to their deaths. Under the direction of von Schirach, children as young as 12 years of age were sent to augment depleted German army units. Again, this is guilt without question.

Von Schirach surrendered at the end of the war in 1945, and was subsequently put on trial at Nuremberg. In the typically cowardly stance of a man trying to save himself, von Schirach denounced Hitler (one of only two men to do so), denying any knowledge of the extermination or death camps.

On 1 October, Baldur von Schirach was found guilty of crimes against humanity and sentenced to twenty years in Spandau Prison. In July 1949, his wife Henriette divorced him. He was released on 30 September 1966, after serving his full sentence. He retired to a quiet life in southern Germany to write his memoirs, which became published under the title, *Iche Glaubte an Hitler* (I believed in Hitler). Again, it seems strange that a man such as von Schirach should escape the hangman's noose. Olga Kirschener says of von Schirach:

This was the man who denied it all, apparently secretly loathing Adolf Hitler and denying all knowledge of the death camps. I don't believe for one minute that there is any truth in this. He was always fawning to Hitler – you only have to look at the photographs and the film reels taken at the various Nazi party rallies. He took great pride in claiming the Hitler Youth, in all its facets, as his creation. He boasted how it had flourished under his personal direction. In my opinion, he certainly knew a lot more than he was prepared to admit. I think he also thought of himself as a bit of a ladies' man, though many thought he was a homosexual, or *blonde arsch* [blonde arse] as they were sometimes called back then. I never met the man, but I felt his influence within the *Jüngmädel Bund* and the *Bund Deutscher Mädel*. Oh, he was guilty of much more than he served sentence for, and he was a coward. Not the best of attributes to be remembered for.

To conclude this chapter, I feel that the testimony given to me by Melitta Schuman is very apt. Melitta, or Litta as she was known to her friends, gives a very different account from that of most followers of the Nazi girls' cult.

The *Jüngmädel Bund* and the *Bund Deutscher Mädel* was not fun at all. When we went on camp into the forest, we were shouted at and ordered about. We had to get up very early in the morning. I used to hate this, as it was often cold, damp and misty in the mornings, and you had to stand to attention, shaking in the cold, while the flag was raised. After this was done, we had to help make breakfast. If we were not quick enough in fetching wood and water, we were scolded by the leaders. You had to totally conform and do and think exactly what you were told. 'Be a good Nazi,' she would shout in your face. They would even strike your face, depending on their mood at the time.

My parents, who were loyal Nazis, pushed me into the *Jüngmädel Bund*, so what choice did I have as a child? Prior to joining the *Jüngmädel Bund*, I filled in the form at school, and told to return the form having been signed by my parents. The *Jüngmädel Bund* meetings were held on Wednesdays and Saturdays. They once asked me what I had done at school that week. When I told them, they laughed at me, telling me that I was wasting my time.

'Why don't you just study your *Mein Kampf* [*Mein Kampf*, or 'My Struggle', was Hitler's political philosophy book, which became the Hitler Youth bible.] It is the only education you will ever require.'

I can't tell you how happy I was when we lost the war, because then it all ended: no more Hitler Youth, no more orders, no more abuse, no more marching and singing, and no more standing in the cold, raising flags. I hated every moment of it. They gave you perks like pocket money. You were permitted to go to the cinema, something that only adults were allowed to do, but it was not worth it, it really wasn't. I burned my uniform and my copy of *Mein Kampf*, much to my parents' disgust. As soon as I was able, I left home because I blamed my parents for it all. They supported and they followed, like thousands of others. We were dragged into that madness and we suffered. In fact, many of us suffered quietly.

When I left home, I could not relate to my mother or father anymore. I did not visit them very much, and when I did, we spoke little. When they passed away, there was little sorrow because there was no love. To grieve there has to be love, so if there was no love, there was no grief.

My life has been wonderful ever since, as I had left Germany and settled in Norway, where I taught children to ski and ice-skate as a means to earn a living. I married and had children, and I am happy that they have choices and can make their own way in life. You should never willingly follow evil. Our elders did and we all suffered as a result, and shame on them.

For those who have only ever lived within a democratic society under a democratically elected government, it is somewhat difficult to understand just how a dictatorship like that of the Third Reich operated. Perhaps a good explanation is that given by Erika Baumann:

In Third Reich Germany, you learned to grow up quickly, because you had to. Our educators were of the view that our parents' attitudes were old and insignificant and were part of the cause of Germany's problems. We were told quite explicitly, 'You cannot learn from a parent who was raised under the old ways. From now on, the only way is that of the current will of our Fuhrer Adolf Hitler.'

I also vividly recall one BDM girl's father scolding her and shouting at her, 'You might be a Hitler Youth, my girl, but in my house I am the boss, not Herr Hitler.'

The next day at school, the girl innocently confided in a friend what her father had said. Her friend then told a teacher, and that same evening the authorities went to the girl's house and threatened her father saying, 'You could hang for high treason for this, or do you realize that you could just disappear?'

On that occasion, it was just a warning, but it served as a reminder that the eyes and the ears of the Nazi state were everywhere and there was no escape. You had to conform even if you didn't agree with what they were doing.

I also knew a boy in the Hitler Youth who would come home every time from those Hitler Youth camps with cut lips and blackened eyes. He told me that they had been forced into gangs. One gang would be on a hilltop, and he and his gang would have to defeat them. They would charge up the hill with their flag and beat the other boys from the top. He said it entailed physical fist fighting and brawling without gloves. Afterwards, some would be unconscious on the ground, having been beaten into a stupor. If any cried, they were ridiculed by the others as being homosexuals or weaklings. He told me he felt as if his life was over. He just wanted to die. Not much of a life for a 13-year-old boy, I used to think to myself. He couldn't cry in front of his parents or brothers either, as they would humiliate him too. He cried in my arms many times, that poor boy. I really did feel for him, as the Hitler Youth was not for him as he was not violent or hard enough. Our friendship continued after the end of the war. I am happy to say he did alright for himself in the end, but he did suffer psychological problems. He had problems with self-confidence, which affected his life in a number of ways.

The Hitler Youth was brutal and contemptuous. The Third Reich was evil beyond comprehension. Those who admire it from historical perspectives have to understand all that went on behind the scenes, both politically and socially. It was nothing of which to be envious; it was cruel, brutal, cold and uncompassionate. Would you want your children to be brought up like that?

15
Angels of Death

The term 'angel of death' has been used often in the past to describe women who have committed crimes such as murder. Many have rightfully earned such a moniker, but none more so than some of the German women who stood trial for unspeakable acts of violence, sadism, brutality and murder during the Second World War. What is perhaps harder to understand from a psychological point, is that their crimes were not crimes of passion as is usually the case with the majority of females who turn to violence or murder. The Nazi angels of death were women who, in most cases, tortured and murdered people under the auspices of duty to the Reich. Yet some would admit they killed for their own pleasure. Their violence and brutality was often unique in severity and explicitly inventive in cruelty. Yet many would give no coherent explanation for their actions when interviewed at the end of the Second World War. Many would use the excuse that they were just following orders or doing their duty.

There will always be a fascination with the German female war criminals. It is difficult to comprehend the scale of cruelty perpetrated by these individuals of the supposed gentler sex, and maybe even harder to understand or judge. They were far from lacking in femininity when not on camp duties. They picked flowers from the fields and forests, enjoyed partying, and flirting with their male SS colleagues.

What is one of the major factors that has to be considered when asking the question why? It is, quite simple, that these women never expected Germany to lose the Second World War. They were utterly convinced that they would never have to face trial for their crimes. In this sense, they felt free to abuse, torture and murder those under their charge. Many were committed Nazis who were prepared to undertake any duty given to them. They were devoid of morality and lacked any sense of human compassion. They were capable of killing with indifference. Men, women, children, babies, the elderly and the sick – in their distorted view, there were no emotional separations.

When brought to trial for their crimes, some showed a degree of remorse. Witnesses at their trials, however, found it difficult to ascertain whether it was remorse for their deeds or remorse at having been caught. Others were unrepentant to the end. Some begged for clemency, while others resigned themselves to their fate. Some appeared to escape justice completely.

All were seduced then indoctrinated into National Socialism via the Hitler Youth organizations. I would argue so were many of the women I interviewed during the writing of the Hitler's Girls book. Yet they did not become brutalized in the system. Many fought in the defence of their communities sometimes killing through the necessities of war. They fought against soldiers not helpless unarmed inmates of a concentration camp. This does not absolve anyone from the act of killing. Yet in war people have to kill or be killed, that is the business of war. It would appear that there was an inherent evil within the character of many of the German women accused of war crime.

No book such as this would be complete without a brief examination of the female Nazi war criminals. In this chapter, we will look at some of them. Some were tracked down, sent for trial and then hanged. Most of the violence and murder that Nazi women became engaged in, was within the concentration-camp system. Some 3,600 women worked in the concentration camps. Of this number, 60 would stand trial at war crimes' tribunals between the years 1945 and 1949. Twenty-one would be sentenced to death. There were a great many other women who displayed the same level of cruelty, being guilty of murdering Jews, gypsies and political opponents to the Nazi regime. Many of them were the wives of serving SS officers. There were many that committed war crimes, but will never be discovered. Some of them still walk among us to this day. To those, one might say what a Catholic priest once said on the subject: 'They may have evaded justice in this life, but they won't in the next.' Here we will, in no particular order, view some of the female monsters of the Nazi concentration camp system.

Irma Grese was born on 7 October 1923, in Wrechen, Free State of Mecklenburg-Strelitz in Germany, to dairy workers Berta and Alfred Grese. She was the third of five children (three girls and two boys).

In 1936, Irma Grese's mother had committed suicide, by drinking hydrochloric acid after discovering that husband Alfred had been having an affair with a local inn owner's daughter. It was possibly this traumatic event in Grese's childhood that sowed the seeds for a warped adulthood.

She left school early (in 1938) at the age of 14, due to lack of scholastic aptitude, bullying by her classmates, and her obsessive preoccupation with the *Bund Deutscher Mädel*. Her father disapproved of her association with the BDM, which led to much verbal conflict between father and daughter. Upon leaving school, she took on a number of casual jobs, including a post as an assistant nurse in an SS-run sanatorium, where she worked for two years.

During this time, she unsuccessfully tried to get an apprenticeship as a nurse. The combination of her mother's suicide, bullying at school, failed academia, and failed career aspirations undoubtedly induced flaws in her adult persona. She would have suffered from a lack of confidence and insecurity, and would have probably been liable to exaggeration. From these few facts on Grese, we can see how, once within the concentration camp as a guard, she would have felt a sense of empowerment. Her seniority over the wretched inmates would have compensated for any previous feelings of low self-esteem.

In her role as a guard, she excelled as one of the most feared, brutal and sadistic of her kind. She was universally feared and despised by the inmates. She attained the rank of *SS-Helferin* serving at Ravensbrück, Auschwitz and Bergen Belsen concentration camps. From mid-1942, she was an *aufseherin* (female camp guard) at Ravensbrück, and in March 1943 she transferred to Auschwitz II-Birkenau. In the second half of 1944, she was promoted to *Rapportfuhrerin*, the second highest rank open to females in the camp system.

In this role, Grese participated in the selections for the gas chambers. Early in 1945, she accompanied a prisoner transport from Auschwitz to Ravensbrück. In March, she transferred to Bergen-Belsen, along with a large transport of inmates from Ravensbrück. She was captured by the British on 17 April 1945 with other SS personnel who had not fled the camp. She stood trial for a catalogue of acts, which included the ill treatment, murder, torture and arbitrary shootings of female camp inmates at Auschwitz and Bergen-Belsen. She was also known for setting her trained and allegedly half-starved dogs onto inmates in the camps, delighting in watching them savage unfortunate victims. She clearly enjoyed shooting inmates in cold blood with her pistol. It was also claimed by witnesses that she beat inmates to death, and also carried a plaited whip that she used to flog others.

During the course of her trial, held under British military law in Lüneburg from 17 September to 17 November 1945, the press labelled Grese 'The Beautiful Beast'. She was also known as 'The

Hyena of Auschwitz'. Her guilt was beyond doubt and she was subsequently sentenced to death.

On Thursday, 13 December 1945, Irma Grese was led from her cell at Hamelin jail to where executioner Albert Pierrepoint awaited her. She was defiant and unapologetic to the end. After entering the execution cell, she gazed around momentarily. She stood firmly on the chalk mark on the floor that indicated where the trap door was. As a white hood was placed over her head, she said '*schnell*.' (quickly). The rope was placed over her head and around her neck. The trap door opened with a crash and Irma Grese was pronounced dead shortly afterwards by a doctor. It is difficult to imagine any young woman's life being snuffed out at just 22 years of age. Judging by Irma Grese's background, once in the service of the Nazi death camps, there could have been no other direction in life. It was sad, but ultimately, she was the instrument of her own destiny.

Dorothea Binz was born 16 March 1920, into a lower, middle-class family in Forsterei Dusterlake. She was an attractive girl, with shoulder-length blonde hair, who attended school up until the age of 15. Her school life and childhood would suggest that it was normal in every sense. She was never denied love or affection by her parents. It is therefore a mystery as to why the monster in this young woman would emerge to such prominence.

Binz volunteered for kitchen work at Ravensbrück concentration camp in August 1939. During her early employment there, she also worked in the camp laundry. In September of 1939, she was appointed position of *aufseherin*. She was also appointed as supervisor of the bunker where women prisoners were tortured and killed. In August 1943, she was promoted to *stellevertretende oberaufseherin* (deputy chief wardress).

In her capacity as director of training for the female camp guards between 1943 and 1945, it had been reported that Binz trained many of the cruellest female camp guards in the system. Her cruelty has been described as the personification of evil itself. She actively sought to inflict pain and suffering on those under her charge. Witnesses testified to her sadistic appetite: beating, kicking, slapping, shooting, whipping, stomping, and generally abusing women prisoners during almost every waking hour. She was particularly feared, often walking among the women prisoners, a whip in one hand and a leashed German Shepherd in the other. At a moment's notice, she would select a prisoner and kick her to death, or select her to be killed. Her eyes, it was said, shone with glee every time she killed someone. It was also reported that SS officer Edmund Brauning was her boyfriend. The two would take 'romantic' strolls around the camp to watch women being flogged. Afterwards, they would stroll away laughing. Up until late 1944, when Brauning was transferred to Buchenwald, the two shared a house outside the camp.

Binz was captured in Hamburg by the British on 3 May 1945. She was held in the Recklinghausen Camp (formerly a Buchenwald sub-camp) and tried with other SS personnel at the Ravensbrück war crimes trial, where she was found guilty of perpetrating war crimes. She was sentenced to death by hanging, meeting her fate on the gallows at Hamelin Prison on 2 May 1947. Before the noose was placed over her head, she took off her necklace and remarked, 'I hope you won't think that we were all evil people.' Her executioner was also Albert Pierrepoint. In the annals of cruelty, Dorothea Binz, whose life ended at the age of 27, has few equals.

Johanna Altvater was a truly unique case in both gravity and the fact that she was twice brought to trial during the years after the Second World War, and acquitted on both occasions due to lack of evidence.

Working for the regional commissar in the Ukraine, she participated in the murder of sick Jewish children in a hospital in one of the ghettos. It was said that she had entered the small hospital where she began to grab the sick children from their beds, before hurling them from the third storey window of the building. Some of the children died instantly, while others were left seriously injured, writhing in agony. The cruelty this woman meted out to children would become her depraved hallmark.

There is little further information on Altvater, other than the two trials at which she was acquitted, the first in 1979, then in 1982. On both occasions the judges ruled that there was insufficient evidence to secure a conviction. It seemed Altvater had covered her tracks very well, literally getting away with murder. The father of one of her child victims testified that 'such sadism from a woman I have never before seen.' Her defence argued that she was only a secretary. This, coupled with the lack of evidence, meant that she walked away to live what remained of her life in relative peace.

Ilse Koch was born on 22 September 1906, in Dresden, to a factory foreman and his wife. She had a happy, joyful home life, and at elementary school, she was described as a happy, polite child. At the age of 15, she enrolled at an accountancy school later, before working as a bookkeeping clerk.

It was sometime in 1932 when she was seduced by the rising Nazi party. In 1934, through acquaintances in both the SA and SS, she met Karl Otto Koch, whom she married two years later. By 1936 she was employed as both a female guard and secretary at the Sachsenhausen concentration camp near Berlin. Her husband was the commandant of the Sachsenhausen camp. When her husband took over as commandant of Buchenwald camp, she followed. It was at here, if allegations are to be believed, that evil would emanate from within this otherwise placid woman.

It was alleged Koch had become involved in sickening experiments, where tattooed prisoners were selected then murdered. They would then be skinned under the direction of Ilse Koch. The purpose of these experiments, it was said, was to aid Doctor Erich Wagner assess how tattooing influenced criminality within an individual. Internal organs were also removed from prisoners' corpses, many being discovered in bizarre display cases at the end of the war. Her husband had been transferred to Lublin in 1941, while Koch remained at Buchenwald, until 24 August 1943 when she and her husband were arrested. SS and police leader, Josias von Waldeck-Pymont, who had supervisory authority over the Buchenwald camp, had issued orders for the two to be arrested.

The charges were embezzlement, private enrichment, and the murders of prisoners to prevent them from giving testimony. Koch was imprisoned until 1944, when she was acquitted because of a lack of evidence. Her husband was found guilty of the charges and was executed by firing squad at Buchenwald.

In 1947, Koch was brought before the American military court at Dachau, where she was charged with participating in a criminal plan, and for aiding, abetting and participating in the murders at Buchenwald. In the courtroom, she announced that she was eight months pregnant. She had already gained a reputation for being promiscuous and having simultaneous relationships with numerous SS officers at Buchenwald. It was also alleged that she had numerous affairs with prisoners while at Buchenwald. Her promiscuity, it is said, was triggered by the fact that her husband Karl had allegedly been a homosexual. Buchenwald records revealed that he had been treated for syphilis.

On 19 August 1947, Koch was sentenced to life imprisonment. On 8 June 1948, this was reduced to four years, due to the fact that there was no clear evidence that she was involved in the murder of prisoners for their tattooed skin.

Due to the pressure of public opinion, Koch was rearrested in 1949 and tried before a West German court. After a lengthy period, where various witnesses were called and her previous conduct during the war examined in some detail, the life sentence was reinstituted.

On 1 September 1967, Ilse Koch was discovered dead in her prison cell at Aichach Women's Prison. She had committed suicide at 60 years of age. Her body lies in an unmarked, unattended grave in the cemetery at Aichach.

Ilse and Karl Koch had two sons, one of whom committed suicide after the war. Another son, conceived in her cell at Dachau by an unknown father, was born in Aichach prison. The baby was taken away from her at birth, but later, discovering who his mother was, he began visiting her at Aichach prison. Koch may have denied having tattooed prisoners killed and skinned, but the reality is that many were killed and their tattooed skins stripped from their bodies. The purpose was to make various pieces of art, the most infamous of which being lampshades. At the end of the Second World War, such gruesome Nazi relics were discovered by the invading Allies. Whether Ilse Koch played any part in this vile practice will never really be known.

Johanna Boorman, born 10 September 1893, in Birkenfelde, East Prussia, is another name that is synonymous with the wartime infliction of pain and suffering. Nicknamed '*Wiesel*' (weasel) and 'the Woman with the Dogs', she had joined the SS as an auxiliary in 1938, in her own words, 'to earn more money'.

Her first appointment was at the Lichtenburg concentration camp in Lichtenburg, Saxony. In 1939, she was assigned to oversee a work party at Ravensbrück women's camp near Berlin. In March 1942, Boorman was one of a handful of female members of the SS to be selected for guard duties at Auschwitz in Poland. Almost as soon as she had arrived, she began to impose cruelty and brutality. She had a large dog that would accompany her as she strolled around the camp. One of her pleasures, was to set the savage dog onto the female prisoners of the camp. She would watch with interest as the dog sometimes savaged the unfortunate victim to death. Although only short in stature, she was a woman with a vicious temper, killing many prisoners by beating them to death. Eventually transferred to Budy, a nearby sub-camp, she continued the abuse and murder of prisoners under her charge with enthusiasm.

Her last post was at the Bergen-Belsen concentration camp. The British liberated the camp on 15 April 1945, where the scenes within the camp shocked and disgusted even the most battle hardened of soldiers. Mike Sewell, a British officer, recalled: 'What I saw that day, entering that hell, were the likes of things that no human being should ever see. Yet human beings were responsible for this. I was sickened then, and I am still sickened by it now.'

Boorman was soon arrested, along with other members of the SS. On 13 December 1945, at the age of 52, Johanna Boorman walked to the hangman's cell. Her executioner, Pierre Pierrepoint, recalled how 'she limped down the corridor, looking old and haggard. Standing just over five feet, she was trembling as she was put on the scales. She then said in German, "I have my feelings."' An interesting statement for someone who had so little regard for the feelings of those she had murdered and abused. Within a few minutes, Johanna Boorman was dead.

Elizabeth Volkenrath was born on 5 September 1919, in Swierzawa, Silesia. Volkenrath began her career of violence and murder when, in October 1941, she volunteered for service at the Ravensbrück concentration camp where she was an *aufseherin*. In March 1942, she was transferred to Auschwitz. It was here that she met SS *Rottenfuhrer* (Corporal) Heinz Volkenrath, who had worked at the camp since 1941 as an SS *Blochfuhrer* (Block leader). The two were married in 1943.

Volkenrath was directly involved in the murder of prisoners both at Ravensbrück and at Auschwitz-Birkenau. She had also been responsible for the selection of prisoners for the gas chambers. She was arrested in April 1945, and subsequently stood trial for war crimes. She was found guilty and sentenced to death by hanging. The sentence was carried out on 13 December 1945. Elizabeth Volkenrath was just 26 years old.

Maria Mandl was born on 10 January 1912, in Münzkirchen, Austria-Hungary. In many respects, one could be forgiven for thinking that Mandl appeared the average school headmistress. Tall, with her dark hair and a not unattractive face, Mandl doesn't fit the description of the average mass murderer. Yet this woman was directly complicit in the murders of 500,000 people.

Earning the nickname of 'The Beast', Mandl is infamous for her central role and participation in the Holocaust. She served in the role of *aufseherin* at Lichtenburg, an *oberaufseherin* at Ravensbrück, and as a *lagerfuhrerin* at Auschwitz II-Birkenau and Dachau concentration camps. Mandl actively participated in the selection of inmates to be murdered. She signed paperwork condemning an estimated 500,000 women and children to death. For her services, Mandl had been awarded the War Merit Cross, Second Class, in November 1944. Her last assignment was at Mühldorf, a sub-camp of Dachau. In May 1945, Mandl fled from Mühldorf and into the mountains of southern Bavaria, back to her birthplace.

On 10 August 1945, Mandl was arrested by members of the United States army. Under interrogation, it was revealed that Mandl was a highly intelligent woman who had been dedicated to her gruesome work. In November 1946, she was handed over to the Republic of Poland where she would stand trial for her crimes.

In November 1947 she was tried in a Krakow courtroom during the Auschwitz trial, found guilty, and sentenced to death by hanging. Maria Mandl was hanged on 28 January 1948. She was 45 years old.

Hildegard Lachert was an interesting character. A notorious, brutal, sadistic SS *aufseherin*, she did not share the same fate as many of her kind. When one considers the gravity of her crimes, this is certainly intriguing. Lachert, who was born on 20 January 1920, served at Ravensbrück, Majdanek and Auschwitz-Birkenau concentration camps. It was in October 1942, that Lachert, then a 22-year-old nurse, was called for duty at Majdanek, where she served as an *aufseherin*.

In 1944, after the birth of her third child, she went on to serve at Auschwitz. It was during her time there that she gained a reputation for ruthlessness. In this context, it is pretty clear what activities she would have been involved. Beatings, cruelty and abuse were all hallmarks of her character.

She fled Auschwitz ahead of the advancing Russian forces in December 1944. It is believed the last position she served in was at Bolzano, a detention camp in northern Italy. She also served at the Mauthausen-Gusen concentration camp in Austria. When Lachert was captured, she appeared before a Polish court in Krakow. The mother of two surviving children was given a sentence of fifteen years' imprisonment. She was released from Krakow prison in 1956.

In 1975, she was arrested again, along with other former SS accomplices from the Majdanek concentration camp. She faced trial in a Dusseldorf court, where a catalogue of testimonies concerning her sadistic behaviour was heard. It was reported by witnesses that she would always beat a prisoner until she drew blood. She had also been given the nickname 'Bloody Brigitte'. Many other witnesses came forward to say that she was one of the worst of the female camp guards. She had often encouraged her dog to attack prisoners, made selection for the gas chambers, and actively abused those under her charge. The court subsequently sentenced Lachert to twelve years in prison, but she never served this time, since her imprisonment in Poland – close to ten years – plus the five years spent in custody awaiting trial, were taken into account. It beggars belief that Lachert then went on to serve with the American Central Intelligence Agency, the CIA, and the West German Federal Intelligence Service, the *Bundesnachrichtendienst*, or BND. She excelled in this work, working extensively against her former Soviet enemy under the auspices of the former Western Allies. She lived a very comfortable existence in Berlin, dying in 1995 at the age of 75.

Ruth Closius was born on 5 July 1920, in Breslau, Germany. After marrying, she became known as Ruth Neudeck or Ruth Closius-Neudeck.

Closius became an SS supervisor in July 1944 when she arrived at Ravensbrück concentration camp for women, where she soon impressed her superiors with her unbending brutality. In July 1944, her dedication soon earned her promotion to *blochfuhrerin*. At Ravensbrück she was known as the most ruthless of female personnel. She once cut the throat of an inmate with the sharp edge of a shovel.

Promotion came again in December 1944, when she was given the rank of *oberaufseherin*, before being transferred to the Uckermark extermination complex down the road from Ravensbrück. In this role, she was directly involved in the extermination of 5,000 women and children. Revelling in her authority, she was both despised and feared by the prisoners.

In March 1945, she became head of the Barth sub-camp, from where she fled the following month, but she was tracked down and arrested. She was incarcerated while the British army conducted investigations into the allegations made against her.

In April 1948, she stood accused at the third Ravensbrück trial along with other SS women. The now 28-year-old former camp guard admitted to all of the accusations made against her. She was found guilty of war crimes and sentenced to death by hanging. On 29 July 1948, she was executed by Pierre Pierrepoint on the gallows at Hamelin Prison. So, came the end of one of the worst female war criminals in the history of the Second World War.

There were many more who had committed equally heinous acts of cruelty and murder, but to examine them all in any detail would be a major undertaking and one that is not possible here. The above women were merely a few cogs within the mechanics of a huge machine. These women were certainly no doves amongst eagles. They had entered into their lives of crime fully prepared and aware of what they were going to do. They carried out their tasks with ruthless efficiency, beyond the comprehension of most civilized individuals. Most were executed with the mark of Kane upon them. In life, and in their passing, they were angels of death, servants to the Holocaust.

16

The Lebensborn Nightmare

The *Lebensborn*, or Fountain of Life, programme, introduced by the Nazis on 12 December 1935, was an SS initiative that became a state-supported, registered association. The objective of the programme was twofold. Firstly to counter the falling birth rate in Germany at the time, and secondly, to significantly raise the birth rate of Aryan children within the Third Reich territories. To achieve this, extramarital relationships between persons classified as being racially pure and possessing the required health criteria, were actively encouraged and endorsed by the state.

To understand the objectives of the *Lebensborn* programme, one also has to examine the Aryan classification in Nazi Germany. The Nazis had misinterpreted the Aryan-race theory within its original context. However, they evolved their own racial theories based on the ancient Nordic and Germanic peoples. The word Aryan was originally applied to describe all Indo-Europeans, in a geographical area stretching from India to Europe. Particular emphasis was placed on the peoples of Persia (modern day Iran) and India. The term Aryan, used to classify these people, was used in the ethno-linguistic sense from the late nineteenth to the mid-twentieth century. The term was also often used by those attempting to promote ideas based upon racial hierarchy.

Aryanism soon developed into a theory, in which those classified as being Aryan were part of a master race. Where the Nazis were concerned, they were convinced that the Germanic people were a master race. It is true that many Germans had strong Nordic ancestral lineages, so the theory of Aryanism, Nordic heraldry and the proposed master race were easily sold to the people.

The physiological differences that separated the Nazi Aryan ideal from that of others, were quite straightforward. The Nazi perception of the perfect Aryan was the blue-eyed, blonde-haired and fair-skinned Germans, both males and females. The possibility of breeding an Aryan master race with these characteristics was one strongly embraced by SS *Reichsfuhrer* Heinrich Himmler.

Himmler became obsessed with the concept, investigating its feasibility well before the *Lebensborn* programme became reality. Himmler surmised that the mating between pure German individuals with blonde hair and blue eyes would then create offspring with the same genetic characteristics. Himmler was eager to put the theory into practise, using males from the ranks of the SS and pure German females, all possessing the Nordic traits. Initially, the *Lebensborn* programme served as a welfare institution for the wives of SS officers. The organization ran maternity homes where women could give birth or receive advice on family issues. The organization soon accepted unmarried women who were either pregnant or had given birth but needed aid. This was provided under the pretext that the woman and the father of the child were classified as racially valuable. Around 60 per cent of the women who became involved in the *Lebensborn* programme were unmarried. Under *Lebensborn*, the women were given protection from the social stigmas of the time. They would be able to give birth secretly, away from their homes. If, after giving birth, a woman decided that she did not want the child, the programme operated an orphanage with its own adoption service.

Prior to entering a *Lebensborn* facility, all non-SS members were subjected to an examination performed by an SS doctor. The first of the *Lebensborn* homes opened in 1936 in Steinhöring, a small village a short distance from Munich. The first home to open outside of Germany was in Norway in 1941. Many of these Nazi facilities were established in confiscated houses and former nursing homes that had been owned by Jews.

Once again, the *Bund Deutscher Mädel*, or League of German Girls, would fall under the evil gaze of their leaders. All leaders within the BDM organization were ordered to actively encourage young women with the right credentials, to become good breeding partners for SS officers. Girls in the BDM with pronounced Nordic appearance were also actively sought. Young girls that fitted the blonde-hair, blue-eyed stereotype were viewed as prize specimens. Many young girls of the BDM, some as young as 15 and 16 years, were exploited by their own male society under the guise of *Lebensborn*.

By 1939, there were 8,000 members enrolled into the *Lebensborn* programme. The final figure by the end of the Second World War is not clear, but it is thought to have been in the tens of thousands.

What is perhaps most tragic about the whole *Lebensborn* programme, was that it created a whole generation of Germans who would have no past. *Lebensborn* was simply a biological production line, in which each child was just a number, and the property of the state unless adopted by a family. When adopted, the children were nameless, their new identities only created in the family that had adopted them.

Many babies and young children in the conquered territories, particularly in Poland and the east, also fell victim to the *Lebensborn* programme. Any children discovered in these regions who possessed Aryan qualities, would be kidnapped if it was thought that they were suitable for Germanization. They would be taken from their birth parents and placed with German families, who would then raise them as their own offspring. There were thousands who went to their graves never knowing their true ancestry or identity. Many would later discover their personal backgrounds, only for the people they viewed as their family refusing to enlighten them. Some of these unfortunate individuals were driven to suicide by the curse of their Nazi past. Most lived out their lives, but suffered all manner of psychological problems, such as depression, low self-esteem, feelings of inadequacy, and self-harm. Lisolotte Feldmayer was one such victim, who had discovered that she had been a *Lebensborn* child. Over the years since, Lisolotte has tried on many occasions to tell her story. To this day, she is still very upset, finding it extremely difficult to talk openly about her past and her experiences. It was only after much time and patience that she shared her darkness with me.

I always felt somewhat different to the other children in my street, but I could give no explanation as to why. It was just a feeling based on how I was treated at home and at school by other children of my own age. In school, there were girls who would gang up on me and shout, 'here's the bastard child.' I did not know what they meant at that time.

When I got home, I would tell my parents, but they told me it was nothing and to just ignore them. The teachers always turned a blind eye to bullying and they did nothing to help. I could not understand why the other kids were so hostile and horrible to me. I was normal in every sense: average height, blue eyes, blonde hair in pigtails, and always nicely dressed with clean shoes. It never occurred to me, either as a child or a young person, that both my parents were dark-haired and had brown eyes. I did not question this quite obvious difference. There was no real resemblance between us.

My earliest recollections were of being collected from a hospital, or similar place, by the people I thought were my parents. My upbringing was not a bad one by any standards. I always had birthdays and Christmas was always enjoyable, though we did not have a lot back then.

My difficulties began in my late teens, when the name calling continued, but I now understood the names and accusations being thrown at me as I walked up our street. People would whisper things if I walked into a shop. It was when one girl called me a 'Nazi girl' that I really lost my temper. I grabbed her and threw her down on the ground. I held her down while demanding why she was calling me a Nazi, and what she meant by it. The girl was almost in tears by this time. I repeated my question. The girl blurted out that her parents had told her that my mother and father were not really my birth parents and that I came from an orphanage in Munich where the SS bred children. I was stunned. I let go of her wrists and got off her. She ran off, no doubt to squeal to her mother that I had hit her. I was just standing there in stunned silence, then, suddenly, everything began to make sense. My heart pounded in my chest and I felt utterly dejected. Was what she had said the truth? I would have to somehow find out for myself. All the teasing I had gone through. All the shouts of 'bastard'. All my parents' avoidance of my questions.

I was seething with anger as I rushed home. I burst through the door shouting out for my mother. She came out of the kitchen, enquiring what the matter was and telling me to immediately stop my shouting.

'I will stop shouting when you stop fucking lying to me? Who the hell am I, and more importantly, who the hell are you?' I demanded. 'Were you Nazis or something?'

Mother responded, 'Don't be so stupid, of course not. Who has told you this rubbish.'

Again, I swore at the woman, demanding that she stop the lying and tell me what's going on. 'Where are my birth records? I want to see them. If what you say is untrue, then you have nothing to hide.'

In the end, she broke down in tears, begging me to stop shouting at her. She said she would tell me everything and we can talk about it over a cup of tea'. I stood in the living room in silence, staring out of the window as she put the kettle on and made tea for us both. She came in with a cup and saucer in each hand and placed them on the table. The woman that for all the years I thought was my mother, looked me in the eyes and began to explain that I was indeed adopted.

She explained that I came from the *Lebensborn* clinic at Munich. She and her husband could not have children, so they adopted me after the authorities had checked their backgrounds and found them to be suitable. There was no record of who my real mother and father were and there was no birth certificate. She then explained to me that I had been born under the Nazi *Lebensborn* project.

I was so shocked that I did not touch the cup of tea. I just wanted to get out of the house. So, I got up, took my coat and went out through the front door. I ran up the road into the fields to find somewhere quiet, where I just cried. I then went to the house of a friend and told her everything. I was so upset that she suggested I stay the night at her house. She telephoned my parents to tell them I was okay and that I would not be coming home until the morning. We sat up late talking in her room about all kinds of things. She made me a hot drink and I shared her bed. I didn't sleep much at all that night, but my friend, bless her, cuddled me all that night. I cried a few times and she did her best to comfort me, but in the morning I felt like I had a hangover. What sleep I did have had been interrupted with nightmare visions of marching soldiers, Swastika flags, concentration camp survivors and dead bodies. I couldn't eat the breakfast that my lovely friend had prepared. She kissed me on the cheek, gave me a hug, and walked home with me. I took a deep breath and walked in through the front door.

Both my parents were there, sitting in the living room. Father asked me to come in and sit down as we needed to talk. They went over the whole story of how they had adopted me. However, they knew nothing of my real parents. They did not wish to discuss the circumstances. They reaffirmed their love for me, and, in their eyes, I was their child. I wasn't happy with that. I needed to know more. I asked them if they had been Nazis. This they denied, saying that they had been childless and just wanted a child they could call their own. Father explained that Mother could not have children after she had suffered a serious childhood accident. He explained that my exact birthdate was unknown, so to them my birthday was the day they had collected me from the orphanage. I accepted their story, but I then stated that my real parents could be war criminals. How would I ever know? I needed to understand all of this, but I guessed that I would not get the truth in its entirety from my adoptive parents.

I made arrangements to visit a professor of history at Munich University. When I arrived at the university, this kindly old gentleman took me to the library, where he selected several books before we sat down. He ordered some tea for us and then he began to explain to me that I was a *Lebensborn* child. He explained in great detail the sort of people involved in this *Lebensborn* thing. The fathers of the babies were almost all SS, but late in the war, girls of the BDM, many under age, were attending the *Lebensborn* clinics to donate their babies that they had conceived in the SS-ran breeding programme.

The professor asked me to show understanding towards those who had adopted me, as they did so in good faith, bringing me up in a good home. I then told him the way I was treated by the other children in our street. They all knew where I came from, as their parents had obviously told them. They also told them that I was no good and that I was a bastard. I explained that my childhood had been full of name calling, which I could never understand. If my adoptive parents had cared that much, then why didn't they move away? The professor did his best to calm my mood, I suppose, but at least I knew where I had come from now.

I left the university feeling numb and withdrawn. Finding the identity of my real parents would be impossible as I had no records, only a single digit number, nothing else. Trying to access records from the Nazi era was impossible. The various archives would apologetically tell me that they didn't have any information.

It was 1958 and I was just 19 years old. I had my whole life ahead of me, but I didn't know who I was anymore. My parents kept on at me to see a doctor. Eventually I agreed, but all he wanted to do was fill me with tablets. I didn't know what the tablets were, so I threw them away.

The relationship with my adoptive parents began to deteriorate and we argued constantly. I began to go out and to stay out late. I began to drink. I would get so drunk, that men would take advantage of me. I would wake up naked in bed with a man lying next to me, not knowing who he was or how I even got there. I would dress as quickly as I could and get away. It got to the point where my parents threatened to have me institutionalized. I told them that they would have to kill me first. The big problem back then in the 1950s, was that if you showed emotional distress and anger, society classed you as having psychiatric problems. They could have you put away in places where they gave you electric shocks to the brain, or even lobotomize you.

My past began to disgust me and I started to inflict self-harm. I would cut myself. This, I felt, was the only way that I could rid myself of the anger and frustration I felt about everything. My parents caught me self-harming, so they tried to get me help. My father was on the telephone talking. I think they were sending some people to our house. Mother tried to keep me talking, but I pushed her away and ran out of the back door to my friend's house. She agreed that if anyone called looking for me, that she would tell them I wasn't there. I couldn't trust my parents anymore, but I knew that, somehow, I had to sort myself out.

My friend arranged for me to leave our village to stay with one of her good friends. She would help me find work so that I could start to support myself. I wrote a letter to my parents explaining I was going away, but I gave them no address to write back to as I was sure they would send the authorities after me.

I ended up working for a kindly old woman, where I helped her with her chores, such as washing and cooking and tidying her house. It was one morning while helping her do her washing, that she noticed the scars on my arms. She stopped what she was doing and invited me to sit down and talk over some tea she then asked about the scars. Initially I lied to her, but she was having none of it. I then told her everything that had happened and about my background. Her reaction was surprising: 'Yes, our generation have much to answer for. It was our generation that embraced the National Socialists, whether we supported or not. We were to blame. At the time, we thought we were doing the right thing, but we were being seduced by evil. Why, poor girl, do you have to carry the burden of our mistakes?'

Sunday was the one day where we did no work, as it was our rest day, or the Lord's day as the old lady used to say. We went to the small local church every Sunday morning. One Sunday, at the end of the service, the priest of the church asked me to stay behind. The old lady had probably spoken to him about me. I was nervous. He reassured me that there was nothing for me to be afraid about. He spoke to me for about thirty minutes, before giving me a phone number to contact.

When I phoned the number later, it was of a young woman who was also born at the same *Lebensborn* clinic as me. We arranged to meet in the local town for some coffee. The night before, I could barely sleep with excitement. When we met, it was as if we had known each other for years. We were both blonde-haired and blue-eyed. We could have been sisters for all we knew. I felt closer to her than anyone else, as we understood each other and where we had come from. She revealed that she had found out who her father was, but it was not a happy ending. She explained that he had been a soldier in the Waffen SS and that he had been involved in some of the heaviest fighting in the east. He had killed people and helped burn down their homes. Her mother was a Hitler Youth member, and was almost ten years younger than what he was. I asked her how she managed to find this information. She explained that the family who had adopted her were proud of her *Lebensborn* roots, and that they were devout Nazis, and wealthy people too. She also revealed that the family had had connections with the facility and that they had also helped to finance it in some way. She explained that she had no names of her biological parents, but basically knew her roots. Spending time with her was a turning point in my life. I knew I had to change and evolve into something bigger, and not to let my past destroy me. I had to build a future, maybe marry, and have my own children and give them the love they deserve.

I hadn't written to my adoptive parents for nearly three months, so decided to do so. I apologized to them for all that had happened, and that I would visit them soon.

I took my new friend with me for support when I went to visit my adoptive parents. There was no animosity.

They just burst out crying, saying how sorry they were for everything and asked for forgiveness. I introduced my friend to them, and, over tea that afternoon, she told them her story. After some time, we did become something of a family again. Although it was not easy, we did get there in the end.

As time went by, more women who were *Lebensborn* babies came forward, forming their own discussion and meeting groups. They printed newsletters and we attended regular meetings, where we would exchange stories and help one another in times of sadness. It was through one of these groups I met my husband to be. We married, had children, and set up a nice home with all the things that most girls only dreamed of back then. My children mean the world to me. I swore when they were born that I would tell them I loved them every single day. They will tell you that I have kept my word. I suppose we spoiled them in some ways, but we gave them everything we could as good parents.

I know that the *Lebensborn* programme created life, but, in the process, it destroyed far more lives than it had ever created. I suppose I was lucky in some ways, as I managed to sort out myself, but not everyone was strong enough or received the help that I had.

Former BDM girl Leena Heike's story is one that is typical of the BDM girls who had been encouraged to sleep with members of the Waffen SS, to produce Aryan children for the madness that was consuming Nazi Germany from the mid-1930s onwards. Now, well into her twilight years, and with children and great grandchildren, she can reflect on what had been a painful youth, tarnished by the evil of *Lebensborn*.

Upon reflection, I was a very stupid 18-year-old young girl. I had joined the BDM, and found my place in the new society. We all used to say to hell with our elders and to hell with the Jews. We are the new generation. We are the new leaders of the world. Oh yes, we used to believe all that, and we used to swallow everything we were told to by our superiors and those in charge of us in the Hitler Youth. Even by 1943, it had become clear that we were losing the war, yet we still believed if we did all we could, we would turn things around.

One BDM meeting in early 1944 was unlike many of the others. Instead of them preaching the virtues of chastity and conformity, the leaders began talking about how we, the girls of the BDM, might contribute to the survival of the German race by having children. Such suggestions were only put to the older girls in the troops. By older, I mean those who were 17 or 18 years old. They found it easier to manipulate younger teenage girls, so it was them who were targeted. The leader explained to us that this would be regarded as one of the highest honours a German female could bestow upon the future Reich. Any girl who volunteered, would receive the best possible maternity care and quality food. Such things could be kept secret from family members if so desired.

In the BDM, it was not referred to as the Fountain of Life or *Lebensborn*. It was often referred to as a 'maternal science project'. Some of the girls were quietly disgusted by the idea, so dismissed it without any further thought. I was one of the stupid ones who put my hand up to say that I will do this for Fuhrer and Fatherland and for the survival of the future German Reich. I did not tell my parents and arrangements had been put in place so that they would be unable to interfere with the pregnancy, if or when it occurred.

I had the idea that they would maybe anesthetize me, and then use a needle or something to inject semen inside me. When I was informed that a partner was available for me, it soon completely dispelled my preconceived ideas. The young man was 19 years old, and had been an SS soldier for around a year and a half, during which time he had earned the Iron Cross Second Class. He was tall with short blonde hair and, of course, with blue eyes – much the same as me really.

It was pretty awkward spending time with this young man whom I didn't even know. I did not know what to say to him, and at that first introduction nothing happened. Naturally, the BDM leader discussed our meeting with me and asked how everything had gone. When I told her that it was okay but nothing happened, her tone changed completely.

'What do you mean nothing happened? All you had to do was be a good girl, lie down, and open your legs. If you are not up to this, I can always find other girls who are.'

That is what she shouted at me and I felt quite down after the verbal bashing she gave me.

At that point, I should have said to hell with this lot and put the stupid idea out of my mind. But I was stupid and easily influenced, and I was determined to show her that I could do it and perform this valuable service to the Reich.

A second meeting was arranged and we went walking in the woods in the dark. With the sound of Allied bombers droning above, we found a secluded spot and I undressed myself. As soon as I was ready, he undressed and I could see he was excited. I lay down and let him have sex with me two times. Afterwards, we both dressed, we talked little and then walked back. From that moment, I belonged to the state even more. I was examined regularly until I discovered our union had been a success – I was pregnant. The only thing that worried me at the time was the thought of the pain of giving birth and if I could handle it all. Another thing was that I would never see the father again. I thought that they may have wanted him involved in some way, but I was told that he had fulfilled his role, and now I must fulfil mine.

He did tell me his name once, but I forgot it. I never saw or heard from him again. If he had survived the war, and the possible prosecution that many SS soldiers had been subjected to, he could easily have tracked me down by the town I was living in. He never did, and I can only assume that he was either killed, or was happy to go around screwing girls for the good of the state. Either way, my problems had only just begun.

Word got back to my parents and they were beside themselves with rage. My mother actually slapped me across the face and called me a whore. My father wanted to beat me too, but I threatened to tell the authorities if they dared hit me again. After that, I was banished from home and was forced to live in the maternity home, where I helped the staff until my time came.

The birth was a long, painful experience, during which I wished I had not done this. I gave birth to a boy, who weighed over 8lb. He was healthy in every respect. After the birth, he was taken away to join the rows of other new born babies in the facility. I had a period of recuperation, and when I was fit, I asked if I could see the child, but was refused. In fact, I begged them to let me see him, but they told me that my work was now done and to go away and continue my duty. I felt as if they had turned their backs on me and I felt a sense of great loss over the child.

I tried to return home, but my parents refused to even see me. I had to go and live with an aunt, as she was the only one who would have anything to do with me. When I arrived at her house, she said, 'You stupid young girl, what have you done? What shame you have brought on the family, do you understand?'

She calmed down after a while and after I had broken down and cried. I felt terrible in the weeks that followed. I began to feel like I did not care about anything anymore. I began to neglect myself and I lost interest in many things. I could not stop crying and things became tough for my aunt and her husband. I just wanted things to go back to how they were before I had done what I had.

One morning I just couldn't take anymore and I decided to take an overdose of tablets. The tablets were sleeping pills prescribed for me by my aunt's doctor. I wrote a letter to my mother and father saying that I was sorry for what I had done and hoped that now they could find some way of forgiving me. I took the tablets and drank some water and went up to my aunt's spare room. My recollections afterwards are somewhat vague. I recall feeling like I was floating, but was aware of someone examining my eyes and the sounds of voices around me.

It was probably a day later when I was aware of being in a hospital bed. I sat up looking around me, wondering if I was dead and this was heaven. The whitewashed walls were almost blinding as I tried to focus around me. I pushed the bed clothes off me and placed my feet on the floor. I tried to stand, but my legs would not do what my brain was telling them and I fell in a heap on the floor. As I fell, I knocked over a chair. The noise alerted a nurse, who came rushing in. She picked me up off the floor and put me back into bed. A doctor then came in and began to examine me, shining a light into my eyes and checking my pulse and heartbeat.

'You are one very lucky girl. Your aunt found you just in time,' he said.

My aunt was called and she and her husband came to the hospital straightaway. When she arrived, she was visibly angry with me, but her anger soon turned to that of concern and compassion. My aunt had contacted my parents and they came to see me after I left hospital a day later. I had forgotten about the note I had written. Both my aunt and my parents had read it. My parents were terribly upset when they saw me. My aunt had ordered me to bedrest, so they came up to my room. We talked for a couple of hours about personal things. Then they asked about the baby and I told them what happened after the birth of the child. My parents visited the *Lebensborn* facility, offering to take the child I had given birth to as their own until they considered me capable enough of raising him on my own. This was to no avail, however, as an SS doctor informed them the child had already been adopted. He was gone and the doctor would not disclose any information, only saying that these were matters of the SS and the state.

I had paid a heavy price for my loyalty and pregnancy. It has haunted me all of my life. I often wonder who had my baby and whether he had a good life where he was now – all of the things that any mother would think and feel. Not knowing is part of my punishment that I will carry with me to my grave.

After the war I tried to move on and live a normal life. I married a good man and had three children with him. I never forgot the child I had all those years ago. I don't even have a photograph or lock of hair with which to remember him by. I did get in touch with an association that helped women who were involved in the *Lebensborn* programme. They were very good and offered all kinds of support, classing us as victims – they never judged us. At the time, I was too young and too foolish to have really understood what I was getting myself into. Against the better judgement of my parents and myself, I sinned in a terrible way. I have prayed that God will forgive me and I have tried to lead a good life, helping others where I could. Ultimately, my day of judgement will arrive and only then will I find out.

Giselle Hirsch, a 16-year-old BDM girl at the time, recalls the story of one of her friends who had given her services to the *Lebensborn* programme:

She was a year older than me and felt pressured by those in the BDM to participate in this programme. I recall her telling me about it and my having a bad feeling that she was making a huge mistake. Many young girls and women offered themselves, but not all were successful. I remember one of the SS doctors saying that if it continued we would need to remove our SS from Russia to keep up with the demand.

Primarily, they wanted girls and women with an Aryan appearance, but others with dark hair and brown eyes were selected too. My friend went along with what was expected of her. She slept with an SS man eight years her senior. She came back all proud about it, but these guys were queuing up to have sex with young girls, many of who were virgins. After they had sex, the men would then return to the front or whatever duties they were doing at the time. The girls were cared for by the state and carefully examined as their pregnancies progressed. When my friend gave birth, she became distraught. All feelings of duty disappeared, as she just wanted to keep the child. They allowed girls that they thought were capable to keep their babies, provided that they had adequate family support. They would, however, and for whatever reason, not let my friend keep hers. She never recovered from her depression, and a few days before her eighteenth birthday, she hanged herself. To this day, I visit her grave once a month to put some flowers down for her. As you now know, the evil that was National Socialism spread into all areas of our lives.

As we can see, the *Lebensborn* programme would have consequences that would reach far beyond the Second World War. Even today, there are still lives that are blighted by its evil. Thankfully, today there is greater recognition, and support groups and specialist counsellors for those who suffered under this evil programme. All of those who have spoken within the pages of this chapter were victims in one form or another. It would appear that there were endless ways in which Germany's females could be exploited or utilized by the Nazi state.

To close, I would like to quote Leena Heike:

A *Lebensborn* nurse once said 'you can call the babies anything you want. They have no names. Here they are just numbers.' The truth is we have no past, no roots as such. The Nazis created us and they are our past. They manufactured us. Many of us are still here, trying to come to terms with our past. There was once many a night where I would have these awful dreams. My dreams would alternate with those of the smiling faces of young German maidens. They would be shouting 'Heil! Heil!' and then they would be like corpses carrying Swastika crosses up the sheer face of a hill. I would wake up feeling physically ill. We will, in a way, carry that crooked cross to our graves.

Afterword

I would like to conclude this work hoping in many ways that both *Hitler's Girl's, Doves Amongst Eagles* and *In Hitler's Shadow* have addressed a great many unanswered questions. I also hope that both volumes have taken the reader on a unique journey. The journey has been somewhat considerable and often sad, with some injection of humour along the way. In many ways, I feel that finally, a brighter light has been shone into the silent, now distant world of Adolf Hitler's Third Reich. The light was switched on in order to find the truth about the lives of young girls of the *Jüngmädel Bund* and *Bund Deutscher Mädel* and, indeed, females in general.

When I first began this work, I was unsure what I would discover. I was even less sure of what the literary world might make of it. In some ways, both volumes represent suffering on an intimate level, especially when compared to other works on the subject. But history itself is littered with false empathy. Upon reflection, it is somewhat difficult to think, that the initial project, which would result in both works, began in 1997, now twenty years ago. Little did I realize that my chance meeting with Kirsten Eckermann on that dreadful winter's morning at Cannock Chase would come to fruition in the way that it has. When the initial work of interviewing began, I asked them to be totally honest in conveying their fears, joy, pain and sadness to me, to not be afraid to speak the unspeakable, or to reveal the things they were told not to. From me there would be no critique or judgement. In doing, so I too faced the demons that these once young women had to face.

What I learned during the gathering of information gave me many sleepless nights. There were many nights in the summertime when I would be going through notes and pages of interviews. Afterwards, I would sit out on the patio, reflecting on things until the sun began to rise. Unable to sleep, I would thumb through the photographs forwarded by contributors. The photographs of the smiling girls are now just ghosts, the landscapes of their youth now long gone or barely recognizable. No previous research project before has ever troubled me to this extent. It has led me to question many things about the supposed community of humanity. The cruelty and destruction of which we human beings are sometimes capable, is truly frightening. Nazi Germany was indeed unique, but it is not alone. From the times we live in, it would seem that humanity has learned very little from the catastrophic mistakes it has made in the past. It seems that conflict is an endemic component of human culture.

I hope that those of you who have joined me on this journey will disembark with a better understanding and clearer perspective. Should what you have read have the same effect upon you as it has on me, please feel free to share your experiences. An easily troubled heart is a compassionate one. The female is the very embodiment of our human community. She loves and nurtures, creating life in a most remarkable way. In some of the most trying environments in history, women have thrived, making their mark through sheer hard work and dedication. The female is a society's most valuable resource. She should never be exploited, abused or sacrificed for anyone's calling. Contrary to the supposed laws of nature, the female has, throughout history and when necessary, risen to the defence of their offspring, family and communities. Many have lived as the lioness, often paying with their lives. If she is to endeavour in enriching the communities of this world, then the world must change in accordance. If anything is to be learned, then it is surely man that requires the teaching. When Adolf Hitler made his proud boast that 'the youth that graduate from my academies will terrify the world,' he was probably correct. As one of the female contributors remarked, 'Did we terrify the world? Yes, for a very short period of time I think we did. For that we paid a high price. For that paltry honour, we all had to walk in Hitler's shadow for the rest of our lives.'

Acknowledgments

I would like to thank the following for their most valued contribution to this work. This book would not have been possible without you: Anna Dann, Monica Vanessa Kieler Dorsche, Theresa Moelle, Dora Brunninghausen, Wiener Katte, Katrina Duvaal, Carly Hendryks, Inge Strauss, Elsa Lantz, Vaida Raab, Anastas Sogiyiev, Heidi Koch, Kirsten Eckermann, Anita Von Schoener, Eleonore Kirschener, Dana Henschelle, Sophia Kortge, Karin Hertz, Gertrud Kretzl, Dana Schmidt, Ingrid Herschteller, Lilla Kallenberg, Kristel Bernd, Lise Hirsch, Marguerite Kopfel, Herbert Kolinger, Gabrielle Haefker, Anita Skorz, Melissa Schroeder, Helga Bassler, Olga Kirschener, Melitta Schuman, Erika Baumann, Lisolotte Feldmayer, Leena Heike, Giselle Hirsch. Many of you are no longer with us. Yet your bravery, resolve and commitment to both the *Hitler's Girls, Doves Amongst Eagles* and *In Hitler's Shadow* projects have been exemplary. May God bless you all. You will live on through the pages of these works.

I would also like to extend thanks to Keith Costa for the use of his great uncle's photograph, and the Bundesarchiv, Germany, for select images that appear in this volume.

My thanks also to Lenny Warren and the Militaria Collectors Network, The National Archives at Kew, Ian Tustin and Jenny Powell of *Vale Magazine*, Chris Warren Photography, and Claire Hopkins, History Commissioning Editor at Pen & Sword Books Ltd, for her unreserved attention and support.

My copy editor and fellow author, Gerry van Tonder, for the beyond exemplary service which he provides.

Jon Wilkinson for his stunning graphics work.

Katie Eaton (marketing) and all the staff at Pen & Sword Books Ltd for their support.

Debbie Jones, you were a true angel during a difficult time, helping to repair damaged foundations. Thank you for your compassion and continued friendship. Thanks to Jody Warner for his work on the indexing for this book.

My partner Paula, who has had to put up with my countless hours on the computer. Providing endless cups of tea, combined with your love, adoration, support and patience is both commendable and a real gift to me as an author and historian. The books could not have been written without the environment with which you have provided me in which to write them.

God bless each and every one of you, with all my love and thanks in abundance.

Index